'. . . an inspiration to thousands of women'

Woman's Day

'She has poured her heart and soul into this book . . . Sally is one of those women that when she comes into your life she brings not only beauty, but kindness and hope.'

Pink Hope

'Sally admits her book was tough to write but wants to share her story with the tens of thousands going through the same experience. Her simple message is "never give up".'

Today Tonight

'But instead of retreating from the public eye to wallow, Obermeder sacrificed her privacy to give others hope . . . Since its release in April, her book has touched many people, both with and without cancer.'

Daily Telegraph

'The beautiful, bright and optimistic Sally Obermeder is a shining example to us all.'

Sunday Telegraph

'. . . written with warmth and candour, telling the inspiring story of triumph in her courageous battle with cancer and her career struggles in the cutthroat world of television.'

MamaMia

'An inspiration to womankind . . . Sally Obermeder tells of her harrowing journey after a routine pregnancy check-up uncovered an aggressive form of breast cancer. Have a box of tissues ready.'

OK! Magazine

'Obermeder . . . never shied away from talking frankly about her battle. This was no doubt **an** inspiration to the many women who were also going through the same thing.'

Sunday Telegraph

'Brimming with raw honesty, laughter and warmth, *Never Stop Believing* is a beautiful memoir that will inspire all on the determination required to overcome unimaginable obstacles.'

Get-It Magazine

Never Stop Believing

Heartache, hope and some
very high heels

SALLY OBERMEDER

ALLEN&UNWIN
SYDNEY • MELBOURNE • AUCKLAND • LONDON

First published in 2013
This edition published in 2014

Allen & Unwin
83 Alexander Street
Crows Nest NSW 2065
Australia
Phone: (61 2) 8425 0100
Email: info@allenandunwin.com
Web: www.allenandunwin.com

Cataloguing-in-Publication details are available
from the National Library of Australia
www.trove.nla.gov.au

ISBN 978 1 74331 968 0

Internal design by Alissa Dinallo
Set in 13.5/17 pt Granjon by Post Pre-press Group, Australia

10 9 8 7 6 5 4

To those who gave me life and those to whom I gave life.
Thank you for giving me the two greatest gifts possible.
I love you. This is for you, and as with everything,
I hope I've done you proud.

'I realised early on that success was tied to not giving up. Most people in this business gave up and went on to other things. If you simply didn't give up, you would outlast the people who came in on the bus with you.' *Harrison Ford*

'You can have whatever you are willing to struggle for. You can't just sit and wait for people to give you that golden dream. You've got to get out there and make it happen for yourself.'

Diana Ross

'I hated every minute of training, but I said "Don't quit. Suffer now and live the rest of your life as a champion."'

Muhammad Ali

'You can't be brave if you've only had wonderful things happen to you.' *Mary Tyler Moore*

'If you're going through hell, keep going.' *Winston Churchill*

'Time passes. The things that terrify you now will someday be part of your past. Remember that, and you can stop beating yourself up, cause yourself a lot less grief and enjoy your life a little bit more.' *Stevie Nicks*

Contents

Foreword

by Larry Emdur

It was the night of Sally's fundraiser. The room was packed with hundreds of friends, family and Sally's mates from TV. Rarely would you see a gaggle of TV and entertainment types from opposing organisations in the one room at the same time . . . voluntarily. But this was a special occasion and we all wanted to help Sally in whatever way we could.

Sure, everyone in the room knew about Sal's story, but to hear it in her words from her heart in her voice was, to put it simply, gut wrenching and earth shattering. From my position as MC on stage I could see everyone—some of the finest news gatherers, journalists, reporters, presenters and communicators in the country. Everyone was crying. Everyone. People who that week had reported on murders, fatal car accidents and deadly fires, custody battles and the tragedies of war were standing, openly weeping, as one of our own, a much-loved industry darling, told us everything we wanted to know and quite a few things we didn't. Some people were prepared with tissues; I could see others regularly lifting a sleeve or cuff to stop the tears. But there was no stopping the tears.

Crying for me wasn't an option up there on stage, I had to hold it together for Sal. We had pre-arranged some secret words and signals in case she wanted to stop the interview or change direction. I wanted to cry, just like everybody else.

As you'll soon discover in this book, Sally has an incredible sense of humour and it co-exists with a delightful sense of the absurd. During her illness she found much strength in laughter. Her contagious and generous laugh often belied the severity of her condition, and while it's a beautiful laugh, you also need to know it is louder than the acceptable Bondi-café-laugh volume.

What occurred to me about halfway through our chat onstage that night at Sally's fundraiser was that it was her jokes or funny stories that made people cry the most. One minute we had her tearfully saying the doctors just didn't know if she'd beat 'it' or 'it' would beat her, the next she'd be telling a very funny story about her baby daughter Annabelle farting in a café. There was something truly amazing about witnessing this woman tell her quirky stories with such verve and enthusiasm; she was in fact laughing in the face of death. All the while these stories, many of which you're about to read, were, I suppose, giving her the strength to live.

We use the word 'journey' a lot in our game. But unlike a 'journey' on some sort of reality show that lasts a few weeks, Sally's journey through work, life, near-death and back to 'fabulous' is as uplifting as it is inspiring.

I continue to learn a lot from Sally; I treasure our friendship. In the synthetic world of television where not everything, or everyone, is as it or they seem, Sally shines as a truly remarkable, beautiful human being.

Treasure the things that bring you happiness, no matter how miniscule they are, and don't waste a moment of your life sweating the small stuff. That's what I've learnt from my friendship with Sally, and I feel sure that's what you'll also get from this book.

Dear Reader,

You will notice that throughout the book there are some short contributions from a few of my nearest and dearest family and friends. Each one of the authors has played an enormously important part in my life, not only standing by me and selflessly supporting me in my battle with breast cancer, but also helping to make me the person I am today. I thank them from the bottom of my heart.

Sally Ode
xx

Before and after

When I woke up on 13 October 2011 I felt like my life was just about perfect. I had a great husband and a great job, my gorgeous Bondi apartment had just been renovated, and we'd recently turned our second bedroom into a nursery. After years of trying, and failing, to get pregnant, we'd succeeded through IVF—on our very first cycle. I'd had a wonderful year at work, filled with great stories and amazing travel, and I was really excited about the series of 'Celebrity Mum' TV segments I was going to do while on maternity leave. I was 41 weeks pregnant, I had my hospital bag packed and ready to go, and I could not wait to give birth. Any day now I was finally going to meet my baby and begin the next wonderful phase of my life: becoming a mother. I didn't think things could get any better.

I can still remember exactly what I wore that day: a fitted electric blue dress with ruching on the side and metallic silver sandals, and I had my hair in a topknot. If you asked me what I wore yesterday, I wouldn't know. But everything about that day is etched in my memory. Because that was the day I left the house happy, full of new life, hope and joy, and came home with a death sentence.

♦ ♦ ♦

I'd worked happily right through my pregnancy, doing stories for *Today Tonight* and *Sydney Weekender* and attending events that sometimes saw me working fifteen-hour days. Now I was on maternity leave, and it was finally time for me to relax, enjoy a bit of me-time and prepare myself for the birth of my baby.

I spent the first few days of my maternity leave doing some of those enjoyable little jobs I needed to get done before my baby arrived, including some pampering and then a quick shopping trip to stock up on my favourite illuminating moisturiser. It has always been my secret weapon against jet lag and late nights because it gives my skin that fresh, glowing, 'alive' look, even when I'm not feeling my best. I wished it came in 1-kg buckets given the sleepless nights I suspected lay ahead.

But I wasn't frightened about what lay ahead. I was loving the anticipation, looking forward to the new experiences, and desperate for my bubba to hurry up and come! It felt like the beginning of a whole new phase of my life, and I was revelling in it.

Four days into my maternity leave, I went to my 41-week appointment with my obstetrician, Dr Stephen Morris. I arrived in his office feeling happy and confident. He did all the usual checks and we talked. Bubba was overdue—did I want to induce? I knew I wanted to have as natural a birth as possible, so I told Stephen I was happy to wait and let bubba come when he or she was ready. We agreed that since we were both doing well, we'd wait and see what happened. The appointment over, I got up, got dressed, and headed for the door—and then I remembered something.

Two weeks earlier I'd felt a minor shooting pain in my right breast. It came and then it went, and at first I thought nothing of it. But it didn't seem to go away. Every couple of days I'd feel this random pain—it was minor, but noticeable. When I investigated I found a lump, but because I was so pregnant, both my breasts felt quite lumpy. I dismissed it as nothing more than my body preparing for breastfeeding. I'd forgotten to mention it at my 39-week appointment and again at my 40-week appointment because it really didn't seem that serious. Now, at my 41-week appointment, I hesitated, standing at the door with my handbag over my shoulder thinking, *Don't bother saying it now, your appointment's over, it's probably nothing, he's got other people waiting.*

For some reason I did mention it. I turned back. 'Sorry, there is just one more thing,' I said. 'I've been getting this funny little pain in my breast. I think I might have some kind of blocked milk duct.' That was the explanation I'd come up with. 'But it's not really bothering me, we can worry about it later.'

'No,' Stephen said, 'we'd better have a look at it now.'

So I hopped back up on the table and he felt my breast, and then said, 'Let's just send you for an ultrasound in the morning and get it checked out. Lex will book you an appointment.'

'Okay,' I said, and skipped out of there none the wiser.

Later, Stephen told me he'd known what it was as soon as he felt it. Now, I know his thoroughness and care saved my life. But that day, nothing in his words or his expression warned me that anything was wrong.

Lex, a beautiful kind woman who is the nurse at Dr Morris's office, rang the Sydney Breast Clinic for me and was told they didn't have any appointments available for two weeks.

'Really, it's fine, I can go later,' I said. I figured I could go after the birth. I had a happy picture in my mind of myself pushing the pram into town, taking my baby with me while I had my ultrasound, then having lunch with my sister or my mum, making an outing of it. Isn't that what new mums did? I'd seen them as I drove to work. They all looked so happy and cheery, pushing prams and drinking coffee and laughing. And I was about to join them.

But Lex insisted. 'No, no, we need a spot tomorrow.'

They gave me an appointment at 9.30 am the next day and I went home without a worry in my head. I thought, wasn't it nice that they were all going to so much trouble to clear up my silly little problem before the baby came? It never occurred to me for one second that it might be anything serious.

◆ ◆ ◆

The next morning, on 13 October, I bounced out of bed early—I still had a whole lot of things I wanted to get done and the baby could come at any time. I hadn't finalised my tax return and when my baby arrived I wanted to be 100 per cent focused on motherhood—not counting receipts and adding up deductions. I went into my friend's office in Bondi Junction and did a whole lot of photocopying, put together all my tax records, and mailed them off to my accountant, then even had time to buy some last-minute baby clothes before my appointment at the Sydney Breast Clinic.

When I got there the waiting room was packed, but I was taken through for my ultrasound quite quickly. After it was finished, the technician told me to sit down and wait for the results. I was happy to wait: I'd brought one of my many baby books with me—strategies for getting your baby to sleep. So, I settled in to read.

After a while the lady came back. 'We'd like to do another ultrasound, if that's alright?'

We did another one.

'Can you do a mammogram too?' the technician asked.

'Yes, of course.'

I had the mammogram, and because my breasts were so huge from the pregnancy it was really quite painful. I remember joking with the technician that a mammogram machine was definitely invented by a man. What guy would readily agree to have his testicles slammed between two bits of steel? So why is it okay for women to have our breasts squashed between two plates like a pancake? And a thin pancake at that. Not a fluffy number. If men had to have mammograms, they would definitely invent something else damn quick.

Then it was back to more waiting.

By this time the morning was over, but they still weren't finished with me.

'Go and have some lunch, but come back straight away because we might need to do a biopsy.'

I'd planned to have lunch with my sister, Maha, that day, so I rang her and said, 'Sorry, I can't make lunch, I've got to have more tests. I'll ring you when I'm done.'

You'd think alarm bells would have been ringing. But they weren't. Seven or eight years earlier I'd sat in that very same clinic, and had the very same ultrasounds and mammograms. They'd found a cyst in my breast, drained it, and that was that. Problem solved.

I went off and grabbed a quick lunch by myself, and when I came back they performed a fine-needle biopsy, and then another one.

While I was waiting to hear how that test had gone, an email came through from my agent. I'd been working on an idea for a book, and now a publisher wanted to commission it. I had a book deal!

I rang my husband, Marcus, straight away to tell him the good news. I was over the moon. A few hours earlier, I couldn't have imagined my life getting any better, but it just had. An author. I would be an author! Oh. My. God. Amazing. And I'd done it while I was pregnant. It's not often I tell myself I've done a good job, or feel good about something I've accomplished. But at that moment I remember sinking into the chair and grinning like an idiot to myself. *I've done it*, I thought. *I've actually done it!* I tried not to make eye contact with anyone else in the waiting room because I didn't think I'd be able to do the polite head nod and look away. My smile was plastered on my face. I felt giddy with joy.

I was still smiling when the nurse came back and told me they were going to do a core biopsy.

A core biopsy is much deeper than a fine-needle biopsy so it's quite painful. They told me I was going to need an anaesthetic. I didn't want one. I wasn't a super-purist about my pregnancy but I'd been careful about what I put in my body—I hadn't even taken paracetamol—so I certainly didn't want to have an anaesthetic when I could be giving birth any day. But the nurse said, 'I'm sorry, you're going to need one.'

So I went in to have the core biopsy. First there were two people in the room, and then another came in, and another.

When you have a bit of a public profile, you sometimes get special treatment: people in shops or restaurants make a fuss because they've seen you on TV or in the social pages. But now I began to realise that these nurses and technicians and doctors weren't fussing over me because I was on TV. And it wasn't because I was very very pregnant either.

I began to get a little weepy, and one of the nurses asked me if I was alright.

'It's four o'clock, I've been here all day, I'm getting a bit tired,' I said tearfully.

'Do you want us to get Marcus for you? We can get him to come over straight away.'

'Yes,' I said, 'that would be good.'

It didn't occur to me that there might be a reason why he needed to be there with me. I thought they were just being helpful and kind.

The test finished, they showed me into a doctor's office to wait for Marcus and get the results. I'd had my little cry and was back to feeling relaxed again. I jumped onto my Blackberry and started sending work emails. (Even though I'd officially finished work, I was trying to line up a Sarah Jessica Parker interview.) They'd sent a nurse in to sit with me, and she kept trying to engage me in conversation, asking me questions like 'How long have you been married?' and 'Do you know whether you're having a boy or a girl?' She was lovely, but I just wished she'd let me get on with my work. I may have been a whole five days into my maternity leave, but I hadn't quite given up my workaholic habits yet—and didn't have time for small talk. I had SJP to lock down before my baby arrived!

At last Marcus arrived, and I could see how relieved everyone was. *That's weird*, I thought. He sat down beside me and took my hand. He didn't say anything. Later, he told me that as soon as they called him, he knew it was bad. The nurse knew, the doctor knew, my obstetrician knew, my husband knew. It seemed as if everyone in the room knew. Except me.

The doctor came in, and there was really very little preamble to what she had to tell us.

'Well, Sally,' she said. 'We've done all the tests and we've had a look at the results, and I'm very sorry to have to tell you this, but you've got breast cancer.'

♦ ♦ ♦

They say that your life changes forever when you're diagnosed with cancer. There's your life before, and your life after.

Cancer shows you things you cannot imagine you'd ever have to experience:

The grief, the fear.

Seeing your husband and parents crying at the thought of losing you.

Confronting the possibility that your baby might grow up without you.

The fear of losing everything you've worked for, hoped for, dreamed for.

And you're sicker than you've ever been in your life: a sickness that affects your entire body—even your elbows, even your feet—and goes on for weeks and months and doesn't end.

But you discover other things too: your strength. Your endurance. The pleasure of finding things to laugh about even in the darkest of times. The true force of friendship. The power of love.

◆ ◆ ◆

This is the story of how I transformed my life.

How I gave up money, status and a safe career at the age of thirty to pursue my dream job in television.

How I struggled to fall pregnant, and was saved from making the worst decision of my life by Angelina Jolie.

And what happened when cancer threatened to take away everything that mattered to me most.

This is the story of how a celebrity-obsessed girl from the suburbs worked her way to her dream job, with nothing to back her up but a lot of self-belief, hard work, a truly amazing husband, and some very high heels.

Something has to give

I think my TV obsession began with Barbie.

When I was a little girl, the only Barbie I wanted was called 'Lights, Camera, Action Barbie'. She came with a toy camera and one of those big Hollywood lights on a stand, and she was the first Barbie to have a huge diamond ring on her finger. She was more expensive than all the other Barbies, and for about six months I used to go into Venture, a discount department store that was around in the early 80s, every Saturday and stand there and gaze at her. I was so in love with the fanciness and the glamour of it all—I wanted that Barbie more than anything in the world. Eventually Mum and Dad gave in and bought her for me—and I loved her.

Growing up, I always wanted to be on TV. I didn't really know how I was going to pull it off. I'm tone-deaf and have two left feet, so *Young Talent Time* was out. But I still dreamed. Sometimes I liked to pretend I was a newsreader. In high school my trick for learning slabs of boring information for exams was to learn them as if they were the news and I was presenting them: 'Today in the human body . . .'

I was a teenager when MTV finally launched in Australia in 1987, and I couldn't get enough of it. It began as a music show, hosted by Richard Wilkins, that aired late on Friday and Saturday nights on Channel 9.

I idolised Richard Wilkins. He always looked like he was having *so much fun*. He was friends with all these amazing, talented, famous people, and he got to spend his time talking to them and hanging out with them. I just couldn't believe that someone actually got *paid* to do that. It looked like the most exciting job in the world.

From the outside, TV looks so glamorous. It seems really fancy and everyone's pretty and perfect. I longed to be part of that world. But when I finished school and it was time to choose a career, being Richard Wilkins did not seem like an option my parents would approve of.

For some people their choice of career is clear: they're really good at science or maths, or they want to be a doctor, or an actress, or a plumber. But I had never really excelled at anything in particular academically, and the things I was interested in just didn't seem like *careers*.

My interests were television, entertainment, celebrities and magazines. Even from a young age I'd spent all my pocket-money on magazines. I used to pore over them, studying the fashion pictures, trying to work out how they made it come together. When I finished school I didn't know that being a stylist was a job. I dreamed of choosing clothes and putting them on models and putting fashion on the page. Creating the illusion. Helping to build those beautiful worlds. Today, everybody knows what a stylist is—TV has taken us behind the scenes of all the glamour industries, from fashion to modelling to magazines and beyond. But when I was growing up, nobody knew those jobs existed, or at least I didn't.

Mum and Dad are both accountants, and to them, back then, those kinds of careers—talking to celebrities or styling magazine shoots—sounded ridiculous. They didn't even sound like *jobs*. So they firmly but gently steered me in a different direction. They warned me that pursuing a career like that would mean I'd be poor and struggling my entire life, and suggested choosing something more stable. Something like law. Or accounting.

I looked at some more stable professions. I did work experience with a dentist, and that seemed like quite a good job, but I really wanted to be able to talk to people, and of course you can't chat to someone who's got a mouthful of instruments, so that wasn't for me. Then I did work experience with my mum, who worked for a trustee firm, and I decided I quite liked the whole corporate thing: getting dressed up in a suit and going into the city. I started a Commerce degree, with two majors: accounting and marketing.

While I was in my first year at uni I got my first ever job, selling clothes at Sussan. I had to fight my Dad quite hard to get that job: I was living at home, he was paying for everything, and giving me a generous allowance. He prided himself on being a good provider and didn't really understand my need to be independent, to start making my way in the world. We had a few arguments about whether I should get a job or not. I decided I'd go out and apply, because once I got a job there was nothing he could say about it.

I started going to Parramatta Westfield, walking around all the stores, putting my name down in case any jobs came up. The place I really wanted to work was Sportsgirl, with all the cool girls. But every time I walked in there I just knew they were looking at me and thinking, *Nope, not cool enough*. It was like high school all over again, all the cool kids looking down on you. Anyway, one day, after being rejected from Sportsgirl yet again, I walked in to Sussan; the lady who ran the store was looking for someone, and I got the job.

I loved everything about that job: I loved the clothes, I loved unpacking the new stock, arranging the displays and dealing with the customers. And I loved my boss. She was one of my first role models. A strong, powerful, stylish, successful woman, she ran that store like it was her own business. She built it up with such passion and dedication, and I just admired her so much. You'd see women on TV and in the movies who were fabulous and smart and successful. She was the first person I'd met who was like that *in real life*. I thought she was so cool, and I really wanted to be like her: strong, driven, and always stylish. I loved her philosophy: never think of yourself as just an employee, always treat what you do as if it's the most important thing in the world, treat it with the respect you would treat your own business and always give it your best. It's a philosophy I made my own.

As much as I loved that early foray into fashion, life was

steering me down a different path. Although I was at uni full time and doing a degree with a double major, I felt like I had a lot of time on my hands, and I wanted to do more with myself. I took a second part-time job as a bank teller at Westpac. That job always made me anxious because it was in the days before they had the screens to protect the tellers, and I was terrified the bank was going to be held up.

One day we got a call from the police. They were following a suspect who'd probably be coming in shortly to bank some money. If he came in, we were supposed to act normally, not tip him off, deal with him just as we would any other customer, but instead of putting his money in the box where we usually kept the notes, we were supposed to put it into a paper envelope, to help preserve any fingerprints. I was terrified when I heard a criminal might come into my branch. I imagined some hard-core crim coming in with the cops chasing after him, guns blazing, the full action-movie scenario.

That morning was particularly quiet, there was no-one else in the branch, and I broke out in a cold sweat worrying about what would happen when this guy arrived. My booth was the last in the row, and I tried to reassure myself that even if he did come in he probably wouldn't come to me. When he finally turned up at the branch he walked straight towards me. Nothing happened, of course: no-one got shot. He banked his money and walked out again. But I'd been so frightened at the prospect of what *might* have happened I felt physically sick. After that, I knew I had to get out from behind the counter. I just didn't have the stomach for it. So I applied for, and got, my first accounting job at Westpac.

Accounting is fine, and, as my parents like to remind me,

there are always jobs in accounting. After I graduated from uni I spent two and a half years as an accountant—first at Westpac, then at a recruitment agency—and over that time I slowly began to realise that accounting wasn't really for me. I do love a spreadsheet, but when it came to things like bank reconciliations I was always having to ring Mum or Dad and ask, 'Debits and credits, which one's which again?' (Yes, it was frightening, given that I'd got a good degree and I was in sole charge of this company's finances.) The job wasn't exactly social, either: I sat in an office with an assistant and did the books while everyone else was recruiting, and from where I sat, that looked really great. The recruiters seemed dynamic, and they were going to meetings and lunches and client conferences, and, obviously, I saw all their salaries, and knew how much money they were making. The top ones were making a killing. Attracted by how exciting it all looked, after a year as the firm's accountant, I switched to being a recruiter.

To be a good recruiter you need to be a great salesperson. You also need the time to build up experience and contacts and a reputation—recruiting is all about relationships. I'm good at building relationships, but I turned out to be terrible at recruiting. Because I was new I wasn't working on any high-end jobs. I was trying to place graduates and people who'd just left school. I'd have some kid tell me, 'I want to be a stockbroker.' And I'd have to say, 'I have the perfect job for you! It's in the mailroom at JP Morgan. If you want to be a stockbroker that's how you get there!'

Today I know that can actually be good advice, and sometimes all you need is a foot in the door at the right place. But at the time I didn't—I thought I was trying to shoehorn these poor people into horrible dead-end jobs no-one would want. But I had to get them to take the job, and then I had to convince them to stay for at least three months, or we wouldn't get paid. My candidates would ring me up and tell me how much they hated their jobs, and I totally felt for them, but I knew if I let them quit, I wouldn't get paid.

All the recruiters were paid on commission. You'd decide when you started how much salary you wanted to get paid, and our boss would advance that amount to me each week, and then at the end of the quarter add up what I'd earned in commissions, and if it was less than I'd been paid, I'd end up owing money, so I'd go into the next quarter needing to make even more. Somehow, I never seemed to make enough in commissions and found myself getting deeper and deeper in debt.

To make things worse, I already had a lot of personal debt to pay off. After I'd made the decision to quit accounting, I went on a three-month trip around the world with my best friend Camilla. We'd first met at uni in 1992 and instantly bonded over our love of neatly written detailed lecture notes (geeky, I know). We've been friends ever since and have gone through births, deaths, marriages and everything in between together. Cam is different to me. She's more conservative, more careful, but we have the same big-picture views of life. She was a brilliant travelling companion and we had an amazing time together—probably a little bit *too* amazing. I knew I was coming back to start my new job as a recruiter, and I'd seen the salaries the top recruiters were getting—some of them were making 200 grand a year—and naively I assumed that was going to be me, so I wasn't very careful with the budget while I was travelling.

I came home tens of thousands of dollars in debt, with no way to pay back what I owed. Westpac and American Express started ringing me at work and at home. I asked the receptionist to say I wasn't in if anybody called looking for me. It was horrible.

Financially, I was going backwards, fast.

Recruitment was also a high-pressure environment. We worked very long hours—early starts, late finishes and I wasn't enjoying it or making any money. I was living with my parents in Baulkham Hills, an hour's commute away. That is, when I say it's an hour's commute away, it's an hour if you leave at 7 am. If you leave at 8.30, it's a two-and-a-half-hour commute because the traffic's so shocking. Maha and I would drag ourselves out of bed at 5.30 and we'd be frantically washing our hair, doing our make-up and getting ourselves dressed and out of the house, saying, 'Oh my God, we're late! We're so late!' And it would still only be 6.30 in the morning. It's just ridiculous how long a commute can take in this town, but when you're expected to be at your desk at eight or else, that's what you have to do.

While it was the worst time for me career-wise, I was fortunate to make some incredible friendships at the recruitment agency. Julia Bradbury managed the temporary recruitment team and our paths crossed heavily for work as it was my job to do the payroll for all the temp staff. I liked Julia the second we met. I would describe Ju as sassy. There aren't too many people who I think fit that description but I think it's spot on for Ju. She's smart, she's strong, she's capable. I hadn't met Lucie at this stage, but years later when I did meet Lucie at *TT* I was immediately struck by a quality that both Lucie and Ju have in spades—they know the right thing to do in just about every situation. Sarah and I call Lucie The Oracle. Years before if I was ever stuck on what to do, I'd ask myself 'What would Ju do in this situation?' and be assured it would be the right thing. Julia was extremely close friends with Tracy Watson and Lizzie Pettit as they had all worked together at Drake Recruitment. So it was through Ju that I met Tracy and Lizzie and our friendship has grown stronger and more solid and more meaningful and quite possibly more fun with every passing year.

My recruitment days were extremely long. And my response to all that pressure was to eat. Not because I was hungry, because I was unhappy. Like so many women, I was stuck in a pattern of comfort eating, and couldn't think of any other way to make myself feel better. I'd eat white bread with butter on both sides. I'd drink copious amounts of juice. I'd eat a big bowl of spaghetti and wash it down with two Cokes. When your work-life makes you miserable you have to find your pleasure wherever you can, and I found it in food.

When I started to put on weight, it happened so gradually that I *almost* didn't notice it. First my clothes stopped fitting, so I bought new ones, and then somehow I was in a size 16 skirt, wearing it unzipped at the back because I couldn't do it up. I went from weighing 58 kilos to 94, and I was extremely uncomfortable with the extra weight.

My weight was already going up when Camilla and I went on that big trip around the world. Maha told me that on the day I came home, when she came with Mum and Dad to pick me up from the airport, she actually didn't recognise me. In her mind I'd always been tall and slender, and then she saw this person walking towards her, dressed all in white with a really dark tan, and this woman was *obese*. Then I waved and ran up to her and she realised the obese woman was me! And she thought, *Oh my*

God, Sal has ballooned. The funny thing is, I was actually feeling pretty good about myself, I'd lost a few kilos and thought I was looking okay. Actually, no.

I remember looking at a photo of myself taken around that time: it was me and a bunch of girlfriends. There were seven of them and only one of me, but I took up half the photo.

My friends could see what was happening, but they didn't want to say anything. I mean, what do you say? Camilla would sometimes say things to me like, 'Hey, we should try and get fit. Let's go on a health kick this week.' Mum and Maha were gently hinting too. I knew I had a problem, but didn't like to be reminded of it. I had to do something about my weight. I just didn't know what.

At uni, if I put a few kilos on I'd watch what I ate for a day or two and the weight would fall off again. Easy.

But when you're talking over 30 kilos, that isn't going to cut it. Naturally, I turned to magazines for advice. I tried every fad diet I could get my hands on. Nothing worked. It was always one step forward, ten steps back. And even if I started my week thinking, *I'm going to eat really well and start walking and I'm going to be really good,* the stress of my job would get to me in no time and by 10 am I'd be tucking into an extra-large satay with white rice.

It's very easy to get stuck in a vicious cycle when you're overweight: your clothes don't fit, so you go out and try to buy more, but because you feel fat, everything looks terrible on you. You feel depressed so you eat half a dozen donuts and put on more weight. I remember going with Maha to buy some suits for my new job as a recruitment consultant, and I was trying on size 16, size 18. It was horrible. They didn't fit and they didn't stock larger sizes. And because I was so broke, I couldn't even pay for them. Maha had to put them on her credit card. She was fresh out of uni, in her first job, and *she* was having to lend *me*—her big sister—money. The combination of all that weight and all that debt was overwhelming. I became really depressed because I thought I'd never get out from under it—and, what's worse, I thought no boy was ever going to like me. And then I'd eat my way through another bucket of KFC to console myself.

I was 25, I was tens of thousands of dollars in debt, horribly overweight, and in the wrong job. Something had to give.

A kickstart

One day, a girl I worked with invited me to go to Weight-Watchers with her. She wanted to lose weight because she was getting married, and I guess she thought I could use some help too. I went along, telling myself it was to support her. It turned out to be the kickstart I needed. The WeightWatchers points system made a lot of sense to me. It was simple and enjoyable and it made eating well so much easier. I picked up some useful tips about exercise too, but the most important thing I took away from it was the realisation that I could do something. If I wanted to lose the weight, I *could* lose the weight.

I started to eat better, and I tried to exercise. But my first attempts at getting fit didn't go too well at all. I got a personal trainer to train me in the mornings before I started my commute.

Because I had to leave by 6.30, I booked the trainer from 4.30 to 5.30, so I'd still have time to get dressed and get off to work. Of course, I was really overweight and really unfit, and the training, plus getting up that early, made me feel so incredibly tired that I only managed to train a couple of times. I went the first time, skipped it the second time, went the third, skipped the fourth. And if you cancel at short notice you still have to pay the trainer. The night before I'd think, *Oh my God, I'm so tired, I can't get up at 4.30 to train tomorrow.* I'd walk in to Mum and Dad and say, 'Guess what? Great news! I've got a trainer coming for you tomorrow! There's only one problem—he's coming at 4.30.'

Mum would say, 'What?! I'm not doing that!' But believe it or not, she did it. In fact both Mum and Dad had a couple of sessions with my trainer. Eventually they said, 'Sal, we're using your trainer more than you are, and we don't even want a personal trainer. And if we did, it wouldn't be at 4.30 in the morning.' It was clear I wasn't ready for that level of commitment, and so I cancelled my trainer.

Realistically, it's very hard to exercise when you weigh 94 kilos. You get puffed and you feel uncomfortable and your joints hurt. But I could walk. That was something I could manage. So I got up at 5 am and walked for an hour every day. And I began to lose weight.

My trick was to break it all down into manageable goals: forget about focusing on the 30-plus kilograms I had to lose, because that was just going to make me feel crazy. It's too huge, too hard. Just think about losing half a kilo to a kilo at a time. Okay done. Next week, try to do that again. It wasn't enough to get me into a size 10 in a hurry, but at least I was moving in the right direction. I celebrated every five and ten kilos I lost as a major achievement.

Losing weight taught me several things that would be very important later on. First, I learned that if I really set my mind to achieve something I could do it. I could stick at something—even though it was hard and relentless and unrewarding—and I would not fail and I would not quit, and I would reach my goal and feel great about it. When I finally hit my goal weight, the sense of accomplishment was immense.

The second thing I learned was that the only person who could do this was me. I couldn't expect my friends to help me or cheer me on or believe in me if I didn't believe in myself. It's like being a top-level tennis player, playing those long matches that last four, five, six hours. They're out there all alone on the court and they have to dig deep: keep going, play just one more set, one more game to get there. In my case, rather than charging down a Grand Slam title, it was getting through one more restaurant meal without buckling, or getting up for one more 5 am start. I admired that kind of mental toughness, and when I lost weight, I discovered that I had it too.

Later, of course, I was going to need it. In spades.

Another really important thing I did was get up the courage to quit the job that I hated—it was torture, and wasn't getting any better. As soon as I resigned, I felt as if a huge weight had lifted off me. All that stress was finally gone. It was like losing an extra five kilos in a single day. For someone who's almost incapable of quitting, it was an important step. Sometimes, if something's doing your head in, it's okay to stop.

◆ ◆ ◆

I had no job to go to, no idea of what I'd do next. I had no money, I was still living at home, and I was massively in debt. I felt lost, and didn't know what to do with myself. I had to find work, any work. When my sister found me a job stuffing envelopes in the dealing room at Bankers Trust (BT), I took it. Although I was probably earning less per hour than I had been when I was selling T-shirts at Sussan, it seemed like the right thing to do. BT was a great funds management firm with an impeccable reputation, and it was a foot in the door. I had to try not to think about all those years I'd spent getting a university degree.

At the same time, I tried my hand at modelling. I did it for about six months, and in that time got an Emirates TV commercial and a few catalogues. The Emirates job paid well and I knew I was lucky to get it. But I didn't really like the agency I was with, and later I heard that the Emirates ad was being run again, which meant I should have been paid an additional fee. The way it works with modelling is that the client pays the agency, and then the agency pays the model. In this case the woman who ran the agency had pocketed the cheque. It was enough to convince me that the industry—or at least her little corner of it—was really dodgy and it wasn't worth persisting.

A more compelling reason for giving up modelling was that I was offered what my parents would call a real job. After I'd been temping at BT for about six months, I scored a job in Funds Management, working as an equity fund business manager. It was exciting and dynamic—nothing like my accounting job was—and I loved it!

◆ ◆ ◆

A surprising upside of working at BT was that the corporate culture was extremely sporty. At lunchtime everyone went running. It was what they did.

Never Stop Believing

At first I thought, *That's not me. Absolutely not. No way. I wasn't built for running.* I'd never been sporty as a kid. I'd played netball, but because I was tall I'd usually been the goalkeeper, so never had to run around. I was that girl at school who always had a note for PE, always had a fake ankle injury. When people had to pick teams, I was picked last. You could see both teams thinking, *Oh not her. We don't want her. She's hopeless.* That was me. When the PE teacher said, 'OK, for a warm-up, two laps of the oval everyone!' and everyone did their two laps, and then they'd all be standing around waiting to start the next thing but they couldn't because I was still trying to finish. I was always miles behind everyone else.

Swimming carnivals were a special form of torture. I was a terrible swimmer and never entered any of the races, but in sixth grade one of the teachers convinced me I had to do it. I chose the shortest race available. I got on the blocks, although I couldn't dive—to this day I'm still terrible at diving—did a kind of bellyflop into the pool, and then tried to swim. It was a freestyle race, but I was doing a dog-paddle at best. Everyone finished and I was still only about halfway along the pool. The next race was about to begin, the kids on the blocks, waiting for me to finish. A teacher walked alongside the pool next to me and shouted encouragingly: 'Come on, Sally, come on, keep going, keep going!'

That was me and sport. Embarrassing is not the word. I was disastrously unfit. Epically unfit. If there had been an anti-Olympics for the unsporty I would have been the champion.

By the time I started my job in finance, I'd managed to get my weight down to around 70 kilos, and I knew I could be doing more. I saw all these people around me running every day and I thought, *You know what? That's what they do here. I'm going to try it too.*

I opened myself up to the possibility of learning to run and getting really, properly fit. Initially I was pretty hopeless, and it was actually embarrassing because everyone was such a good runner. But I discovered that one of the secretaries was at the same level as me, so she and I would meet at 6 am in the city, and we would run. We figured if we could only run 100 metres, then walk 100 metres, then run another 100 metres, there was no-one in the park to see us so it didn't matter. Maha was also working at BT, so I dragged her along as well. This is what always happens in our relationship: whatever I'm into, I inevitably end up dragging her into it too, saying, 'It's really good for you! You'll love it! Trust me!' Often she'll have to be dragged kicking and screaming, but I usually get my way. And we always end up laughing about it afterwards. Eventually I got to the point where I didn't feel embarrassed to run at lunchtime. I still wasn't very fast—it was jogging and it was a little bit ploddy—but at least I was doing it.

It was my first major step towards getting really fit, and it was hard, but I learned to love it.

There is a four-and-a-half-year age gap between Maha and me and for most of my childhood I found her to be an annoying interference in my life. A younger sister. What good are they *anyway?* I would wonder. Brothers. They're far more handy. An older brother even better so he can bring all his good-looking friends over. But a younger *sister?* The unhappiness was exacerbated by the fact that she had far more toys, including far more Barbie dolls, than I ever had. I also deeply resented that Mum and Dad let her do just about everything years before I was allowed to do it. They had mellowed and I wasn't happy about it one bit. I lay the blame fairly and squarely on her. Having said all that, we got on well enough. But it wasn't until perhaps she was around thirteen and I was seventeen that we bonded tightly and I was completely and utterly hooked.

What the *hell* had I been thinking? An older brother? What good is that? As if he can come for manicures. As if he would take the same shoe size. As if he wanted to eat popcorn and watch rom coms. As if he could ever fill my heart with as much joy, love and happiness.

Together we've been through so much in the way sisters do: disease, diets, careers, clothes, friends, enemies, houses, haircuts, money, men, renovations, and a baby. We speak ten times a day, from the trivial to the absolutely vital—all of it is discussed.

Sometimes our conversations sound like this:

Me: 'So I was thinking about that thing–'

Maha: 'Yeah, totally, me too.'

Me: 'You know we should–'

Maha: 'I don't thing that's a good idea, it would–'

Me: 'Yeah, yeah, you're right, so then instead–'

Maha: 'Exactly, so will you–'

Me: 'Yeah, for sure, I'll get right on it.'

We've spent so much time together we hardly need to talk and yet we will often say at the end of a three-hour lunch, 'I feel as if we have so much more we haven't covered yet!'

◆ ◆ ◆

Towards the end of my time at BT, I started working out with a personal trainer—again—this time, something clicked. There were no last-minute cancellations or fobbing my trainer off onto my poor parents. I began strength training, I learned a huge amount about health and fitness, and I began to transform my body: I developed lean muscle and strong, slim arms. I had strength. I could do push-ups and squats and lunges. I could do sprints. I felt like I could do anything, that my body and I were connected, and that, if I treated it well, it would perform and do amazing things. That was a wonderful high, and it completely changed the way I felt about myself.

From being the girl who couldn't get round the oval without puffing, I'd become fit and powerful and strong. The sense of achievement was almost overwhelming, and it was more than just looking better and feeling better. It showed me that I didn't have to be that hopeless girl. I had the power to transform myself, and all it took was effort and commitment, combined with the right advice. It was a powerful realisation, and one that would help me through the experiences that were to come.

Once I knew what it was like to be really fit, I never wanted to give that up again. I think that's one reason being diagnosed with cancer came as such a shock—I was fit, and healthy and in tune with my body, and I treated it well. I felt so good. I felt amazing. So how could I possibly have cancer?

I didn't understand then that *anyone* can get cancer. You can be a couch potato or a triathlete: cancer doesn't care whether you ate that doughnut or not. Cancer follows its own rules.

◆ ◆ ◆

While I was at BT, I met the man who would change my life: Marcus.

At school, the only girls who attracted any attention from the boys were the blonde-haired, blue-eyed ones—and obviously that wasn't me—so nobody ever looked twice at me. Once I got to uni, however, that changed. I started getting heaps of attention from boys, but didn't know what to do with it. As far as I was concerned, nothing had really changed: I'd finished school, had six weeks' summer holidays, and now suddenly guys were writing me love letters in class and asking me to parties. It took me about a year to even realise the rules had changed; I wasn't being ostracised, I was actually kind of popular. It was a little weird and I didn't know what to make of it. I was very shy, still trying to find myself, and wasn't interested in having a boyfriend while at uni, so I didn't really date much.

By the time I was ready to start dating, I was putting on weight and disappointed to discover no-one wanted to go out with me. That was quite a painful period for me, because all my friends were being asked out, and it was such an exciting, fun time for them. I was still socialising with my friends, of course, but I was always the odd one out—they were pairing up and I had no-one. I felt trapped and by being neither healthy or comfortable in my body, I was very unhappy. Then once I started to lose weight, and began to feel better about myself, I finally went out on some dates. I'd dated a few guys before I found someone I became a little more serious about. He was a guy I worked with at BT, and things were good, but it wasn't right long term, and I called it off. Not long after that, in June 2000, I met Marcus.

I had set up my friend Jack, a colleague at BT, with a girl-friend of mine, and it had worked out so well he wanted to return the favour. He told me he had a friend who was exactly my type, he was a lawyer, and I was going to love him. Jack organised drinks at his place and mentioned the lawyer was going to bring along some other mate of his. But all I heard was 'Lawyer! Cha-ching!' So I said, 'Fantastic, I've always wanted to date a lawyer. That sounds great!'

Saturday night rolled around and I went to Jack's place. The doorbell rang, and Jack said, 'Oh, this is them!'

I ran to the front door so I could scope them out through the peephole. There were two guys. I turned to Jack and said, 'Oh my God, perfect! Perfect! He's the one on the left?'

Jack looked through and said, 'Oh. He's the one on the right.'

Oh.

Jack let them in, and introduced us. The guy Jack had been hoping to set me up with was Yury. Marcus was his mate, and all three of them, Jack, Yury and Marcus, used to work together at Arthur Andersen as accountants.

Yury and I are really good friends now, and we laugh about the idea that anyone could think we were right for each other. He always says, 'I'm not going out with someone like you. Please! In the part of Russia where I grew up, everyone looks like you! I want someone who's the opposite of everyone I know!' These days Yury is married to a blonde bombshell, Anna—I am *so* not his type. Now I think, *That is* so *fine*! Because he's really not my type either. Nowadays, we holiday together and we're all very close. But that night it was all a bit awkward.

But I was hopeful the evening might not be a total waste of time. As soon as Marcus saw me I noticed his eyes light up, so I thought there might be something there. I flirted with him— and kept circling back trying to get him to talk to me, offering drinks, food, anything I could think of to start a conversation, but he wouldn't have a bar of it. After the initial eye contact, he'd barely look at me. (Of course that's not how Marcus remembers it. He says he wasn't ignoring me. He was just being polite and talking to the other people at the party, friends he hadn't seen for a while, because it would have been rude not to.) Whatever the explanation, I eventually thought, *I give up, this is just not happening*, and went to talk to somebody else. Then, just as I was about to leave, Marcus started to chat to me, and we had this really long, really great conversation.

On Monday, Jack said, 'Oh, Marcus has rung me, he wants to know if it's okay if I give him your number.'

'Sure,' I said eagerly. 'That'd be great.'

Jack was just being polite. Marcus had already got my phone number from Jack before he left the party.

Not long afterwards we went on our first date—lunch at Church Point. And that was it! Within the first seven or eight weeks of knowing him, I knew he was the one for me.

I remember once when we were still dating, we went to visit friends of ours, Rob and Loretta—who lived in a big house in the suburbs—and on the way back, I said to Marcus, 'I really want that.'

'You want a big house in the suburbs?'

'No, I really just want to have that life like Rob and Loretta, you know. Be settled together. I just feel like things are taking ages.'

He looked at me and said, 'It's been eight weeks. You haven't even met my parents!' His parents were away on holidays. 'If you could just be *slightly* patient, and meet my parents, then we can get on with it.'

Afterwards I thought, *I can't believe I said that out loud!*

Marcus proposed after six months, and we were married six months later, in June 2001. It was a year to the day after we met.

We got married in the Rose Gardens at the Botanical Gardens. It was a simple ceremony with a celebrant, although it almost didn't happen—I was running late (about 45 minutes late) because I was still having photos taken at home with Mum, Dad and Maha, and the celebrant kept threatening to leave because she had back-to-back weddings lined up. But I made it in the end.

We'd decided to write the vows ourselves, which caused me a lot of angst. Marcus had suggested we should go away and write them separately. Being the kind of person who needs to get things done right away, I got on my computer and fired up a search engine—these were the days before Google was popular—and started looking for vows online. I wanted to research them thoroughly so I'd know what I needed to say. And I found a series of different things and cut and pasted them together until I'd formed a combination I was happy with. I kept asking Marcus, 'Have you done yours?' And he kept saying, 'No, the inspiration hasn't come.' A few more days went by. Inspiration still hadn't come. I was becoming more impatient. I needed to get this ticked off my to-do list. For me, this story sums up the differences in our temperaments. When there's a deadline, I feel like I *must* stick to it; whereas Marcus will say stop focusing on the deadline, inspiration comes when it's ready.

Finally he rang me and said, 'I've got it.' I grabbed a pen, he read his words out to me, and I copied them down. And when he'd finished I thought, *Oh shit, that's so good.* And then he asked, 'So what have you got?'

I was so embarrassed. Even though I'd really thought about it while I was doing it, my vows were still kind of Hallmarky. There was no personal touch—there wasn't anything from within. So we went with the vows Marcus had written.

I still have the piece of paper with the vows scrawled on it, and for years I've carried the printed version of them with me in my wallet. I love our vows, Marcus wrote them so beautifully.

And as the finishing touch, Marcus sang 'Amazing Grace' all alone, unaccompanied, no music to back him up. It was absolutely phenomenal. Beautiful. All of our guests were crying.

We had the reception at Fort Denison. When I was a kid living at Castle Hill, every Sunday was picnic day. Mum and Dad would always take us somewhere different—like Lane Cove National Park or Watsons Bay or Clifton Gardens. And every Sunday we'd drive over the Harbour Bridge, I would look out at Fort Denison, and wonder, *What is that thing?* As the years went on, I'd look at it and think, *That would be such a good place to get married.* I don't think I realised then that it used to be a prison. To me, it looked like a romantic castle but it was closed to the public. The year we became engaged Fort Denison was opened for events. I booked it for our wedding reception, and I'm so happy I did, because it was such a unique, special place. I've never been to another wedding there. We organised a boat to take all our guests across and bring them back again.

Here's the thing about me: even though it was a beautiful wedding, and everybody had a wonderful day, at the time, and for a long time afterwards, I couldn't accept that it had been a gorgeous wedding and appreciate it for what it was. I had to critique it; I just can't help myself. Everything I do, I mark out of ten. Even our wedding! For the record, I gave it a six out of ten. And to this day, Marcus still teases me about it. This was long before I started attending a lot of events, but I rated our wedding the way I'd rate a work function: I was really happy, but I think the speeches were a bit long—minus one point. Okay, I also wasn't really that happy with the entertainment—minus two points. And I didn't get enough time to dance—minus another point. Okay, that leaves my wedding with a total score of six. That's how I rated everything in my life.

And it was crazy, because I couldn't treat myself the same way I treated other people. If someone cooked a meal for me, I'd say, 'That's fantastic! I love it and I'm so excited about it.' I'd look for the good in everything, especially when it's something done out of love. Whereas, if I cooked a meal for my friends, or even for myself, I'd always give it a mark. I always had to judge. I was incredibly hard on myself about everything, and I couldn't see it.

Metamorphosis

My marriage to Marcus sparked a new period of transformation in my life. I think one of the reasons it was so transformative was because we're so different from each other. Sometimes I look at him and think, *I don't even understand how we got married because we're so different.* If you asked Marcus what his favourite topics of conversation were, they would be history, religions of the world, science, philosophy ... Whereas if I never spoke about any of those things ever again, I would be happy.

We approach new things in very different ways. When we meet someone for the first time, I absolutely love them—I love everyone!—until they do something wrong, or say something I don't like, and then they start to come down in my estimation a little, until the feelings reach a more normal level. Marcus can meet the same person, and I'll be talking about how much I love them, and he'll say, 'I don't know, I haven't got to know them yet.' I think everything's marvellous and exciting until proven otherwise; whereas he thinks everything needs to be substantiated, the evidence weighed, before you can make up your mind.

We're different in other ways too: if we want to go on holiday or buy a car, I'll go out and do tonnes of research and look at a million different options; whereas he'll just go to people he trusts, ask for their opinion, and then make a decision.

But we are in sync with a lot of other things that are fundamental: our values and our morals, and what we want from life. And I think over time we've started to become more in sync in many ways. Most of the time, I think we get along just because we laugh a lot.

One very important difference between us is our family background, and the attitudes it bred in us about our paths through life, particularly our careers.

My parents were naturally cautious people who had always worked for large companies in secure jobs. That's what they knew, that's what all their friends did, and they couldn't imagine an alternative. Marcus's parents had always been more entrepreneurial. They started their own business, which has grown and been successful for amost 40 years now. Within their company, they'd come up with and tried many new ideas. It had never occurred to me that you could live your life like that—have an idea, back yourself and just do it—but to Marcus it seemed unsurprising. He'd grown up surrounded by people who had their own businesses and to him, this was normal.

Marcus has a great deal of courage, in so many ways; the

courage to see what he wants, decide to do it, and then follow it through. He has the flexibility to succeed in any kind of environment: he has the structure and discipline required for a corporate job, but enough courage and bravery to be entrepreneurial. I had never known anyone like that before. A great thing about him is he's not afraid to take risks or to encourage other people to take them. He's not reckless, but he's not going to find a million reasons why he wouldn't succeed and shouldn't try. His attitude has always been, to hell with what makes sense, sometimes you just gotta go with your instincts and follow your dreams—and, look, if it doesn't work, you can try something else. At least you won't die wondering. For him, that would be the worst thing: to go to his grave thinking, *I could have . . . but I didn't, and now I'll never know.*

No-one in my life had ever thought that way before. He believes dreams are something you should try to realise, not ignore because they seem too risky.

Many of us have that spark inside—the possibility of something wonderful—but it takes someone brave to come along and give us that first push. We need someone to say, 'Yes, this is possible, you can do this. Give it a go.'

Once I received that first encouragement from Marcus, that was all I needed. Everything else I found within me. I know without him I would never have had the courage to take even a single step towards realising my dreams.

♦ ♦ ♦

When Marcus and I married in June 2001, we both had steady jobs in large organisations: I was at BT, Marcus was at NAB; we were making a decent living and were keen to buy our first home as a couple. Marcus had managed to put together a deposit for a house through the sale of his coffee business and some advantageous property deals he'd made before we were married.

Early the following year we found a house in Kirribilli we loved. It was too big for us, but Marcus was very clear from the start that a family was part of the plan, and I'd always imagined myself with a huge parcel of kids someday. We decided we'd buy it, sit tight, and when the time came, fill it with kids. But it was expensive—more expensive than we could afford—and when we decided to buy it, Marcus said, 'If we do this, we have to stay in our jobs. We can't just leave. We can't afford to. We're going to be working to pay for this house forever.' We solemnly agreed that there would be no question of either of us switching jobs.

Within months I was becoming restless.

I loved my work, but I'd reached a plateau: either I stayed at my current level until my boss retired and then, maybe, I could be promoted; or I could take a step to the next level and become an equity analyst. That would have been a really interesting job and the money was fantastic, but the guys and girls who do that are regularly pumping out 15-hour days. I wasn't sure I was ready for that kind of commitment. BT was also going through a period of upheaval; the company had been bought and sold, there were a lot of internal changes, and it looked like we were all going to be made redundant. I began to wonder whether I should consider trying something completely different.

All those dreams I'd had about working in a world of glamour and beauty and excitement, being on TV with beautiful people, came back in force. I'd spent my 20s moving around different careers, trying to find one that fitted, and there'd been positive things about all of them (well, nearly all of them) but something in me wasn't satisfied. Inspired by Marcus, I'd begun to realise it wasn't enough for me to have a job that was safe and well paid. I wanted to feel really passionate about what I was doing. I wanted to be able to throw my heart and soul into it. And I wanted a chance to be in the spotlight, and to prove that I belonged there.

I'd already been through one transformation: with my body, losing weight and getting really fit for the first time in my life. It was time for another metamorphosis: with my professional life.

When I told Marcus I wanted to become a TV presenter, he shook his head over the whole house debacle, but said, 'If you've got a dream, you have to have a crack. You can't die wondering. But we'll have to sell the house.'

At the start of 2002 I returned to modelling. Although my earlier experience hadn't been entirely positive, I decided at 28 years old, practically geriatric for a model, it wasn't too late to have another shot.

Lizzie, one of my besties, had worked as a model years before in Japan, and she loves the razzle dazzle of showbiz possibly more than anyone I know. I knew she was the right person to come with me to see five or six different modelling agencies. They all asked, 'How old are you?'

I asked Lizzie if she thought I could get away with 22, and she said 'Oh darling of course!' That's why I love Lizzie, she's so kind to me, even if it's a lie!

'Twenty-two,' I told them, perfectly straight-faced.

I must've got away with it because I found an agency. I signed with Gordon Charles. He told me, 'You've got quite a commercial look. You're not going to do *Vogue*. But you'll probably get catalogues and commercials.' That was enough for me. And he put me on the books. Then BT was sold, our division wound up, and we were all made redundant, and I received a payout that would sustain us for a few months so I could begin modelling full-time.

What that actually meant was going to regular castings.

The agency would ring and say, 'They're casting for a tooth-paste commercial' or 'They're casting for a catalogue' so I'd dress up, attend the casting, show them my book of photos and do whatever they wanted me to do. If you've seen those episodes of *Next Top Model* where they send the girls out to five different go-sees in some foreign city with nothing but a map, you know the drill. I'd have days where I went to seven, eight, nine castings in a day. I'd be driving from Darlinghurst to Surry Hills to Alexandria to the Northern Beaches, all over the place, trying to win these jobs. And of course no-one pays you to go to castings. You only get paid if you score the job. More often than not, I wouldn't get the job. And everywhere I went they'd always be running late.

Sometimes they'd tell me they wanted a certain kind of look, and that I should dress accordingly. I was a bit of a goody-two-shoes and I'd always follow the instructions to a tee. I'd have it all in the back of the car—a business suit and sports gear and mumsy clothes or whatever else they wanted to see—and I'd dress myself and do my hair and make-up so carefully. After a while it dawned on me that the girls who were a bit more seasoned never bothered to turn up dressed for the part, that's not actually what gets you the job. You're either going to get it or you're not. It doesn't matter whether you brought your yoga pants or your corporate outfit. If you have what they're looking for, you'll get it.

Usually they're looking for someone who can do some very specific thing. Once I went to a casting for a job for an American TV station. They were shooting it here, and they said, 'We want someone who can hula-hoop. Can you hula-hoop?'

'Oh yeah, yeah, yeah, definitely.'

'Okay great! Do you mind showing us?'

They passed me a hula-hoop and I started hula-hooping frantically, working up a sweat and thinking, *Oh my God oh my God, I might actually have a chance!*

Then they said, 'That's pretty good. Do you know how to belly-dance?'

Now, conveniently, I actually do. It's not great. It's not technically perfect, but it's passable. 'Oh my God. Yes, yes, of course I can!'

But the people at the casting obviously didn't know much more than I did, and loved my belly-dancing, 'That's so impressive. That's amazing!' they said.

I was there hula-hooping and belly-dancing for about 45 minutes, and they seemed really keen on me. They kept asking, 'Are you free next week? Are you *sure* you're free next week?'

Definitely, *definitely*. 'I'm free next week.' I was free for the next five years. I had no jobs booked.

That night I went home to Marcus and said, 'You won't believe what I did today. I think I've got this job and it pays really well and it's marvellous.'

I told him about everything I'd had to do for them, and by the time I'd finished Marcus was rolling around on the floor laughing, saying 'Oh my God. Do you think they really need any of that for the commercial or do you think they were just laughing at you?'

And I thought, *Oh my God, maybe they were.*

Needless to say, I didn't get the job.

It's like the old line: 'Dance monkey dance'. That's what you have to do sometimes to get the job. You can't be too worried about dignity if you want to be a model. Some of the things they ask you to do are ridiculous.

There were times when it was tough to keep a sense of humour. I'd turn up and see the girls who were there for the same job, and couldn't help comparing myself. I'd start thinking, I should be skinnier, I should be blonder, I should be prettier. For someone like me, who had a long history of being a little insecure about my looks, it was probably not the ideal job. Every day was like trying to get that job at Sportsgirl, turning up and getting rejected.

Modelling is really tough. It's all about how you look, and you have absolutely no control over the outcome, no real way to monitor how well you've done, no ability to improve. You either book the job or you don't. I'd come home from a casting call and Marcus would ask me how it went—and I'd never know. I'd go to a casting and think it had gone amazingly well, the people would tell me, 'Definitely, wonderful, we'll call you.' But they wouldn't call, and I'd find out the job went to someone else. At other times, they'd glance at my book and then at me and say, 'Okay, thank you.' And next day they'd ring to tell me I'd booked it.

I did win some modelling jobs. I booked catalogues that paid decently, and I hit the jackpot with an ad for Oral-B. I turned up to the shoot, did the ad and they gave me a nice little cheque for $3000. I thought I was so cool and so rich. And what I hadn't realised was that cheque was just my performance fee for the shoot day. There was also a usage fee on top of that, which meant that every time the ad ran, I was paid. Plus this was an international campaign and I received a separate payment for each region—the States, Europe, South America. After twelve months were up, they ran it again, and the cheques rolled in. I felt so lucky to have won that job, and it was really from nothing more than having good teeth and a half-decent face. The money that one ad brought in really helped us.

Jennifer Hawkins was with the same agency, and long before she became famous we did a few jobs together and developed a friendship. One job was an important campaign for Rosehill Races. Another was a job for Harvey Norman, walking up and down Martin Place holding cardboard cut-outs of a new kind of flatscreen TV. It was just awful. The job was supposed to last two days, but after a couple of hours—with all the businessmen watching us and yelling, 'Hey, nice set!'—we agreed we weren't coming back for the second day. As we were saying goodbye, Jen told me she was going off to do something a little bit different. She said, 'I don't know what'll happen but hopefully it'll be a good experience.' It was the Miss Universe pageant. And a week later, she was crowned Miss Universe.

Jen and I often cross paths and it's always great. It makes me so happy to see how well she's done. One of the first stories I did when I got to *Today Tonight* was an interview with her, and as soon as I walked in the room, she looked at me and I looked at her, and I felt so proud of her—of both of us, really—and so happy. Because we both knew how hard we'd worked to achieve our goals. I knew Jen when she was driving up from Newcastle to attend castings, and cheerleading on the weekend.

◆ ◆ ◆

After I'd been modelling for about six months I realised I couldn't keep pretending I was 22 or 23. More importantly, I wasn't finding it terribly satisfying. I wanted to do something that showcased more of my personality, and allowed me to be myself, rather than just a face or a body in someone else's story. That's when I decided to have a real crack at TV.

Around that time I'd run into friends and they'd say, 'What are you up to?'

'I'm trying to get into television.'

'Whoa! Right.'

And I'd say, 'Yeah, I know, it's crazy. But that's what I want to do.'

Then they would nod, and say, 'So do you know anyone in TV?'

'No.'

'Do you have any experience?'

'No.'

'Have you studied it?'

'No.'

They'd nod again, and smile, and say, 'Riiight.'

I understood. It was like I'd suddenly decided I wanted to be an astronaut. And my friends definitely had a point: I had no relevant experience or training or contacts. I had no easy way in. If you opened the employment section of the newspaper—this was in the days before Seek—there were no job ads for TV presenters. But I wasn't going to let that put me off. People had laughed and said, 'Riiiight!' when I told them I was going to lose 30 kilos. But I'd managed that. And I was determined to pull this off, too.

My first stop was my agent, to see if he could give me some

guidance. He was quick to tell me about the models he repre-
sented who'd made it on TV—Jen wasn't on TV then, but he
had some other girls who were—but he was a little vague about
how they'd actually got there. Although he didn't come out and
say it, I imagined he thought it was a miracle I'd landed that
Oral-B job, and I should be grateful for that and go away quietly.
I could tell he rated my chances of breaking into TV as pretty
close to nil.

It wouldn't be the first time I'd experience that attitude. And
I didn't let him put me off. I knew I was just going to have to
work it out on my own.

I found a TV course run by a company called TV Pro Global
in Chatswood. I had to audition to get in, although looking back
I suspect they would have let anyone in if they were willing to
pay. I told them I wanted to work in entertainment. For my
audition they got someone to pretend to be a celebrity, and
I had to interview them. It was my first real attempt at it,
and I was really surprised by how good I was. I wasn't particularly polished, but I wasn't nervous at all. I felt great in front of
the camera. I just loved it.

'You were great,' they told me. 'You can do the course.'

So I did, and I started to learn some presenting skills, and
they helped me put together a show-reel.

When you sign up for these courses, they always tell you
they're going to help you find a job, but they don't. They can't,
because there are no advertised jobs.

Once I'd finished the course, all I could do was get copies of
my show-reel copied onto videotapes and send the tapes out to
every TV show and production house I could find.

A show-reel is a TV resumé, a series of segments showing

the different things you can do. When you've actually got a real TV job, it's a mix of all the segments you've done that showcase your work. When you're a beginner and you haven't ever done anything, you need to go out and replicate those segments. For example, if you wanted to show yourself talking about healthy eating, you'd have to organise a cameraman and a sound guy, write your own scripts, and find somewhere to film, because it can't be in your apartment. So, you go to your local fruit shop and say, 'Hi, do you mind if I stand here near the apples and film something?' And it's awkward when you're not really from a TV station. A lot of people don't want their businesses filmed. Then you'll try and do something actiony to show that you can do something and talk at the same time—I've got some footage of myself riding a skateboard. Once you've filmed your segments, and paid the cameraman and the sound guy, you then have to find an editor to put it all together. Multiple copies of your reel are an additional cost.

When I started out, everything was on VHS. Later DVDs came around and I really wanted to show that I was cool and committed to this career. So I stepped it up and had some DVDs burnt. I commissioned a graphic designer to create labels with a picture of myself so that they'd look professional.

I was pouring thousands of dollars into copying and sending videotapes and DVDs that no-one ever watched. No-one ever called me back. I'd ring up all the places on my list and ask, 'Just wondering if you got my show-reel?' And no-one would ever know who I was.

Now I know from being on the inside how many thousands of show-reels come in. You think yours is the only one, or maybe there's a handful of others. But there are hundreds every day.

It's no wonder no-one ever calls you back. They'd never get any work done.

I was getting nowhere, but I wasn't willing to give up. I kept signing up for courses, and at one of these someone mentioned a show running on Channel 31. The show is called *Joy's World*.

Joy's World, run by Joy Hruby, who's in her 80s, has been running on community TV for more than 20 years. It's a collection of segments presented by different people—and it's the weirdest thing you've ever seen. There'd be a guy doing a piece on taxation, then someone else would do something with a puppet. After that a story on herb gardens. There was no money for editing and no possibility of re-takes. If you made a mistake it went to air. It was like live TV. And if you were keen, you could go and see Joy and audition for a spot.

Joy's World is filmed every Saturday morning at the South Sydney Leagues Club. I got there at 9 am and already there were people there drinking, and there was a transvestite behind the bar, and off in a corner were the budding TV stars. It was an odd combination, a mish mash of alcohol, gambling and TV wannabes all in the same room on a Saturday morning. You had to come along for a few weeks to get a feel for the show before they'd let you audition. And this is how crazy the world of TV is: no-one was getting paid on *Joy's World*. There's probably no audience but you still have to beg to get a gig.

Eventually Joy let me on, and I had to find somebody to interview. Do you know how hard it is to find someone who will come out on a Saturday morning to be interviewed on a show about nothing that's watched by no-one?

I did my best. I interviewed my sister about her work-life balance. My sister worked in HR and is basically a workaholic.

Marcus had owned his own coffee brand, so I interviewed Marcus about coffee. I got my friend Yury, the man my friend Jack had tried to set me up with, to come on the show and talk about his travels. Normally Yury can talk underwater, but as soon as I got him in front of a camera he froze.

'So, Yury, what was it like when you were in Uzbekistan?'

'Well . . . there's a lot of culture and . . . churches.'

'What about when you were in Russia?'

'Well . . . there's a lot of culture, a lot of churches.'

Every week I felt like I was learning more and more, and gaining valuable experience. Looking back, I realise I wasn't actually *that* good; but at the time I could see a progression. I'd watch each show as it went to air, tuning in so I could critique myself and work out how I could get better.

Often it's just little things that you don't realise you're doing. I used to nod frantically all the time—because I was so interested in what I was being told—but I realised it made me look like I had this wild twitch. So I had to train myself not to do that.

Every week I was getting a little bit better. But I wasn't making any money, it wasn't a real job, no-one was watching, and I was still getting nowhere fast.

Living within

our means

As you read this, you're probably assuming that I could do all this because I didn't have to worry about money. You probably think my parents were supporting me, or Marcus had a great job, so it wasn't an issue. I wish that were true.

Six months after we'd bought the house in Kirribilli—the one we could barely afford on *two* salaries—I was made redundant by BT. I was modelling a little bit and trying to get into TV, but was hardly bringing in anything. Less than a year later, Marcus left his job at NAB to start up his own finance business. From two secure jobs, we were down to none. Instead we had two start-up businesses, with all the costs that involved, and not much coming in—at all. Times were tough.

I've always been a fairly driven kind of person—I've always felt the need to do more, work harder, keep proving myself—but now I found I was lifting the bar even higher. When you add major financial pressure to the urge to succeed, nothing you do ever feels as though it's enough. The ultimate goal was career satisfaction, but the short-term goal was survival: living from one bill to the next. Even that wasn't easy. I'm not the kind of person who can just relax and go with the flow when things get tough. I was desperate to make this TV thing work, but there seemed to be endless money going out—on courses, DVDs and postage, on the video camera I hired so I could practise every day—and nothing coming in.

I realised I was going to need a back-up plan, in case TV didn't work. I decided I'd try and build up a side business as a personal trainer because I loved my own training so much and was so inspired by it. I also hoped it might help me get into TV. Back then there was a TV show called *Body and Soul* that was affiliated with a newspaper liftout of the same name. I loved that show and dreamed of being on it. Maybe I could communicate my passion for health and fitness, and somehow translate it into a TV career. I was trying to think from every angle and find my niche, find my way in.

But there are start-up costs involved in becoming a personal trainer: you have to do courses (expensive ones) and you have to get certified, you have to join gyms, you have to advertise, you have to get insurance—and it all takes time and money. A *lot* of money.

Eventually I did achieve my certification as a personal trainer and built my business from scratch. I would run it until my third year at *Sydney Weekender*—it did quite well.

To make things even more complicated, not long after Marcus started his new business, he got sick. He was struck by Bell's Palsy, a form of facial paralysis caused when the blood flow is cut off to the facial nerves and the nerves die. It happened very suddenly and meant that Marcus couldn't control any of the muscles down one side of his face. It was awful: he couldn't blink, couldn't eat or talk properly. He was off work for two months, he lost a huge amount of weight, and that led to medical complications. There were endless appointments with doctors, eye specialists, and neurologists. It was an incredibly stressful time for us, emotionally and financially. Marcus was so unwell, and I just had to try and make sure I kept everything together—earning money, paying the bills, paying the mortgage, running the household, organising everything—so he could have a chance to recover.

It was the first time either of us had ever had to deal with a serious health crisis, and an experience like that can sometimes break a relationship. It came close to breaking ours. Even before he got sick we'd been arguing a lot, and that really scared me. I grew up in a house where there was no confrontation. My parents didn't argue with each other and I didn't argue with them, which was lovely in a way, but it meant that I had never learned how to express my negative feelings—and that started to become a real problem for us. It also meant I had some unrealistic ideas about what goes on in a marriage. I began to think, *Oh my goodness, I've made a mistake. Our marriage is all wrong. We probably should just get divorced. This is not how it's supposed to be. It's supposed to be a fairytale. You're supposed to get along perfectly all the time and be ridiculously in love—permanently.* And things got more and more difficult between us, to the point where I began to think, *I've made a big mistake. I don't think I can make this work. I need to leave. We need to get divorced.* And then, just a couple of days later, Marcus got sick. I thought, *Well, I can't leave now. I'll wait till he gets better, he's back on his feet and then I'll go.*

But I was lucky in the man I'd chosen. Unlike me, Marcus is very good at identifying and articulating his feelings, and gradually, over time, he taught me how to do it too. Marcus would ask if I was upset with him because he was sick, and I would tell him of course not, how could I blame him for being sick, I wasn't upset with him. Marcus knew me, he could tell I was upset, and he told me we should talk about it. But for a long time I couldn't. It was a very difficult thing for me to learn: how to be honest with someone when you have something uncomfortable to say. But, as he was always pointing out, it's better to say what you're feeling and get it out there than let it all keep simmering away under the surface until it explodes, and the situation is beyond repair.

Gradually I learned how to argue, and how to do it in a healthy way: expressing how I felt, acknowledging those feelings and moving on. It was a difficult process, and it was a period of real personal adjustment for us as a couple. We had so many arguments during that time, and I'd never quarrelled so much with anyone in my life—it's crazy to think I could've got to 30 without arguing with anyone. For the first time I understood that arguing didn't have to mean something was wrong with the relationship. The point of arguing was to move forward: I had to learn to say what I felt so we could make things better between us. And I'm so grateful to Marcus for showing me how to do that.

Now I can see we were lucky, because that crisis forced me to learn some skills that helped make our relationship stronger, which meant we were much better prepared when a far greater health crisis came along: my cancer.

◆ ◆ ◆

With neither of us earning the kind of money we needed, we could no longer afford our dream house. We slipped further and further behind with the mortgage payments. My parents tried to help us out, but in the end we realised that hanging on to the house was killing us. We decided to cut our losses and sell. It was devastating; luckily in the end we came out about even, but there was no way we could hang onto it any longer.

Looking back, I can see that we bought that house for the wrong reasons. We were newlyweds, and wanted to make each other happy. Marcus thought he was giving me what I truly wanted—the whole suburban package with the big house. I thought it was a beautiful house and loved it, but it wasn't the key to my dreams by any means. I agreed to buy it because I thought that was what *Marcus* wanted: a family home.

After the house was sold, we looked at each other and thought, *How did we end up with a million-dollar mortgage on a place that neither of us wanted? What on earth were we thinking?* It was actually a really good lesson for our marriage. It showed us both that we had to be honest or we could end up in another situation like that, doing dumb things for dumb reasons.

Twelve years on, we still haven't forgotten that lesson; our home is a small two-bedroom unit in Bondi. We love it—and we're living within our means.

◆ ◆ ◆

Meanwhile, my parents were so worried about us and all the financial pressure we were under, they kept sending me job ads and asking, 'When are you going to get a real job, darling?' My mum and dad are old-school. The way they see it, they moved to this country so we could have a better life. You get a good job, you save up, you buy a house, because that's stability. The life I was living made no sense to them. My friends were telling me I was crazy too, because as far as they could see, I was getting nowhere fast.

But it's a funny thing about confidence: once Marcus gave me the impetus to get started, I didn't need anyone else to believe in me. Self-belief was enough. I knew I'd make it—because I had to. And I simply wasn't prepared to give up now.

I did another TV course run by two guys called Peter Kirk and Ben Rose, who had their own show on Channel 31 called *Not the Movie Show*. Some of their star pupils were chosen to appear on the show. I was determined to get on their show— even though, again, it was Community TV and there was no money and probably no-one except the hosts' mums were watching—but I wasn't their favourite. There were two other girls called Nicky and Kelly doing the course who they liked much better than me. Every week they'd say, 'Nicky's the stand-out,' 'Kelly's a superstar.' Me? I was okay. Just not as good. I tried not to get despondent about their lack of encouragement and instead thought 'Suck it up and keep trying'. I had to work so hard just to compete for the chance to work for free! But I fought, and I eventually made it onto their show.

Not the Movie Show was a lifestyle show, with segments on all sorts of things like food festivals, parades, and red-carpet movie premieres. Each week they'd hand out the stories, and say,

'There's a Spanish food festival on. Okay, Nicky, great, you're going to cover that. There's some red-carpet event. Kelly, you're doing that.' So those two girls would do most of the segments, and everything else was shot once a week inside a restaurant in Crows Nest. Those bits—called the links—attach the segments together, like, 'Coming up next, Nicky explores the Spanish food festival', 'After the break, Kelly meets all the latest stars on the red carpet.' They were the bits that we would do as a group—and occasionally somebody would be granted a lucky one line to say by themselves. You might get the chance to say, 'Next week make sure you join us because blah-blah-blah's on.' And every week I'd be thinking, *Is that me? Do I get it?* And you know, nine times out of ten it wasn't me.

James Tobin, who now works at *Weekend Sunrise*, also started on *Not the Movie Show*. I knew him because he lived in my building, and his cousin, who he lived with, worked with me at BT. So our paths crossed, and they crossed for many years as we both tried to make it in TV. James is a really good friend of mine and he's a great guy. And it's so nice when you see people you've worked with through the years, and with whom you've come up the ranks, become successful.

◆ ◆ ◆

For a long time it was really tough, and I was working like a dog: while I was trying to find an opening in TV, I was working just as hard on my personal training business. I got a job in a gym that paid $12 an hour, just so I could have a bit of money coming in, because sometimes $12 an hour is better than nothing. They gave me the most menial duties, and there'd be times when I'd be checking the toilets had toilet paper and

I'd be thinking to myself, I'm so glad I did those two degrees at uni . . . But I kept going—I didn't really have an alternative.

Once I got accredited as a personal trainer I had to build up some clients so I could make a bit of money. I had pamphlets printed and did letterbox drops. I walked the streets for eight or nine hours at a time, delivering thousands and thousands and thousands of pamphlets. It was the height of summer, and pamphlets are really heavy, and I'd be trudging the streets, sweating. And anyone who's ever done a pamphlet drop would tell you that the conversion ratio is so small. You'll do 10 000 pamphlets and get two calls. But I didn't care. I just thought, well, those two calls are two clients I didn't have before. I'll take it, that's great. And very slowly I built up that business.

It took a long time before I really made any money at all. Because I was so new I didn't feel I could charge the same prices as all the cool trainers who'd been around for ages. I had to charge less, much less. And people aren't afraid to ask you for a cheaper price. I think I was asking $60, which was quite cheap, and people would say, what about $50? I had no clients, I was hardly in a position to say no. So I'd end up saying, 'Okay, yes, $50,' and then thinking, Oh my God, what is happening here? I'm barely scraping anything together.

And even when I did get some clients I still had a lot of costs to cover—home bills, business bills, rent to the gyms where I trained my clients. I was always looking for ways I could become a better trainer, find more to offer. It was the attitude I brought to everything: do more, achieve more, make yourself better. I decided to become a Pilates Instructor.

Before you can become a Pilates instructor, you have to be certified, not just to teach Pilates, but to teach a group class. The certification test to teach a group is done to music. I am so bad with music, which is why I like Pilates—it's generally not to music. There's a practical and a theory component to the group instructor test, and I passed the theory, but failed the practical test because I wasn't in time with the music. The examiner came up to me afterwards and asked, 'Can you hear the beat?'

And I was like, 'Ah, no.'

She said, 'You know, I really think you should go home and actually try and listen to the beat.'

I went home to Marcus and said, 'Oh my God, I failed because I can't hear the beat.'

He bought me a metronome. I practised the routine for hours in the lounge room. And then I went back and hosted a class again, and I passed. My examiner was the same woman and she said, 'Oh, that was much better. You can hear the beat now, obviously.'

And I thought to myself, *Mmm, no. I still can't hear it, I basically just practised it so many times I knew it by heart.*

So I became a Pilates instructor. But even *that* wasn't enough to satisfy my need to keep improving myself and boosting my professional credentials. I did a Diploma of Journalism to help build my skills as a reporter, in case I should ever be in the running for a TV reporter's job. I started a Naturopathy degree, so I'd have something else to fall back on if personal training became too gruelling when I got older. I was preparing for three careers at once: the one I wanted in TV, my back-up career as a personal trainer, and the back-up to my back-up, as a naturopath. I was working every hour of the day.

To me it all made sense. Personal training was something I was passionate about, and it was a flexible career that gave me the freedom to pursue other opportunities. I could even imagine a time when they might intersect at some point in the future. There were trainers and fitness experts on TV—why couldn't I be one of them?

Every day at home I was practising presenting with the video camera I'd hired. I'd set it up in the lounge room, pull out my *Famous* and *Who* magazines, and do my own entertainment stories based on their articles. I was seeing a voice coach. I was working for free for *Joy's World* and *Not the Movie Show*. I was *busy*.

Those years really did have a profound effect on me, fuelling my need to validate myself through work. The path to success was so long, and it wasn't as if there were many milestones along the way where I could see how far I'd progressed. It was just a long, long slog, and every time I achieved something—an accreditation or I found more clients—there was always more I needed to do. I still wasn't making money, I still wasn't on TV, but I couldn't let go of the belief that if I just worked a *little bit harder*, I'd finally crack it, the break I needed would arrive. Every day, I'd wake up and think, *What more can I do?* And over time, those habits became ingrained, until my every waking thought was about pushing myself harder. I didn't even realise that's what I was doing—I was working too hard to stop and reflect. The way I saw it, I didn't have a choice. I was out there without a safety net. I just had to keep going.

What I really needed was a lucky break.

Luck is when . . .

In 2004 I went to a wedding and ran into a girl I used to work with at BT. She had gone to work at Channel 7, so I asked her for a favour. I told her I had a show-reel and wondered if she'd show it to somebody, anybody, at the network so I could get some feedback and maybe line up some work experience. My friend took my show-reel away and looked at it, and was honest enough to tell me it wasn't good enough to show anyone yet. I needed to get more experience, more polish, and then get a new show-reel done. Obviously, that was pretty tough to hear after two years of hard slog, but I kept working on *Not the Movie Show* and on my own, and six months later I put together a new show-reel. This time she liked what I'd done, and very generously showed it to the Executive Producer of *The Great*

Outdoors. He offered me a week's work experience. At last I had a foot in the door!

I still remember the first time I drove in the gates of Channel 7. I was so excited to finally be there, walking down the corridors lined with portraits of people I'd grown up watching. This was where the magic happened. I had butterflies just being there— and was hungry to be a part of it.

◆ ◆ ◆

My week at *The Great Outdoors* turned into a month. I loved it there. My job—unpaid, of course—was to do research for their stories. If they were doing something on South America, I'd go hunting around looking for absorbing details about the destination: the history, the food, the stats, the cool places. It was interesting work, and I loved being in a place where they were *actually making real television*. The first time I saw Tom Williams walking down the corridor gave me a huge thrill, and when he *spoke* to me, I felt like the earth had stopped spinning. I couldn't believe how nice he was, humble, down to earth and funny. (He still is.) There's a saying I love: 'You can tell the measure of a person by how they treat someone who can do nothing for them.' It's so apt and important to me because often when you're at the bottom, people treat you like you're at the bottom, then when you begin to rise up in the world, suddenly they want to be best friends. Not Tom. I was nothing more than a work experience girl he would most likely never see again. The respect and the genuineness that he showed me have stayed with me over the years. In fact, I remember thinking, 'I hope I am just like that one day—successful and humble.' That moment has stayed with me since then. This was the world I'd dreamed of: at last, I was walking the same halls as the glamorous people on television, although if you've ever been behind the scenes at a TV station, you'll know there's nothing glamorous about it. The offices can be shabby and the studios are often like dusty old warehouses. But it was real television, and I was in it!

When my month of work experience was over I knew I had to find a way to stay. I'd also realised there was no point hanging around trying to break into *The Great Outdoors*. It was just about the most glamorous show on TV: who *wouldn't* want a job as a travel reporter? I had no chance. I'd be better off on a much smaller show, educating myself, learning the ropes, and working my way up from there.

Sydney Weekender was perfect for me. It wasn't in prime time and it wasn't national, but it was about travel and lifestyle, a perfect fit for my interests and passions. My boss from *The Great Outdoors* put me in touch with Alan Dungey, the Executive Producer of *Sydney Weekender*, and in January 2005 Alan offered me a month of work experience.

Sydney Weekender was a fantastic place to work. It was a small team with beautiful people, and after my month was up, I begged Al to let me stay.

'I can't pay you,' Al said.

'I know, that's okay, I just really want to stay.'

'Okay, you can stay.'

I stayed for three and a half years.

◆ ◆ ◆

This was what my day looked like: I'd train my personal training clients from 5 am until 8 am. Then I'd get changed in my car and do the hour's drive from the gym in Potts Point to the Channel 7 studios, which were, back then, at Epping. I'd do a full day's work researching for *Sydney Weekender*, then I'd get back in the car, get back into my gym gear, and go back to the gym to train clients until 10 at night. Then I'd go home and go to bed.

Yes, it was gruelling. But I finally felt like I was getting somewhere.

After I'd been at *Sydney Weekender* for about six weeks, my boss, Al, asked me why I was working for him and what I wanted to do.

'I want to be on TV,' I said.

'Everyone wants to be on TV,' he said.

'I know. But I *really* want to be on TV.'

'Okay. Why don't you go out tomorrow, record a couple of lines and come show me what you can do.'

I was thrilled. It was my chance!

Oprah Winfrey once said: 'Luck is when hard work and opportunity meet.' What she meant was, you've got to do all the hard work first so that when someone says to you, *go out and show me what you can do*, you're ready. I felt like after two and a half years of *Joy's World*, *Not the Movie Show* and interviewing invisible celebrities in my lounge room, I had to be ready. It was only two lines, but this was make or break.

The next day I went out on the shoot with Mike Whitney, the host of *Sydney Weekender*. He has hosted *Sydney Weekender* since 1994. He's a former Australian cricketer whose face is instantly recognisable everywhere he goes around the country. Men love him—they want to talk cricket. Women? Well the women swoon. It's the funniest thing to watch. Women flock to Mike like seagulls to chips. They fawn and flirt and then ask for a hug because Mike's like a teddy bear. So warm and gracious, he makes everyone feel special. Mike's also famous for hosting *Who Dares Wins*. 'Dare me, Mike. Dare me,' people will say, whether we're in Taree or Turramurra. He's an Aussie icon. People always want to know whether Mike is just as outgoing in real life. And he is. He's lively, gregarious and has the funniest stories you'll ever hear. He can have you in stitches for hours until you're begging for the stories to end. I love that about Mike. He's also a softie—I hope he doesn't mind me saying that. I cry easily and often. Mike was the only other person in our *Sydney Weekender* office who was the same. If I ever shed a tear I could guarantee that Mike would be too. We'd pass the tissue box backwards and forwards to each other as we shook our heads at our inability to control our tears. We started at 7.30 in the morning, and I was so nervous about doing my lines I jumped every time someone called my name. Finally, at 6.30 pm, when my nerves had been shot to pieces, it was my turn. I recorded my two lines and then we all went home for the day.

The next day, Al said, 'Hey, I've got that tape.'

'Oh, okay. Great!' I said. I didn't ask him if he'd had a chance to watch it. I didn't want to be pushy.

A day went by. Several days. Then weeks. Al didn't say a word. I was completely freaking out, thinking I must have been so abysmally terrible he didn't even want to talk to me about it. At last, five weeks after recording my two lines, I mentioned it to Joanne Hodgson, a colleague and researcher who was showing me the ropes, and she said, 'He's probably forgotten about it. Why don't you just ask him?'

I went into his office. 'I wonder if you've had a chance to look at my tape?'

Blank look. 'What tape?'

'Remember when I did those two lines?'

Slow realisation. 'Oh.'

I'd spent five weeks unable to sleep, feeling like my life was hanging in the balance, and all he could say was 'Oh'?

He pulled the tape out, stuck it in, and watched me say my two lines. He turned to me and nodded and said, 'Yeah, it's fine.'

Fine? After all that trauma, was that all he was going to say? But at least he didn't think it was total crap.

He then told me that obviously they had heaps of presenters, and there were no positions available. But if all the other presenters were hit by a bus and they'd asked the cleaner and the cleaner wasn't available, then *maybe* I could do something.

'Okay!' I squeaked. 'That's fine!' It was all the encouragement I needed.

I continued with my five-days-a-week researching 'job'. I didn't care I wasn't getting paid. To me it was as if I was on a job that was paying handsomely, and I treated it as such.

After I'd been researching on *Sydney Weekender* for seven months, I got my first paid job. They created a three-part spin-off series called *Mike Whitney's Walkabout* and needed a researcher, and they hired me. At the end of the year, after production on *Walkabout* finished, *Sydney Weekender* lost one of its researchers, and I went back to work for them as a full-time researcher.

I worked five days a week finding new travel and lifestyle stories for Mike and the other presenters. And in addition to that, I put my hand up to work on the *Sydney Weekender* magazine that was published quarterly. It was a compilation of the best stories that had been on the show, turned into magazine articles. It was my job to pull out the old tapes, look at the script, and then turn the stories into an article. After I had been at *Sydney Weekender* for about two years, I had established a niche—I was the food, fashion and shopping specialist and I got my own little section in the magazine where I wrote about those subjects. The magazine wasn't part of my regular job, it was something I did after hours. Even though I felt overworked, I relished the opportunity to learn something new and expand my skills and knowledge.

◆ ◆ ◆

In the months of working on my income-free *Sydney Weekender* job, I was hoping and praying that a presenting spot would open up and I'd get my lucky break.

At last it came. They needed a girl to do a story at the Manly Aquarium and Waterworks. The presenter pulled out late on Friday afternoon and they needed a presenter first thing on Saturday morning. I was available. I got to do the segment. I was delirious with excitement.

It was an enjoyable story. I had to slide down a waterslide while delivering my lines. Then I patted a snake. It was a day of many firsts. I did my best, and thought I did a pretty reasonable job for a first-timer.

At the shoot I'd taken my rings off and given them to the producer so they wouldn't get lost while I was in the water, and then I forgot to get them back from her. On Sunday she rang me.

'I've got your rings,' she said.

'Oh, yeah, thanks,' I said. 'Can I get them from you tomorrow?'

'Sure. Look, I'm going to be honest with you. I saw Al last night at a function, and he asked me how you went. And I didn't want to lie to him. I told him you were terrible.'

I wasn't expecting that at all. 'Oh.'

'You've got no strength in front of the camera. You really can't present and I just don't think you're ready for this. If you want some advice, I think you should try going out to regional New South Wales, somewhere like Wagga or Goulburn, and do two or three years out there. And then maybe if you get much, much better, you could possibly come back here and try again.'

I was just floored. There was no solid constructive criticism—nothing specific about my technique that I could take away and work on—she'd just told me that everything I did was bad and I was hopeless. I hadn't expected to be perfect on my first real assignment, but I hadn't expected to have such a crushingly negative assessment of my performance either. Had I really been that bad? Had I ruined my big chance? I'd waited years for this. I'd worked years for this. The thought that it might have all gone wrong was a massive disappointment.

I hung up the phone and sobbed all night. I'd been working towards this for so long, and I had so much of my sense of self-worth riding on the outcome of this one little segment, that the thought that I might actually have been terrible was more than I could bear. This was my first real test as a TV presenter on a major network, and I knew opportunities like this didn't come along all that often. It felt like everything I'd dreamed about was hanging by a silk thread.

The next day I went in to see Al. 'The producer told me what she told you,' I said. 'And, um, I don't really know what to say.'

'I've taken her comments on board,' Al said, 'but it's up to me to decide. I'll have a look at it when it goes into editing, and then I'll let you know what I think.'

There was a six-week lag between shooting the story and editing, which usually took place the day before we went to air. I was going to have to wait six weeks to know whether I had a future as a presenter.

Those six weeks were horribly stressful. I'd sustained myself through years of struggle, hard work and sacrifice with the strength of my self-belief, but now the voices of doubt began to nag at me. Those little voices in your head that tell you you're not good enough, you don't deserve to succeed, you didn't work hard enough, you should have done more . . . For six weeks they gnawed away until I felt half-crazy.

At last, Al came back—with the good news. 'I've had a look at it, and it's fine. Of course it's not great, it's your first time, but you'll get better. I can see something in you, and I think it's going to develop.'

The day it went to air, Maha, Camilla and some other close friends came over to watch the show with Marcus and me. We had a viewing party to celebrate my first real story on a real TV show. It felt brilliant!

◆ ◆ ◆

The situation hadn't changed, though. I was still the girl they called when there was nobody else who could possibly do the job. For three months I didn't get in front of the camera again. Two months after that I got my third story, about swimming with dolphins.

Al rang me late on a Friday night. 'I'm in the edit suite and I'm watching the dolphin story,' he said.

I thought, *Oh no, here we go.*

'You've got it!' he said. 'That thing that I saw in you, that potential—it's there now. You've relaxed into yourself and you've found your groove. You're not "presenting", you're just chatting, and it's really working.'

I was so happy—actually 'happy' doesn't begin to describe it. I was elated.

'You can be on the permanent rotation. Welcome to the team!'

The memory of that phone call is still so clear. When I got the call, Maha and I were hosting a girls dinner with Lizzie, Julia and Tracy, to celebrate my birthday and Julia and Tracy selling their recruitment business. After I got off the phone and told the girls what Al had said we all cheered and went out nightclubbing. A celebration was firmly in order.

◆ ◆ ◆

It was only a chance to record two stories a month. My full-time role was still as a researcher, and I would shoot my stories on Saturdays. My friends still asked me why I'd given up a stable career and good money for the chance to earn a tiny salary and get my face on TV twice a month. But I was absolutely over the moon at how things were working out. I was a real presenter, on a real TV show.

After all that work, all those sacrifices, I was finally on my way.

Persistence pays off

Sydney Weekender was one of the best places I've ever worked: it was like a family, with no office politics, just a small, happy team. Alan Dungey, our Executive Producer, was a very special kind of boss, because he made everyone feel like equals, working towards the same goal. He never made me feel like we were boss and employee, and he's become a lifelong friend. It was so good I could see myself staying there for ten years, then waking up one day and thinking, *Oops, I forgot to leave.*

During my time on the show I learned an incredible amount and earned the kind of experience in front of the camera I'd been so hungry for. After three and a half years, however, I knew I'd learned as much as I possibly could. Even as a regular member of the presenting team my opportunities to keep learning and developing were somewhat limited, simply due to the nature of the show. I needed more on-camera time, and the opportunity to rise to bigger challenges professionally. And, even though it was an amazing place to work, I still wasn't really making a decent living. Marcus would sometimes ask me, 'How long will you keep going with this before you decide it's not realistic? You're not a full-time reporter yet and that just might never happen.'

I was outraged at the question. 'How can you ask that? I'll never quit! Don't you believe in me?'

'Well, you've been doing this for three and a half years now and three years before that. Isn't there going to be some point, eventually, when you decide this isn't going to work out?' His business had really taken off by now and I think he wanted me to work with him there.

'I can't quit now.'

There was an analogy I used quite a lot at the time. Imagine you're in a queue at a nightclub, and it's very long, and it's not really moving, but you can't ever get out of the queue, because if you decide to get back in again you'll have to go right to the back and start again. 'I just have to continue until I get there. When I get there, that's when I'll stop. It's as simple as that.'

It was time for me to take the next step and try something new.

I went to have a chat with Al. I wanted to be totally upfront with him: our industry's pretty small, and I believe you shouldn't go looking for jobs behind your boss's back. I had a job on a show that meant everything to me and I wanted to do the right thing by the person who had so kindly given me such a huge opportunity: my first real job in TV. You don't thank someone for changing your life by running off behind their back. I told Al I wanted to start looking for a new job, and I wanted to go with his blessing. Luckily for me, Al was understanding and supportive. So I started looking around to see what other opportunities were out there.

There weren't that many.

As well as *Sydney Weekender* there were four other shows in production at the Epping Studios: *Saturday Disney, The Great Outdoors*, plus two dramas, *Home and Away* and *All Saints*. I'm not an actor, so obviously the dramas were out. And I'd already decided *The Great Outdoors* was not an option. Leaving aside the question of the cut-throat competition, if by some miracle I got a job there I'd be away six months out of the year, and I doubted that my marriage could survive that strain. I was going to have to do what I'd done three and a half years earlier: choose a show, offer to do some work experience, then work hard to make my own opportunity.

As a viewer, I'd always been a fan of *Today Tonight* (*TT*) because they show the kinds of stories I love: fashion, celebrities, beauty. I'd see promos for 'the new skinny jean' or 'the dress you can wear a hundred ways' or 'the best moisturisers in the supermarket' and I'd always make sure I was home to watch them. I couldn't get enough of that kind of segment. *Today Tonight* seemed like the perfect fit for me.

Sydney Weekender had a production break over summer, and I knew I had six or seven weeks off when I could do work experience for someone else. I had been thinking about putting in a

call to *TT* when I went to Melbourne for the Melbourne Cup
with my friend James Tobin. James and I had worked together
at Community TV and he'd become a reporter for *Sunrise*.
I found myself travelling in a car from the hotel to the races with
James and Craig McPherson, the then Executive Producer of *TT*.
As soon as Craig introduced himself I realised who he was, and
I couldn't believe my luck.

'Hi, I'm Sally Obermeder,' I said. 'It's great to meet you. I love
the show and I was actually going to ring you this week because
I was wondering if I could come and do some work experience
with you this summer.'

Craig just said, 'Yeah, yeah, yeah, call me next week.'

So the next week I called him. 'Hi, it's Sally Obermeder.'

'Who?'

'We met at the Melbourne Cup, I'd love to come and do some
work experience with you.'

'Oh yeah, right. I haven't done the summer rosters yet. Call
me back in a month.'

Now after being on the inside, I know there aren't any summer rosters and he was just trying to put me off. But I didn't
know, so I didn't take the hint.

A month later I called him back. 'Hi, it's Sally Obermeder.'

'Who?'

'We met at the races. Remember me? I'd like to come and do
some work experience with you this summer?'

'Oh. Right. Yeah. Ring me in a few weeks.'

By this time it was the end of the year. Channel 7 always
throws a big Christmas party for all their employees, and when I
spotted Craig at the Christmas party I approached him and said
hello again. Would you believe it? He *still* didn't remember me.

I can't tell you how embarrassing it was to keep giving him the same spiel and he never remembered me. Any normal person would have given up.

'Hi. I'm Sally Obermeder. We met at Melbourne Cup. I wanted to come and do some work experience with you at *Today Tonight*.'

This time, to my surprise, instead of brushing me off with a 'Call me in the New Year', he started to grill me.

'Why do you want to be on camera?' he asked.

I was shocked and flustered by the question, unsure what kind of answer he was really looking for. Was he asking me about my career progression plans? I started to explain what I'd been doing at *Sydney Weekender* and where I wanted to go next, but Craig interrupted me.

'No, no, *why?* Why do you want to be on camera?' Then he spelled out what he meant. 'Most people I've met who want to be on camera have some deep-seated insecurity or personal problem. What's yours?'

So I tried to answer him by saying 'I like to connect with viewers' and 'I enjoy finding stories and sharing my experiences,' which were true, but sounded like clichés out of a TV 101 handbook. Craig wasn't interested in my textbook answers. He wanted something more personal.

Marcus is also the kind of person who likes to know the reason behind things. Sometimes he reminds me of a kid going through the 'why' stage: he's always asking me why I want to do something, why I want to go somewhere. Back when we were broke and working so hard, he sometimes used to ask me the same thing: Why do you want this so much? Why does it mean so much to you? The question used to frustrate the hell out of me, because I thought it was idiotic. I mean, the answer was obvious: just because! Over time, though, I began to understand that I needed to look deeper, to understand what it was that motivated my actions, what drove me to do what I did.

So thanks to Marcus, I did have an answer to Craig's question.

'I think I want to be on TV because I'm trying to make good,' I said. 'I was picked on when I was growing up, and I never felt like I was good enough or cool enough or pretty enough. So I think I want this because it's some kind of affirmation that I *am* good enough.'

It's funny the things that leave a mark on you. I grew up in a close, wonderful, loving family, but when I went to school I always felt different, and not in a good way. Castle Hill was very Anglo-Saxon, so I felt like the only girl with olive skin. When I was in primary school the other little girls used to pick on me; they'd shout obscenely racial taunts that are too terrible to repeat. It was kid stuff, I know, but at the time it hurt. I couldn't understand why they'd say those horrible things to me. Those girls made me feel as if there was something wrong with me just because I didn't look the same as everyone else.

Growing up I certainly wasn't crying myself to sleep every night about what a few cruel girls said to me at school. But once that idea gets under your skin—that there's something wrong with you, that you're not good enough—it can be hard to shake off. There's always some distant ideal that you're trying to live up to, and for me, it was the world of the people I saw on television. They were always poised and pretty and smiling. No-one could ever say you weren't good enough, or pretty enough, or special enough, if you were on television. If you were on television, you'd made it. Simple as that.

Looking back, it sounds like a pretty good reason for *not* hiring someone. But all Craig said was, 'Call me next week.'

So I did, and he *still* didn't remember who I was, and then when he did remember he finally told me he didn't need anyone.

It was not the answer I'd been hoping for, and I was so disappointed. I felt like I was right back where I was years ago. I couldn't get Craig to take me on for free, even with three and a half years of actual TV work under my belt.

But not long after that a job *did* come up, and my persistence paid off, because Craig remembered me. He approached James Tobin and said, 'Hey, remember that friend of yours from the Melbourne Cup? I've got a job going. I don't think she'll get it, but I promised I'd let her know. Get her to email me.'

I was so excited when I heard they wanted me to come in for an interview. I *knew* this was the right job for me. It was very different to the work I'd been doing at *Sydney Weekender*; *Today Tonight* was offering a full-time, five-days-a-week job on a two-year contract for a general reporter who could report on a full range of stories, from hard news to finance to entertainment and lifestyle. But I decided to be upfront. In addition to Craig, Sarah Stinson the then Chief of Staff of *TT*, was interviewing me. I told them my passion was for entertainment, fashion, lifestyle and beauty stories: that's what I love and that's what I wanted to do. They asked me if I watched the show and whether I could think of any stories done in that area. I happily rattled off a bunch of recent stories I'd seen and loved. I think my years of researching also worked in my favour, because it meant I knew what was involved in putting a story together. They questioned me on whether I could cope with the pace and the pressure. A nightly current affairs show is very different to a weekly lifestyle program. I can't recall exactly what I said, but whatever it was, they seemed pleased with it. I proved to them in that interview that I understood the show and I understood the audience, and my show-reel proved I could present (although later I came to realise that the *Sydney Weekender* style was totally different from that of *Today Tonight*). I walked out of the interview on such a high, because I knew I'd nailed it. That job was mine: I was 100 per cent sure.

That same afternoon, Sarah rang me and said, 'The job is yours.'

I was beyond happy. I felt as if I was floating, as if everything I'd done in my career had been for this opportunity. And now I was here I was insanely happy. I knew I had to make the most of it.

◆ ◆ ◆

For some people, getting that job probably would have been enough. National show? Tick. Prime time? Tick. Ratings-winner? Tick. I've made the team? Tick tick tick! But I couldn't rest on my laurels. I still didn't actually feel like I'd made it. It was more like I'd progressed to the next level of a game, and now I had to start proving myself all over again.

Obviously there were many new skills for me to learn, and I had to prove to Craig that I was worthy of his trust. It was time to lift the bar even higher: do more, achieve more. I was 35 years old; I felt as if I was ten years behind everyone else, ten years behind the position I should be in. After the initial elation, I felt I couldn't waste time revelling—there was more at stake than ever. This was the most significant opportunity

I'd had yet. There was no way I was going to mess this up. Whatever it took to succeed, I would do it. And then I would do some more.

◆ ◆ ◆

It was a super-steep learning curve. At *Sydney Weekender* I'd been a researcher, but the business of turning my research into an on-air story was done by the producer. My other role as a presenter was also put together by a producer. I just had to turn up and do the pieces to camera. It was a straight presenting role. At *Today Tonight*, I had to learn how to produce my own stories, how to pull together all the individual elements to create the final on-air package.

My very first story was about coffee. I'd been assigned a producer, Darren Ally, or D-man as we call him. D-man had worked at *TT* for years—he's fun, gregarious and cheeky, and always keen for a meal. We hit it off instantly and he's become a good mate. (This has been a pattern of mine ever since I left school. Everywhere I go, every time I start a new job, I collect a new group of friends, and then I carry them with me through life. I've still got close friends from uni, from the recruitment agency, from BT. I love having so many people around me who've been there through all the changes in my life, and I've loved being there for them.) It was D-man's job to get me up to speed with all the elements of my new role. He'd arranged for us to shoot that first story in a café—and I'd shot a *Sydney Weekender* story in the same café, so I felt like I was on familiar ground. The cameras rolled and I did my piece to camera. I was happy with it—this was the part of the job I was comfortable doing. When I was finished, Darren came over and said, 'That's great, excellent stuff. You did really well! . . . Umm . . . maybe . . . Umm . . . how can I say this? Maybe smile less—a *lot* less.'

I realised I was still doing my very upbeat weekend lifestyle presenter thing: 'Hey, here's something GREAT you should try!' Whereas this was a serious story about how Starbucks and other big companies were chewing up all these little gourmet coffee houses. Okay, this is serious. Not so smiley. Gotcha.

The next story was about as serious as it gets: a woman whose ex-partner had gassed their three children and himself in a car. I interviewed her and I felt heartbroken. I was at a loss. It was so wrong and so unfair. I interviewed her dad, who'd just lost his grandkids. He cried. I cried. Other reporters can do those kinds of stories, but not me. I'm openly emotional. I don't think the reporter is supposed to cry too.

After that they didn't give me any tough stories to cover. It was all lipsticks and diets and jeans, which suits me just fine.

◆ ◆ ◆

I learned a great deal in that first year: working out what we needed to shoot, organising all the people (my crew, interview subjects, models, products), then going out and shooting everything. I quickly discovered that I had to be very clear with the cameraman about what I wanted to shoot: I might be doing a fashion story, but we're a current affairs program, so I couldn't rely on the cameraman to know he needed to get the criss-cross detail on the swimsuit, or that the shoes were an essential part of the look. I had to develop an understanding of how a story fitted together, how to get the right balance between the vision and the talent, the best way to make the story entertaining and memorable. I wrote my own scripts, tying all the elements I'd shot together. Then I found I also needed to sit down with the editor and help pick the shots so the story came together exactly as I'd imagined it. Editors don't necessarily get Planet Fashion either.

Sound controlling? Maybe. But I still remembered what I'd learned from my first boss at Sussan: if you're going to do something, do it to the very best of your ability. Don't leave the details to someone else. I knew every story I put to air reflected on me. I wanted to be sure it was right.

◆ ◆ ◆

I had to step up my presenting skills, from interviewing to doing pieces to camera, but the really big challenge was that I had real responsibility and ownership of my stories from start to finish. For the first time, I felt like I was in a job that utilised *all* my skills, *all* the things I was passionate about: my love of entertainment, celebrities and fashion; my passion for presenting; but also my ability to analyse material and turn it into a great story; my organisational skills; my stamina and appetite for hard work; and my people skills. To me, that's the definition of a great job: one that lets you do all the things you love and all the things you're good at. The fact that I also got to be on TV was the icing on the cake.

◆ ◆ ◆

I also had to learn how to find stories. Sometimes Craig or Sarah would give me something they wanted me to cover, but just as often I pitched stories to them. One of the things that made Craig a fantastic boss was the autonomy and freedom he gave his team. I felt entrusted to deliver a great story. I felt that he had faith in me, and that in turn made me want to give him the best story I could. He's one of those rare people who cares only about your work. He judges you on your work ethic, your commitment, and your output. He's not swayed by how you look or publicity or hype. I was determined to show that his faith in me hadn't been misplaced.

Sometimes stories are easy to find: a Hollywood star's in town to promote their new movie, or a band's touring, so you ring up their publicist and try to get an interview.

But that's when it starts to get tricky. First, you need an exclusive. On a daily prime time current affairs show, you've got to have the news first, and you've got to have it exclusively. If it was on *Sunrise* that morning, we won't show it on *TT* that evening.

Access to the stars is always controlled by someone else: a record company, a production company, a PR agency or a manager. You have to convince them that you're going to do a better job with their star or movie or band or fashion label than any of the other journalists who are vying for access, and when you're a brand new junior reporter, that can be really tough.

When I was starting out, this was how it usually went:

Sony would announce, for example, that Britney Spears was touring. I'd ring and say, 'Hi, I'm Sally Obermeder from *Today Tonight*. We'd love to do an interview with Britney.'

'Who are you and what do you do?'

'I'm a reporter on *Today Tonight*.'

'Oh.' Pause. '*Today Tonight*?'

'That's right.'

'That could be good. Do you think Kochie could do the interview?'

'No, he works on *Sunrise*.'

'What about Kylie Gillies?'

'No. She's the co-host of *The Morning Show*.'

'What about James Tobin?'

'No, he works on *Weekend Sunrise*.'

'What about Andrew O'Keefe?'

'No. He hosts *Deal or No Deal* and *Weekend Sunrise* with Sam Armytage.'

'Oh great. Yeah. Sam Armytage, we'd like her.'

'Um, no. She's not at *Today Tonight*.'

'Oh, I see, well who hosts *TT*?'

'Anna Coren.'

'Can she do it?'

'No, she's the host.'

I may have been on a top-rating show, but because they didn't know *me* it was really hard to get access to anyone. Why should they choose me over someone like my childhood idol, Richard Wilkins, or the lovely and talented Angela Bishop, who've been in the industry for years? It was a classic double bind: you can't get the stars until you've proven what you can do. But you can't prove what you can do without access to the stars.

So, I did what I always do: I persisted until I made a breakthrough.

I'd ring up a record company, trying to get time with the latest hot act, and the record company would tell me I couldn't have them, but I *could* have some tiny little pub band no-one had ever heard of. I'd turn them down because there was no way Craig would ever put the story to air. But I kept ringing all the record and movie companies; I wouldn't give up. I begged them to give me a chance just so I could show them what I could do. I remember one promoter said, 'Okay, you can have Cliff Richard,

Sally Obermeder

on the proviso the story runs on a particular night.' I went back
to Craig and begged him to let me do it. I told him that if I did
this story and did a good job they'd give us more. Craig was
really good about it, he knew the situation I was in. He approved
and assured me it would run on the night they'd requested. I
went back to my contacts and gave them my word—it would
all go ahead as they'd requested. But when that particular day
rolled around there'd unfortunately been terrible bushfires and
Craig told me he was going to have to bump my story to another
night. I knew mine wasn't the most important story of the night;
if something major happens, the fashion or entertainment story
is always going to get bumped. I begged Craig: 'I've been calling
these people for *two years*, I *promised* them it would run, if you
bump this now they will *never* trust me again.' My story ran.

Left: Aged four, February 1977. *Right*: Aged five, with one-year-old Maha, June 1979.

Aged six, playing frisbee with Maha.

Left: With Maha in Wollongong during the summer holidays, aged about sixteen. *Right:* Sporting a great 80s hairdo at school. *Bottom*: Recruitment days.

Top: With Camilla at the Grand Canyon. *Bottom left:* With Camilla.
Bottom right: Halfway through my transformation, with my best friend Camilla.

With Marcus on our wedding day, June 2001. *Bottom*: A photo taken at our
wedding reception. It beautifully sums up my relationship with Marcus.

Top: Proud new home owners, Kirribilli, 2002. *Bottom:* During my days working for BT Funds Management.

Top left: With Jennifer Hawkins during my modelling days. *Top right*: *Sydney Weekender* publicity shot. *Bottom*: With my bestie Lizzie Pettit on her wedding day.

Top: Shooting *Mike Whitney's Walkabout* in Queenstown, New Zealand, 2005.
Bottom: Kissing a dolphin while shooting a story for *Sydney Weekender*,
August 2005.

Top: Celebrating with Marcus about an hour after I'd been offered the job at *Today Tonight*. *Bottom left:* It may look like a Chanel handbag but it's actually the cake my *Sydney Weekender* colleagues gave me to celebrate my new job at *Today Tonight*. *Bottom right*: Photo taken after my interview with Beyoncé in July 2009.

A star act

One of my first really big interviews was with the magician David Copperfield. That was a sensational experience and gave me a taste of how wonderful and surreal working in TV can be. David Copperfield has his own private museum dedicated to the history of magic, and it's filled with one of the world's largest collections of magic props, books and artefacts, including some that used to belong to Houdini. David gave me a personal tour of the museum and told me the stories behind the objects—as well as playing a trick on me with a collapsing chair that caught me by surprise, and made for some hilarious television. It was a fascinating day and the kind of experience that money can't buy.

Then we went to see his Vegas show. He got us seats in the front row, and I was his assistant for one of the tricks. That was such a thrill! I love watching magic shows on TV and wondering, *How do they do that?* I'm always looking for the strings or the body double. And when he got me up to help I thought *for sure* I'm going to be able to see how he does it.

He handed me a box with a scorpion in it. The box was right there in my hands. Then he put something over it and before I knew it the scorpion was gone and I was holding a deck of cards, and, I swear, I have no idea what happened. It wasn't like he was holding it, *I* was holding it. It's moments like that that make me love my job.

That interview worked in my favour in a number of ways. David was an excellent interviewee, heaps of fun and very cheeky. The story came together really well. It was memorable, which was great for my profile, and it meant people felt more relaxed about trusting me with a star.

My next stroke of luck was scoring an interview with Beyoncé, one of the biggest stars in the world. And once I'd interviewed her, nobody could say I wasn't ready to do the big interviews. Out of over 100 celebrity interviews I've done since then, I've only ever had two fall into my lap, and this was one of them. Matt White, the then host of *TT* and a good friend of mine, was supposed to do the interview, but he was on *Dancing with the Stars* and couldn't go to the States, so I got the call-up.

Beyoncé was on tour and we'd been given a 15-minute window to interview her backstage at the concert venue in Sacramento, California. (Fifteen minutes doesn't sound like much, but it's actually a luxury. Sometimes you might have flown around the world for the interview, and they give you only two minutes.) When we're interviewing celebrities, we like to do it in hotel suites. We order flowers and candles and dress the room up to make it look really fabulous. But sometimes it doesn't matter how many times you explain what you want to the agent or the record company, when you're there on location you just have to take what you can get.

My producer on that story was David Dutton. After my time with D-man, I was teamed with Dutton because he did a lot of entertainment stories and they knew I'd learn a lot from him and we'd get along well together. They were right. Dutton is one of my closest friends and the source of many side-splittingly funny nights. When we reached the location, we discovered we'd been given an empty room the size of a toilet, behind the main stage in the stadium, which was right next to the public toilets. You could hear *everything*. Sound is a big issue when doing an interview, but I couldn't exactly say, 'Excuse me Beyoncé, would you mind waiting while they flush?' David and I just looked at each other, convinced it was going to be a disaster. Somehow we had to make it work.

We had an hour before Beyoncé arrived, and we were panicking. She's famously punctual: not one of those celebs who'll make you wait. If she says she's coming at four, she's coming at four. We left the boys to start setting up. It was to be a two-camera shoot, which meant one camera would be filming Beyoncé, the other filming me, so the crew had to set up the gear, link it up to the sound equipment and find angles where they weren't going to be filming each other. And David and I sprinted out of the stadium to find something we could use to dress up this terrible room.

The stadium was in the middle of nowhere, so we couldn't just pop down the road to the shops. We jumped in a taxi, drove off to a super-centre and started buying decorative items: fake plants, real plants, tall plants, short plants, candles, statues, lamps. When we got back, it looked like we were doing one of those *Better Homes and Gardens* make-overs, we had so much stuff. Then we had to dress the room, and it was a mad panic. I'd shout, 'We need a plant! Get a plant!' and he'd shove a plant in a corner and I'd shout, 'No, a statue! No, candles!' In between all that I was trying to do my make-up and get dressed. I hadn't come made up. I'd figured I had an hour to get ready—I wasn't counting on going shopping for homewares.

At four on the dot, Beyoncé turned up.

And she was fabulous. There are some people who just want to be famous, but Beyoncé really has something special. She's clearly a talented artist, but she's also a businesswoman. She's driven, motivated, organised. Some celebs you talk to are just drifting aimlessly like sheep, waiting for their PR people to tell them what they're doing next. Not Beyoncé. She was completely on top of everything: she knew she was coming to an interview with us, she knew we were from Australia, she knew we had 15 minutes.

And she turned out to be a great interview subject because she was appropriately open and she didn't dodge the questions. She showed me how she does her own make-up backstage. She truly looked phenomenal. I asked her why she didn't use a make-up artist, and she said, 'I've done my make-up for so long now, I can do it just as well if not better than any make-up artist.' By the end of the interview I felt genuinely inspired and motivated, especially when she said, 'I can never *ever* not give 100 per cent—it's against my nature.' That's something I've always tried to do in my own life, but hearing it from her made me think, *Yes! I've really got to try and do that too!* I walked away from that interview thinking, *How can I take some of what I've learned from her and channel that into my own life?* She is fierce, just like her alter ego, Sasha Fierce. It's the perfect name for her.

And the toilet-flushing problem? Mostly we got around that with music and editing, but if you listen really carefully, you can hear just one tiny little flush.

Razzle dazzle

It wasn't all smooth sailing. About nine months into the job, the Oscars rolled around. It was the first time I'd ever had a chance to do an Oscars story and I was really excited about it. I had been doing a lot of fashion stories, and had already lined up two commentators to talk about the red-carpet fashion. At 6 on the morning of the Oscars I was at the gym, testing out Power Plate—the newest gym equipment all the celebrities were using—when I got a call from Sarah.

'Look, don't get upset,' she said.

When anyone starts a conversation with 'Don't get upset', you just know you're going to get upset.

'Don't get upset, but you're not going to do the Oscars story. The Oscars story will be the lead and Craig feels that your voice isn't strong enough and you're just not ready for it. But don't worry, you can help Lucie and Sluggo pull the story together and give them some guidance about which fashion things to do.'

Lucie McGeoch, who was to become one of my closest friends, was producing the story. David Richardson, or Sluggo, would be the reporter. Not me. And it's true, David Richardson has the smoothest voice you've ever heard, it's a voice that's made for television and radio. With that voice he could sell you anything.

'OK,' I said, 'I understand.'

I did understand, but that didn't prevent the tears from flowing. I sat there in the gym and thought, *Even though I've done nine months, I still have to keep proving myself. Even though you think you've come a long way, you've still got further to go.*

I headed to work feeling upset, but put on a brave face. Lucie told me, 'I know you're upset, but try to use this to motivate yourself, so that next year it won't be like this.' I thought, *Yep, this is my goal. Never again will this happen to me. Never again will they say, 'You can't do this story, we'll have to give it to somebody else.'* And it was the first and only time I didn't get to do an Oscars story. After that they were all mine.

♦ ♦ ♦

Many of the people I meet are inspiring, but there are some who are truly exceptional. It's what I call the Hugh Jackman Factor.

Hugh Jackman has these incredible abilities—performing, singing and dancing and acting—but he's also just an awesome human being. He's sincere and genuine, and he seems really confident within himself. He doesn't need to impress you. He's not an amazing person because he's a superstar—he's a superstar because he's an amazing person. If Hugh Jackman worked at your local post office you'd still be wowed by him. He is mesmerising. It's something special within him—a gift.

One of the things I love about interviewing celebrities is seeing the common themes in the questions that my friends and people I meet ask me about them. So while with Mike Whitney everyone wants to know if he's just as outgoing in real life as he is on TV, with Hugh everyone wants to know about his wife Deborah Lee Furness and their marriage.

Hugh and Deborah have been married since 1996. In our interview we spoke a great deal about both Deb and their kids. Hugh is one of the most open and gracious interviewees you could ever hope for. What I recall above all else is Hugh describing a special gesture he and Deborah use to signal to each other when in public. Hugh had just hosted the Oscars, and when he first came on stage he patted his heart twice. The cameras panned to Deb and she did the same thing in return. That's their gesture to each other. I melted then and there.

Another celebrity who really impressed me was Rob Thomas from Matchbox 20. My sister is a huge fan of their music; before I met him I could take it or leave it, but I came away from that interview thinking, *I will always buy your music, because you're a really fantastic person. You're not shallow, you're not up yourself, you really love the music for the music's sake, and you love meeting people.* Even though he's a rock star, he was normal and so genuine and interested in other people. He's not interested in you because you're there to do a story on him. It's because he's just a fabulous human who wants to share and connect with you. You can't fake that sincerity, no matter how good an actor you are.

I think Rob Thomas should be an honorary Aussie because

he takes the piss out of himself the whole time. I love a celeb who doesn't take themselves too seriously. My motto is take your work seriously but don't take yourself seriously.

He had recently written a new song which sounded similar to an INXS song, so I asked him if he was 'inspired' by INXS. 'Oh no, it's not inspired by them,' he said. I wasn't surprised, I had fully expected him to deny it. 'I ripped it off completely, it's a total INXS copy.' He laughed. I loved it. That's what I mean about honest. What celebrity says that? I still laugh about that.

Mark Wahlberg is great, too. Despite having done thousands and thousands of interviews, you sense that he's listening to every question like it's the first time it's ever been put to him, which it's clearly not. And he gives a genuine answer, not a rote answer. He's not just saying, 'Yeah, yeah, I love my kids, I love my wife.' He's actually trying to connect with you. I think it's a gift to be able to do that with someone you don't really know, especially in such a short space of time—sometimes a five-minute interview. So you walk away thinking, *I felt how he loves his kids. I felt how he's serious about this or I felt how he regrets that.* You walk away with a real insight into that person.

I don't know if that's what people mean by the X factor, but that's what it means to me. It's more than what you do on the stage or screen. It's about your qualities as a human. And that's what makes those people so special.

Those are my favourite interviews: the ones where I meet someone and think, *What a great person. I'd like to be like that.*

◆ ◆ ◆

Another thing that makes this job fulfilling is the chance to meet childhood idols.

Growing up, I loved Jon Bon Jovi. Bon Jovi was my favourite band—I was obsessed with them. They toured when I was 13, and I was *desperate* to see them perform. Maha was only nine, but she put on a big song and dance about wanting to go too. Maha was the kind of little sister who loved everything I loved and wanted to do everything I did. And it drove me a little bit crazy—I used to shout at her, 'You can't like *all* the same bands as me!' But Mum and Dad said that if I wanted to go, I had to take her with me. I would have agreed to just about anything for a chance to see my idol. That concert's still fresh in my mind: it was the first one I ever went to and the seats I got were incredible. I don't know how I did it, it was such a fluke, but we got seats right up close to the stage, only three or four rows back. Mum and Dad let us take the camera and we took all these hopelessly fuzzy photos. And then at the end when the concert was over, the bass player threw his guitar pick into the audience, and I caught it. For a thirteen year old, things don't get much better than that.

And when Bon Jovi toured again at the end of 2010, there was absolutely no way I was not going to cover that story. I got the exclusive—I visited the stadium, stood on their stage and looked at their guitars, *and* I got to interview Jon Bon Jovi. A childhood dream had come true. Sometimes it can be fraught with danger meeting the people you admire, but I'm pleased to say that he didn't disappoint. He was charming, sweet, humble, and still really good-looking. The highlight—he was also funny. A real bonus. I wanted to know if it was tough to transition from Rock God one night to dad the next. 'No,' he said. 'I just make the kids scream my name and cheer every time I enter the room.' See what I mean? Funny. Now that's something that money and fame can't buy.

◆ ◆ ◆

When you're dealing with celebrities there's often some sensational piece of gossip they don't want to talk about: maybe it's been rumoured they've cheated on their partner or they're pregnant or they're getting divorced or they've just been arrested. Often, the gossip is a significant reason you're doing the story. But this job is all about trust—they have to trust you to do the right thing by them, and that means you never make promises you can't keep or tell lies to get a story, because if you do, they'll never trust you again. You have to be upfront before the interview's even started and tell the star's PR or manager: 'Look, I'm going to have to ask them about the drugs/pregnancy rumours/ alien abduction, because people want to know and if I don't ask I'm not doing my job. But I promise I'll do it as sensitively as possible.' It's no good saying you won't ask a particular question when you know you're going to, because then the celeb will scream about you to the PR, and the PR won't work with you again.

I interviewed Kristy Hinze once and yes she is insanely gorgeous in person, more than you can imagine is possible. She had a new fashion range she was promoting, but all anyone really wanted to know about was her recent marriage to a billionaire 36 years her senior. There had been a lot of media discussion about it, with some people more or less accusing her of marrying for the money. And I had to find a way that wouldn't upset or offend her to ask about her marriage. Obviously she would rather *not* have talked about it. But I warned her PR person in advance so there would be no misunderstanding and she could think about what she wanted to disclose. She said something like, 'He's an amazing person. He's smart. He's interesting. I learn so much from him. He makes me want to learn more and do more and I love and respect the person that he is.' She was really warm and heartfelt and her answer was so genuine that you just felt the love in her answer, and I think a lot of the criticism went away after that. But that's the kind of balancing act you have to do every day.

People have long memories. When I first started calling contacts, there were plenty of examples where I was warned, 'Don't bother calling them. They won't speak to us.' So I called them and discovered they wouldn't take my call, usually over something that had happened many years ago. But I persisted. And persisted. And persisted. And slowly, very slowly, I won people over.

One of my many challenges was David Jones. When I started at *TT* I was warned the marketing team were not too keen on us, so whenever the stores did their fashion launches each season, we would get the Myer story and Channel 9 would get the DJs story. Simple as that. Craig would ask me whether we were covering the DJs fashion launch and I'd have to say, 'No, they don't seem to be big fans.' I couldn't get a meeting with them. I couldn't even take them to lunch. I was paying and they still wouldn't come! It took me a good three years of endlessly trying and constantly being rejected before they finally agreed to a breakfast meeting with me. At last I was getting somewhere. I took them to breakfast and they couldn't give me a story, but they agreed to let us shoot the fashion parade and cover the red carpet. It was the first chance they'd given us in years. I was thrilled, but, as luck would have it, I had to cover something else on the night of the parade, so one of our other reporters went instead. That fashion parade took place just as the scandal erupted over sexual harassment allegations against David Jones

CEO Mark McInnes, and the $37 million lawsuit that was being brought against him and the store by former employee Kristy Fraser-Kirk. To me, the red carpet is not the place to start grilling fashion designers and celebrities about their views on sexual harassment, but unfortunately my colleague didn't see it that way. He asked a lot of questions and made the guests feel awkward. Surprise surprise: the DJs team was upset to say the least. I was furious: it wasn't a situation I'd created, but I was the one who ended up apologising, and I was afraid all my hard work and years of trying to get a foot in the door had been wasted.

Fortunately, while they were upset, they realised it wasn't my doing; it took me more effort to get back into their good books, but I managed it. And later, when I fell ill, one of my biggest and happiest surprises was how kind and giving and incredibly supportive the DJs team was.

◆ ◆ ◆

But there's more to the job than just arranging interviews with the stars. I can't just *react* to stories: I have to *find* them too. That means looking at all the press releases I am sent, all the new products being launched, reading all the magazines to find that one thing that's really exciting, unique and new. Obviously there are a million new products being launched every month, but it's my job to work out why *this* product is news. The time I'd spent as a researcher had helped me to hone my skills at finding stories. The questions I always asked myself were: How is this thing going to make people's lives better? Why should we put it on our TV show? Why should people care? I was always looking for the hidden gems: fun, versatile, clever ideas from little companies or designers nobody had heard about.

Reversible jeans that were black on one side, blue on the other. Shoes you could wear sixteen ways because you could tie them up differently. They're the stories I love—and viewers love them too—because they're about being creative, doing things in new ways, and looking great on a budget.

I'm always on the hunt. Sarah and Craig would get up every day at 4 am to read the papers, and even though my job's not exactly cutting edge, I need to be across everything that's happening in my world of fashion and entertainment. That means reading all the mags and watching all the big shows—like *X Factor* and *MasterChef* and *Australia's Next Top Model*—and following everyone on Facebook and Twitter, in case something happens. There *are* occasionally breaking stories in the world of fashion and entertainment!

Sometimes I can't believe how lucky I am that I've finally found a way to turn all my favourite things into my job. Then I remember that luck didn't have much to do with it.

◆ ◆ ◆

You don't always get a lot of respect when you're an entertainment reporter—even if you're the National Entertainment and Lifestyle Reporter, a title I happily earned after 18 months of hard work. The stories I do are very rarely the lead story of the night. But that doesn't mean they're not important in their own way.

This is how the lead story is chosen. After Craig and Sarah have read the morning papers, they pull together what's called the rundown, which is the list of stories that will go to air that night. They allocate those stories, and they work out how long each story should be. The first story of the night is always considered the most important, and entertainment, fashion, beauty and lifestyle stories are almost never the lead, which is fair enough.

Once, one of the reporters I work with, who can be a bit smug, said to me, 'So, what have you been working on? Have you been busy?'

It happened to have been a two- or three-week stretch where I had been really busy. I said, innocently, 'Yeah, yeah, I've been really busy, I've had a story on almost every night.'

'Oh really?' he said. 'I hadn't noticed. I actually only ever tune in for the lead.' He was implying that because my stories were never the lead, they weren't important. I was surprised that someone who worked on the same show felt the need to have a dig. I thought, *You know what? Mock all you want my stories about jeans and diets and lipsticks, but I love what I do despite your opinion.*

I don't allow people to look down on me because what I do isn't hard news. Maybe a lipstick isn't going to change the world, but it's what a lot of people actually want to know about at the end of a tough day.

◆ ◆ ◆

When you look at this job from the outside, it looks like it's glamorous, all champagne and parties. When I was first trying to break into TV I'd read the newspaper social pages, and they'd be full of socialites and starlets, and think, *God, I would KILL to go to an event like that! How do they get invitations? Who decides?* It seemed like this magical world I'd never be able to get access to.

Now I know it isn't magic. It's just contacts.

I never imagined that going to a party might feel like work.

But when you've just done a ten-hour day, the last thing you feel like is changing your outfit, doing your hair and make-up (no, I didn't have a team to do that for me), and attending an event. But I had to, because it was a part of my job: because the people throwing the parties were the same people I was ringing every day to get stories, and I wanted them to know they had my support and I wanted them to get to know and trust me.

Okay, a party's a party, and I love parties. But when I was starting out I found it tough.

First, there's the clothes problem. If you're a well-known celebrity, designers are happy to lend you clothes for events. The celebs are photographed, the clothes get free publicity, and everybody's happy. But when you're a nobody, no-one wants to lend you clothes. So, I had to wear my own, and I certainly wasn't getting paid enough to have a wardrobe full of evening wear. One of the first events I was invited to was a new store opening for Leona Edmiston. I'd never been to anything like that before but I knew it'd be full of fashion people and I would have to step it up. I bought a new dress for the event and even though it was cheap, it was very trendy and I loved it. However, it was made from polyester. So every time I moved, the dress made this *shhh, shhh, shhh* sound and everyone would turn around to see what the noise was. I'd stop dead in my tracks. Then when they resumed their conversations and returned to their drinks, I kept walking, *shhh*, *shhh*, *shhh*. More heads turning on their part, more dying of embarrassment on mine. Everyone else at this event looked incredibly chic, and I was there completely out of my depth, rustling with every step. They looked at me as if they thought I had crashed the party.

And that brings me to the second problem: other people.

Have you ever been to a party where you don't know anyone? Not a single soul. And everyone else there already knows each other. It's enough to make you stay home, right? But if you don't show up, you won't get invited again. You've got to go. I went, and it was hell. I stood there awkwardly, with a drink in my hand, trying to look like I belonged. I got my phone out and pretended I was busy answering emails or making a call when, really, all I was trying to do was not look like a complete loser. Photographers would ask me to step out of the way so I wouldn't spoil their shot of other, more interesting people.

I developed a string of tricks to help me kill time and look less like an outsider. I remember one party I went to when I was at *Sydney Weekender*. As usual, I knew no-one, and had no-one to speak to. My first trick was to go to the bar and get a drink. Then it was on to my second trick: I walked around pretending I was looking for someone. Fortunately, this party was at a large venue so it took me about two minutes to do a lap. (Parties inside boutiques are the worst because let's face it, it only takes about 15 seconds to do a lap. And once you've done eight laps, people start looking at you very strangely!) Time for my third trick: ditching my drink—in a pot plant, on a nearby table, in the toilets, anywhere—and going to the bar to get a new one. Always let everyone who's waiting go before you. Make sure you get served last. This cycle of get drink—walk—ditch drink get drink took a good five minutes. Right, now what to do with the other hour and 55 minutes? When I still had no-one to talk to, I went to the bathroom and called my sister from the cubicle.

'Oh my God,' I said, 'this is a nightmare. I know no-one. I don't even know the party organiser so I can't thank them for inviting me.'

Maha was at dinner and didn't have time to indulge me in a long conversation. I hung up and thought, *Now what? It's too awkward to be the only person standing on their own. I know what I'll do. I'll just sit here.* So I sat in the cubicle for about 15 minutes. Wondering if I'd ever get anywhere. Wondering if it would always be like this. Eventually I left the cubicle and decided to go home.

Don't worry, I said to myself, *It feels like you're not getting anywhere but you are. Every little step is an achievement and when you look back you'll realise how far you've come.*

I can't even tell you how many parties I've been to by myself, how many painful experiences I've had. Maybe 100, maybe 200. And I'd always think, *Why am I here? Why do I torture myself like this?*

I'd come home and Marcus would say, 'Did you have fun?'

'Fun? Fun? Are you kidding? Do you understand what it's like? I don't know anyone! No-one knows me. No-one wants to speak to me. It's clear I don't belong!'

He'd say the obvious thing: 'If you're having a terrible time, why go?'

I'd look at him like *he* was the crazy one. 'Not go? As if!'

I knew I had to suck it up, endure the pain and push on. No-one gets anywhere worth going without a struggle.

After a while I did get to know people and make friends. I began to feel like I belonged. And after I'd been doing it for a *long* time, designers would sometimes lend me clothes. Awesome! The only drawback? You have to be able to wear sample sizes. So forget about the deep-fried finger food.

And then there's the stress.

I remember doing a story with Sophie Monk, who was in

town to promote a new brand of body-shaping underwear. It was a same day story, which meant we had to choose models (who were the right size, right look and available at a moment's notice), book the models, find a location (that was big enough, suitable for camera and sound requirements and also available at a moment's notice), book extra talent (for instance, a fashion designer to give their opinion on the range, who could also drop everything and come to the shoot), film all the models in all the multitude of shapewear and interview Sophie. Then we would need to find another range of shapewear (that was also brand new, had never been featured, and was somehow exciting and different) and do all of the above all over again for that range. Oh, and have it ready to go to air at 6.30 pm!

Miraculously, thanks to endless stress, swearing, coffee and running—make that sprinting—around in heels, David Dutton and I got it all shot and scripted. We took it to the editor, who cut it and rendered it, which means feeding it down from the editor to the control room and then putting it to air. The editor was having problems with his computer, so we urgently rang IT, and they were able to fix it, but it kept breaking down. IT would then return, it would break down again and on and on this went. All this stopping and starting was causing huge problems.

The story wasn't finished when it hit 6.30 and the show went to air. We were in the rundown as the fourth story of the night and were still frantically trying to get the segment finished. The first story went to air, and David and I were freaking out, screaming at the editor, who was shouting at the computer. I was sweating so much it was like a fountain under my armpits, convinced I was going to be fired and David too. The second story went to air and the control room called us, yelling, 'Where's your story?' It still wasn't finished, we had to fill three minutes and there were black empty spots throughout the story. We were screaming 'Use this bra shot', 'Get that slimming corset', 'Get some vision of Sophie' at the editor, as he frantically attempted to cut the vision and insert it in the right places. The third story went to air and they were going berserk in the control room. And, even though I know they always have an extra story on standby in case something like this happens, I was visualising the people of Australia sitting in their lounge rooms watching an empty screen. Our story was due to go to air at 6.41; at 6.40 we finished editing and started rendering. It was still rendering as it went to air. If the editor's computer had broken down again, the viewers really would have seen dead air. Luckily it went through without a glitch. David and I looked at each other after it was all over and I said, 'Oh my God, seriously, how could a story about Sophie Monk and shapewear be so stressful?'

Fashion Week

Sometimes it can be hard to see how far you've really come. For me, the benchmark is Fashion Week every year. Fashion Week used to be this wonderful fantasy world that I thought I could never have access to. Beautiful models wore beautiful clothes, created by beautiful designers, while beautiful people watched the shows. And only special people were invited to Fashion Week. The rest of us could read about it afterwards in the glossy mags and salivate. Then I started at *Today Tonight*, and I actually got *inside* the shows.

My first year, we covered a handful of stories; no-one knew who I was, and I sat in the back row, if I sat down at all. (Just in case you don't know, there's a very clear hierarchy at Fashion Week. The most important people sit in the front row; the further back you are, the less important you supposedly are. There's also a lot of careful thought that goes into deciding who sits next to whom. Rival magazines don't sit next to each other, and neither do rival department stores. There are feuding celebs, wives and mistresses to separate. It's very complicated.) I thought it was phenomenal—and was so excited to be part of it all, so nervous about getting it right, desperate to do a good job. I'd never spent so much time worrying about what to wear to work. I was thrilled to be right there in the thick of it all, with the stunning models, gorgeous clothes, fascinating people and rowdy photographers. No-one wanted to photograph me, of course, but I was at Fashion Week! Wow!

The next year rolled around, and this time I wasn't in the back row, I was in the middle row, and a couple of the photographers were greeting me by name and asking if they could photograph my outfit.

The following year, I was moved up to the second row. And then the year arrived when I was in the front row. Me!

Now I know for a fact that if you're in the back row, you are one hundred per cent guaranteed to see the same show as the people in the front row. Amazing, huh? So it's not the rows or which one I'm sitting in that I care about. This was just an indicator of the progress I'd made in terms of my career and it was a way for me to measure that advancement over the years to see where I'd been and how far I'd come metaphorically speaking (because literally I'd progressed about three metres from the last row to the first).

It is at Fashion Week each year when I stop and reflect and think, *Is this actually happening? To me? Little old me? The dorky kid who got picked on? The fat girl who ate her way through tough times? She's in the front row? How did that happen?*

I just sit there watching everything buzz around me and it's like an out-of-body experience. From above I look at myself sitting there, and I smile from ear to ear. If I was still looking for proof that I am good enough, then this is it: all I have to do is look back and count the rows to see how far I've come.

IVF:
the next step

When you read about everything I did to build a new career for myself, it might sound like I'm the most career-obsessed woman in the world. And it's true, my career is important to me. I worked hard to get where I am, and once I got there I worked even harder.

But I always wanted to have kids. In fact, I always pictured myself as a mother of four, which is weird, because you'd think if I did the maths I would have started a lot earlier.

When Marcus and I were married in 2001, I was just about to turn 28 but felt as if I had plenty of time: we'd have a few years together, we'd travel, and *then* we'd try to have children.

As it turned out, those first few years of our marriage were so intense neither of us was even thinking about kids. We were working day and night to try and build our respective businesses, our finances were a nightmare, we were stressed, it was crazy. Kids just weren't an option. For me, this felt like my one chance to really go for it and build my career—it was now or never. I knew that once I started a family I'd have to slow down, because, more than anything, I wanted to be a good mum. But as I entered my thirties, I wasn't ready to slow down. I felt like I was ten years behind everybody else, still standing in that queue, waiting to get my lucky break.

And besides, we were still young. We thought we had plenty of time to worry about that later.

But the idea of having kids never really went away. In 2005, when I started working at *Sydney Weekender*, I was 32 years old, and I finally felt like I was getting somewhere in my chosen career—I was a researcher, and while I hadn't yet done a single story as a presenter, my goal looked like it was in sight. It seemed like the right time to start trying for a family.

All my girlfriends were getting pregnant and having babies, and from what they'd told me I knew it could take ages to conceive—as long as a year. I think part of me hoped it *would* take that long, because it would give me just a little more time to make an impact at work. But another part of me was very excited about the prospect of getting pregnant. I remember the first time we tried, we looked at each other and said, 'Here we go, we're making a baby!' It was funny, exciting too, and I remember thinking with a thrill, *I'll probably be pregnant next month.*

But I wasn't.

I look back now and laugh at myself, because I had no idea. When you're young, people are always warning you, 'Be careful, you'll fall pregnant,' so you assume that every time you try, you'll fall pregnant. Back then I didn't know there were only a couple of days when you *could* get pregnant. So, we were trying wherever and whenever we felt like it, and hoping we'd make a baby. Marcus liked to joke, 'More practice! More practice!'

But the months kept passing, and I didn't fall pregnant. And every month was a little like an emotional roller-coaster. I'd go to the chemist and buy a pregnancy test full of optimism, enjoying that little window of hope, thinking, *This is it, oh my God, I might be pregnant!* I'd walk home from the chemist, thinking, *Ten minutes from now I might be celebrating.* I was already starting to believe it'd worked, I could see the future, me with a baby, I could feel that joy. And then ten minutes later, I'd peed on the stick and discovered I wasn't pregnant after all. And all my dreams came crashing down again. This happened month after month.

I've always had a super-regular cycle, and assumed I'd fall pregnant eventually. But after about two years Marcus began to worry that something might actually be wrong. It was all taking too long and it certainly wasn't like we weren't trying! We decided it was time to get some help.

We saw a doctor and got ourselves checked to see whether there was any physical reason why we couldn't fall pregnant. By now I was 34; the doctor told us we were both fine, and there was no reason we shouldn't be able to have kids, but if we were worried, he could give us a referral for IVF. I said no, we wanted to do it the natural way. The doctor's only recommendation was that Marcus should start wearing boxers instead of briefs.

A new, more proactive phase in our baby quest began. I went

to see a naturopath for advice. I am a big fan of naturopathy—I'd done part of a degree in naturopathy—and I loved my naturopath, Christine. She prescribed herbs and vitamins and an array of pills to take. I happened to mention that if that didn't work, perhaps we could try IVF. She gave me a piece of advice that was to haunt me later. 'Really try and avoid IVF if you can,' she said, looking very serious. 'I've known women who've done it, and they've ended up getting breast cancer.' I didn't know the first thing about IVF, and the thought that it might put me at risk of cancer terrified me. If there was any possibility I might get cancer, I didn't want anything to do with IVF.

Besides, I didn't believe I was going to need it. I was sure that if I followed Christine's advice, I'd be pregnant in no time. I happily went out and bought everything she'd prescribed. It was expensive, but I didn't care; following her advice made me feel incredibly healthy, and I felt sure it was going to make the difference. How could I not fall pregnant when I felt this good?

I did not fall pregnant.

We weren't prepared to give up. We'd realised it was time to get serious about this. We started doing our research into what we needed to do to get pregnant. Who knew there were so many theories? So many different things you could try? I read dozens of books and scoured the internet.

We discovered there were all these different positions which were supposed to help you conceive. Naturally, we tried them all, from A to Z, even the rather strange ones. Desperation will do that to you. Some people swore that if you lay with your legs in the air afterwards it would help the sperm reach its destination, others swore it didn't help, while some said it only works on horses. At any rate, it didn't work for us.

After I discovered that women have only a small number of days in each cycle when they can actually conceive, we began to focus our efforts on those days. First, that meant charting my cycle (after a while, charting it obsessively) so I'd know exactly when my best opportunities were. Then I got a saliva kit that helped me identify when I was ovulating. Nothing says 'romance' like spitting on a stick. It was about as sexy as *CSI*.

And while it was good to have that knowledge about when we needed to hit the mattress, it kind of took the magic out of things. I like my life to be very structured. I love systems and order. But there are some things which ideally stay fun and spontaneous, and surely sex is one of them. Perhaps it's an inevitable part of trying to conceive, but when you're aiming to make a baby, sex can seem a bit like a mechanical chore: 'Today's Wednesday, time to clean the oven, collect my dry-cleaning, and make a baby.' It's supposed to be an act of love, not an item to tick off your to-do list.

Undeterred, we kept going, and a number of times we thought it had really worked. Marcus always thought this month was going to be the month. We knew that one of the first signs of pregnancy was that your breasts started to get bigger, so he'd be checking out my breasts as the month went on. 'They're definitely bigger!' he'd say. 'This time you're pregnant for sure.'

I never was. When my period arrived again, it was always a huge disappointment for both of us. A family was something we wanted so much, and it didn't get any easier as time went on—it just got harder and harder. The disappointment built up, with every failure we felt more disheartened, more frustrated, and ever more desperate for it to work. We invested more and more in it—more time, more effort, more emotional energy—and the failures made us feel more determined than ever to make it happen, any way we could. Because this wasn't some insignificant thing we were trying to do. It went right to the heart of our marriage and our relationship and where we wanted to be as a couple. And the more we struggled, the more painful it became. For Marcus, every time was like a kick in the stomach. Every month there'd be a loss of hope, and he began to believe it would never happen for us. He began to feel he was going to miss out, be forced to live a childless life and say goodbye to a long-cherished dream.

◆ ◆ ◆

The fact that all my girlfriends were getting pregnant effortlessly made it harder. They'd only have to *look* at their partners and they'd be knocked up. I found myself watching my pregnant friends, glowing and blooming, and they'd swap stories and advice, and I'd have nothing to contribute. I went to baby showers, visited my friends with their newborns in the hospital, went to christenings, first birthday parties, and while I was always happy for my friends, because I love them and I was glad to see them and their beautiful families, it was always bittersweet. They had what I desperately wanted; they'd moved on to a new phase of their lives, and Marcus and I couldn't follow them there.

And I couldn't see any reason why I was different. We were all roughly the same age, why was it so easy for them but so difficult for me? I was fit and healthy, I knew I didn't have any medical problem that was interfering with my fertility. I just couldn't get pregnant.

I told myself that this was just another example of what I've always believed: Nothing I've really wanted has ever fallen into my lap. If you really want something, you have to work for it. So why should having a baby be any different? I really thought I just had to work harder.

My close girlfriends were aware of all that we were going through, and they had plenty of ideas and advice. They knew about things that had worked for less fortunate women like me. They'd say:

'My friend went on holiday and fell pregnant straight away.'

And I'd think, *Great! Let's go on holiday! It's the perfect excuse!* We'd go away and have a holiday. No luck.

Then someone else would say, 'My friend did acupuncture and she fell pregnant straight away.'

I'd think, *Why not? It's an ancient time-honoured method, I've heard it works for all kinds of things, I'll bet that's what I need.* So, off I'd go and have acupuncture. After I'd been going for a while, my acupuncturist convinced me that really Marcus ought to be having it too. Poor Marcus! He has an immense dislike of needles. But he was willing to try and overcome this aversion if it meant we could finally have this baby we wanted so much. He gamely came along and let them stick him full of needles. Now *that's* commitment!

And still the advice kept coming.

Chinese herbs that tasted like dirt mixed with manure? Yep, I'll have them. Reflexology? Yes, fine. I convinced Marcus to give up coffee—for two whole years!—in the hope it would help his sperm health. For Marcus, giving up coffee was like giving up breathing—his parents have been in the coffee industry since he was four years old, so coffee is in his blood—but he did it. We kept trying more and more things, always believing the next thing would be the one that finally worked for us. And it wasn't cheap, all this effort: the consultation fees and the herbs and vitamins and Chinese medicine and all the rest of it was costing us a small fortune.

And then there were the gadgets.

I'd heard about something called an ovulation watch. It took your temperature and it beeped to tell you when you were at your most fertile. I went on a trip to LA, where I knew you could get these watches, and I had a crazy-expensive day catching cabs all over the city trying to track one down. I must have dropped $100 just on one cab fare! Finally I found one, and, because I'd decided I needed it, I bought it. But that watch was the ugliest thing of all time and I didn't want to be seen wearing it publicly: not because of what it was (although it would have been kind of embarrassing to have to explain, if anyone asked) but because I'd hate anyone to think I'd actually choose to have something that hideous on my wrist! I compromised and wore a lot of long-sleeved tops. I look back now and think what a waste of $200. I kept on hoping that every new gadget would be the one that made the difference, every new suggestion might be the missing piece of the puzzle, the magical solution to our problem. I had faith that we could beat this thing through sheer force of effort.

But as time passed, it became harder to stay upbeat. Children I'd seen as tiny babies were growing up and starting school, and I still wasn't pregnant. My friends kept offering advice, all of it totally contradictory. Some people would tell me I was too focused on having a baby, others would tell me I wasn't focused enough.

'You're trying too hard.'

'You're not trying hard enough.'

'Maybe it's because you travel for work.'

'Maybe it's because you're too stressed.'

'Maybe you just need to relax.'

Can you think of anything *less* relaxing than being told to relax?

I know my friends were only trying to help, because they knew how much we wanted this, and they really wanted to see us succeed. But I couldn't help feeling that I was subtly being blamed for our failure to get pregnant, as if I was doing something wrong. I know some of my friends thought I was working too hard, and that was the real cause of our problems, and that I should put all my dreams and aspirations on hold—maybe not forever, just for as long as it took to make a baby. Funnily enough, no-one ever seemed to think that Marcus should quit his job and go on a yoga retreat in order to make a baby!

And no-one seemed to understand that one of the reasons I was working so hard was to avoid facing the pain of my failure to conceive. Work had become a kind of shield. It was somewhere I could go to retreat from the pain of my failure. At least when I went to work there seemed to be some connection between effort and outcome. If I worked hard, I got results. Working harder, doing more, actually got me rewards. And working a fifteen-hour day, I didn't have a spare moment to contemplate where my life might be going. Having a child was so fundamental to my sense of self as a woman that I just couldn't bear to think about what it might mean to fail in that regard. I was still telling myself I hadn't failed—it just hadn't worked yet. But with the years going by and me not falling pregnant, my fears were growing.

Not having a child wasn't just about me and my feelings. It was also a problem for my marriage, for Marcus, and for our future together.

It's a funny thing that once you hit your mid to late thirties, that make-or-break time for starting a family, some women with children become a little cool or frosty or stand-offish towards you if you don't have children. (I'm not talking about my friends—it tended to be people I met professionally who don't know me well.) They never said anything to my face, but I couldn't help feeling that they were judging me—as if I was shallow and selfish because I hadn't given up my 'carefree' lifestyle—even though they had no idea what my personal circumstances were, and how much grief it might be causing me that I didn't have children.

I was all tied up in knots, ashamed and guilty that I'd failed, anxious about the future, and sick with disappointment that nothing we were trying seemed to work. I was filling my days up with work so I wouldn't have to think too much about where my life was going. But I was still too frightened to take the next step: IVF.

Marcus and I had the same conversations over and over. I'd tell him how bad I felt that I was failing him by not being able to get pregnant, and how much I wanted to put things right. So he'd say we should go and see the IVF doctors. There were plenty of intervening steps we could take along the way, we wouldn't have to go directly to full-on IVF. I always refused, suggesting we do more of what we were already doing—herbs and acupuncture and iridology and all the rest of it—and we'd be right back where we started.

Looking back, it's hard to understand why I was so scared, but that warning from Christine, my naturopath, had really struck a chord with me. I was so resistant to IVF I even suggested trying for adoption before trying IVF. Marcus didn't want to go down that route when we hadn't exhausted all the options that were still available to us to have a child of our own.

He couldn't understand why I objected to IVF. For him, it was just a solution to the problem. For me, it felt like an admission of failure. I couldn't bear to think that I couldn't produce a child, supposedly the most natural thing in the world that people have been doing since the beginning of time.

The pressure was building. It was obvious by now that nothing we were trying was working: Marcus could see it, and, if I'm being honest, I could see it too. I was being hounded by my parents. They wanted to be grandparents and they were really afraid that if I didn't get a move on, I was going to miss out.

I felt trapped; I was desperate for a baby but, for some reason I was ashamed. My inability to get pregnant didn't feel like a simple medical issue; it felt like a personal failure. It was devastating that the thing that mattered most to me—having a child—was the thing I couldn't make happen. The strategies that had always worked for me before—doing more research, finding out the answers, working hard, being disciplined—were failing. It was so deeply upsetting that I almost couldn't bear to think about it.

IVF was our last chance. Finally, reluctantly, I agreed to have an initial consultation with Dr Costello, a fertility doctor at IVF Australia. He confirmed what our previous doctor had told us: 'Technically you're both fine. You should be able to have a child. There's no obvious reason why you can't.' This should have been good news—at least he wasn't telling us we *couldn't* have children—but it didn't give us the answers we'd been hoping for either. And then he told us that at my age and given our track record with trying—by now I was 36—I had only a 5 per cent chance of falling pregnant naturally.

People go on about biological clocks and remind you that your fertility falls off a cliff after the age of 35, but that didn't feel like something that applied to *me*. I was fit, I was healthy, I was full of vitality. I didn't feel 36. I felt much younger. I wasn't ready to admit, to myself or to anyone else, that I might actually be getting *old*—too old to have a baby.

We left the fertility clinic feeling downcast and frustrated. There was nothing physically wrong with us, nothing we could fix. I couldn't say to Marcus, 'Well, your sperm count's down.' He couldn't say anything to me about my eggs. Nevertheless the blame game began: 'It's your fault', 'No, it's your fault.'

That's when you start to blame psychological factors.

People had been telling me for a while that I needed to work less, stress less, slow down, chill out, relax. The subtext was always that I was too busy, too stressed, too uptight to get pregnant. I've always been hard-working, so it felt like I was being criticised for being the person I am, and that who I am was the problem. Obviously that's not easy to live with, and I'd always resisted it when people said that to me.

But now, I began to wonder. If there was nothing *physically* wrong with either of us, and there was nothing wrong with our *technique,* then maybe we had to start looking elsewhere. Maybe, subconsciously, something *was* going on that was preventing us from conceiving. I knew I couldn't will a pregnancy into existence, but was it possible I was willing it away? I didn't think that I was, but how could I be sure?

I knew Marcus thought at times I was too obsessed with my

job, and that there may be the real possibility we couldn't get pregnant because I didn't really want it. And I couldn't help wondering whether he was right. I felt torn: I really wanted a baby, so I was willing to do everything I could to try to make it happen, but I also struggled with the idea of cutting off my career opportunities too early.

A message from a superstar

I'd been trying to conceive for four years when I got my biggest break yet: my job at *Today Tonight*.

Much as I longed for a baby, I didn't want to risk going on maternity leave when I'd only just started there. I needed time to learn the ropes, to prove myself, to make myself an invaluable part of the team. I didn't feel that I could roll into my boss's office after three months or even six months and say, 'Surprise! I'm having a baby.'

So I told Marcus I wanted to put our baby plans on hold for just a bit longer. He wasn't happy about that. We both knew that the longer we put it off, the higher the stakes became. We'd been told very clearly by the IVF doctor that our chances were already low, and getting lower with every month that passed. More delays now might mean the difference between having a child and never having one. It caused a lot of friction between us and put a huge strain on our relationship. Marcus made it clear that if I kept putting this off indefinitely, it could be a deal-breaker. He told me he loved me and he wanted to spend his life with me, but for him, that had always included a family too. If it was impossible, so be it, we'd have to find ways to live with that. But if we never had kids simply because I'd refused to try IVF, then he wasn't sure he could live with that. He wanted to know that we'd tried everything within our power to make it happen.

My marriage is the most important thing to me; more important than any career. I've always known how crucial it is to strike a balance between channelling my time and energy into my work and putting it into my relationship. There have been plenty of times during our marriage when I've been working so much our relationship has suffered; whenever that's happened, I've always made sure I took a step back from work and put my time, focus and energy into my relationship with the man I love. It's always been a delicate balance, and the balancing act was never more difficult than it was at this time.

I know how incredibly lucky I am to have a husband like Marcus. He's always been totally supportive of me and my dreams. He's stuck by me through all the work and the struggle, and helped me to realise my goals, just as I've helped him to realise his. But a family was something that really mattered to him. If I kept putting it off for too long, it could end up having serious consequences for our marriage.

This was the horrible situation I found myself in: it was make-or-break time, for me professionally, *and* for my fertility. I wouldn't get a job opportunity like this again. It was now or never. I just had to hope that if we pushed the IVF decision out just a little bit longer we'd be one of the lucky couples: the gamble would pay off and we'd still be able to get pregnant.

With the fertility doctor's warnings ringing in my ears, we decided we'd take the risk. IVF would have to wait while I got established in my new role. We agreed that we wouldn't give up trying entirely—we'd just keep doing what we'd already been doing, unsuccessfully, for the last four years. After all, the doctor had said it *might* work. I was still only 36—in my mind I now pushed out the fertility cliff from 35 to 40, so as long as we started before then, I believed we still had some time up our sleeves.

◆ ◆ ◆

My first months at *TT* were an exciting, exhausting, exhilarating time. I was working extremely long days and throwing myself into my new role. But at the back of my mind I knew I was going to have to make a decision about IVF. Realistically I knew it was our only option.

Many people, especially my parents, struggled to understand what I was doing. To them, having a baby was far more important than some job as a TV reporter. I felt I'd worked too hard for too long, and made too many sacrifices, to give it all away now, when I was so close to achieving the goal I'd dreamed of. I was terrified that if I had a baby too soon I'd have to start at the bottom again when I came back from maternity leave. After all I'd been through to reach my goal, I knew I couldn't go through all that again. It was tough, time was running out, and I felt I was being made to choose between two things I desperately wanted: my career and a baby.

To me, it seems that the decision to start a family really is different for women and men. For Marcus, having a baby would be just one more, very exciting, part of his life. He was ready to be a dad, and I knew that he'd be a great one. But the impact on his life was going to be minor, compared to what it would do to mine. He wouldn't have to spend nine months trying to work while he was pregnant, he wouldn't have to give birth, he wouldn't have to take time out from his job, or turn down career opportunities. I would. And this is a problem most women face: even though many fathers are doing way more parenting than they ever have before, it's still mothers who are generally the primary carers, and it's still mothers who generally take career breaks to look after young children. And when we do go back to work, it's usually the mothers who have to stop working long hours and take time off when the kids get sick. Dads fit kids around their work lives, whereas mums fit their work lives around their kids. We do it because we want to, and because taking the best care of our kids feels right. But we can't ignore the fact that there are sacrifices involved.

However, it wasn't really the thought of sacrifices that made me pause. If I could have conceived naturally, I would have been there like a shot. The problem was, on a deep level, IVF felt wrong to me. Producing a baby is supposed to be an act of love, not an act of science. The whole process seemed so foreign, so artificial, so unnatural. And I couldn't ignore the niggling idea that women who had IVF got breast cancer. I had no family history of breast cancer, no reason to think it would ever happen to me. But the idea haunted me. Marcus did some research and reassured me there were loads of women who'd done IVF and who hadn't got breast cancer, but I simply couldn't get past my fear and discomfort. I couldn't feel comfortable about the injections, the hormones, the invasive tests, having to put my body in the care of doctors. And apart from that, it seemed really *unfair* that it was all falling on me. 'No-one's asking *you* to pump yourself full of hormones,' I'd grumble to Marcus. 'What if it was *you* who had to have all those needles and blood tests?'

In fact, back then I wasn't particularly bothered by needles. Later I'd come to hate them. But really, in my mind, I had created a completely unfair and irrational stigma about IVF. It was what all the women who couldn't have babies naturally turned to, and I didn't want to include myself in that group. It would mean admitting that I'd failed, and that thought was gut-wrenching.

Maybe if I'd had a friend who'd been through it, and who could help me get my head around the idea, then it might have been less frightening. Of course I could name some celebrities who'd used IVF: Celine Dion, Marcia Cross, Courteney Cox. But I didn't know them personally. And celebrities never come clean about the details.

Slowly I began to realise that if I didn't ask for help there was a chance I might miss out altogether. By now I was 37, and, although I didn't feel 37 or look 37, there was no question that my eggs were 37, and if I didn't make a decision soon, it might be made for me.

I told Marcus, 'Okay, I know I've been hiding from this. What I need to do is get a whole bunch of books and start reading, and just try to wrap my head around it.' I had to get past my fears and anxiety about IVF and try to make an informed decision. I still wasn't sure it was right for me. But time was running out.

◆ ◆ ◆

As luck would have it, I had to go away on a long trip for work. I'd secured a whole package of celebrity interviews, and I was thrilled to have so many exclusives for the show. I would be interviewing Julia Roberts, Mark Wahlberg, Salma Hayek, Adam Sandler, Eva Mendes, Emma Stone, Andrew Garfield, The Rock, and more. It was going to be an amazing but gruelling trip. Usually when I travel for work, if it's a long trip I go with a team—a camera operator, a sound person, and maybe a producer—but this time I was away for two and a half weeks by myself. That meant when the work day was done, I could go back to my hotel room and tackle my huge pile of IVF books. I hoped that once I'd read them I could get a real understanding of what it would all mean, conquer my fear, and ready myself to take the plunge.

A week into the trip I was scheduled to interview Angelina Jolie in Cancun. It was part of the worldwide campaign to promote her movie, *Salt*, and I was one of many journalists from print, TV, and digital who were all there to interview her. That trip was what's called a junket: a trip paid for by the promoters where you interview the stars to help promote and build excitement around the launch of the movie. Cancun's main hotel strip is one long street filled with amazing 5-star hotels, overlooking the ocean, and it's so beautiful—it's just like a postcard, and you can immediately see why it's a popular choice for tourists, retirees, honeymooners, families and American college kids on spring break. Some people think it's too touristy—like the Gold

Coast of Mexico—but I disagree totally, it's postcard perfect and I loved it. I was staying in a fabulous hotel in a room overlooking the ocean. Every morning I got up early and went running on the beach, then I did my interviews, and when the day's work was done I'd sit on my Juliet balcony drinking coffee and reading IVF books while the sun went down. The organisers had arranged social events in the evenings so you could mingle with the other print and TV journalists but I skipped most of them so I could focus on getting my head around this IVF thing. I really needed a bit of time to be by myself and think, and that was what I got on that trip. It was a gift.

The day I was scheduled to interview Angelina, I walked down to the lobby wondering what she'd be like. Would she be a diva who refused to share any details of her life? Or the earth mother she's portrayed as in the tabloids? As one half of *the* most famous and magnetic couple in Hollywood, I was prepared to meet a diva, but my expectations were totally turned upside down.

In person, Angelina is surprisingly tiny, elegant, undoubtedly beautiful, but there's something more—she exudes a gentle warmth. Immediately I took a liking to her and it grew by the second as she answered question after question honestly and genuinely. I've done a lot of celebrity interviews and I can pick rehearsed answers a million miles away, but this time, if I was being fed PR spin, it certainly didn't feel like it.

I approached the subject of motherhood with some trepidation. Most celebs generally fall into one of two camps when you ask them about being a parent: either it's the generic 'I love being a mum, every day is nothing but joy and sunshine,' or 'I don't discuss my personal life.' I expected Angelina to fall into the second group, but when I asked her how she felt she'd changed since becoming a mother, she explained how adopting her first child, Maddox, caused a monumental shift within her, opening up a part of her she didn't realise was there. Once that happened, it made her yearn for a larger family. Whenever she talked about her children I saw her face light up, and could tell they were her whole world.

At that time the question of celebrities adopting babies had been making the news. Some people seemed to think it was unfair that celebrities could adopt babies, so quickly and easily, when regular people couldn't, while other critics thought it showed an inflated sense of entitlement: that these rich, famous people were acquiring babies, almost as if they were accessories. Angelina, who has three adopted children as well as three biological children, was at the centre of this media frenzy.

I didn't ask her about any of that in the interview, and she didn't comment on it, but she said something that really struck a chord with me: 'Sally, it doesn't matter how children come into your life. There's no one method, no right or wrong way.'

And that's when I finally understood. For the first time, it all seemed so clear: it didn't matter *how* I had the baby, what mattered was that I just *had* one.

It was a strange moment. I knew she was talking about her own life, and she didn't have the first idea about me and my baby dilemmas, but I heard what I wanted to hear when I needed to hear it. I felt as though it was a message meant just for me—as though the universe was trying to tell me something via the Queen of Hollywood.

◆ ◆ ◆

It seems funny to me now that when a celebrity-obsessed girl from the suburbs needs advice, she doesn't listen to her husband, or her mother, or her sister or her best friend. No, she listens to Hollywood.

I came home from that trip feeling as if a weight had been lifted off my shoulders. I'd had the time I needed to read and research and think and absorb. IVF no longer seemed like this scary, dangerous, weird, unnatural thing. It was a means to an end, no more, no less, and we were lucky to have that option. My conversation with Angelina had been like the end-point to that thought process: her words had helped to crystallise everything. We wanted a baby, and this was a way to make it happen. It was as simple as that.

In fact it was suddenly *so* simple I couldn't believe I'd been resisting for so long. I was now so ready I was actually looking forward to it! What a change: in two weeks I'd done a complete 180.

Marcus was thrilled to hear that I was finally happy to go ahead with IVF, even if he did think the whole Angelina-told-me-to-have-a-baby thing was a touch over the top.

At last, we had a plan: I'd see out the year in my job, and then in the new year, while we were on holiday, we'd start our first cycle of IVF.

The ultimate phone call

We began our IVF treatment on New Year's Day, 2011.

After resisting for so long, going to the clinic to begin our treatment was really exciting. At last I felt I was doing something really proactive. I wasn't burying my head in the sand or waiting for a miracle to happen. I felt as if I'd finally taken control, and not just in a herbs/ovulation watch/saliva kit kind of way. *Real* control. *Really* proactive. We were getting *real* help. I knew having a baby was my priority, it was something I really wanted and I was going to do all I could to make it happen.

The summer holidays had begun, and I had a month off

work. I'd decided I wanted to do that first cycle while I was on holidays so I could focus on it. I had heard that some women found the process physically and emotionally demanding, because of reactions to the drugs and hormonal mood swings, along with all the regular anxiety that comes along with trying to conceive. If the process turned out to be too overwhelming, I didn't want to be juggling my feelings with a ten-hour day at work.

Even though I was excited, I was nervous about what was going to happen, anxious about what it would be like, and generally a bit teary because it was such a big thing. And when we got there, there were all these other people sitting in the waiting room *with their children*. I turned to Marcus and whispered, jokingly, 'Who are these people who come to an IVF clinic with children?'

'Obviously, they're here because they're also trying to have a child,' Marcus said.

'Well, they already have a child. They shouldn't be here. It's like flaunting a bucket of KFC in front of someone who's starving!'

I was kidding, but underneath the jokes I realised that I actually did feel jealous, even if we were sitting in the IVF clinic together. We all wanted children, but they had a child, and I didn't. Up until that point I'd been in denial about how desperately I wanted a baby, and how much I envied couples who already had one. I'd cried plenty of times when a pregnancy test had come back negative, or another natural remedy had failed. But this was the first time I'd really confronted how terrible it would be if I never had a baby.

Sitting there, I felt it hit me with full force: I want a baby.

I really want a baby. I don't care how many cycles I have to do. I really want this.

And I looked at these people with children, who were obviously coming back to try to have a second or a third. And I thought, *Oh my god, what if I miss out?* Because this was it for us. If this didn't work, we had no other option. There was nothing else to try.

◆ ◆ ◆

The clinic we'd chosen was Sydney IVF (it's now known as Genea), and our doctor, Mark Bowman, had helped to guide us through all the different options available. Dr Bowman is a lovely kind man, nurturing and understanding and gentle, as well as being super-smart. He was the perfect person for such a full-on job that requires smarts, skill and the ultimate bedside manner.

We'd decided to try ICSI for our first attempt. ICSI is a more intrusive form of IVF where the sperm are injected into the egg manually, rather than letting it happen naturally, as with regular IVF. An IVF treatment cycle takes about four weeks. Once you've had your initial consultations, the treatment starts with a visit to the fertility nurse. She gave us the medication I was going to need, took us through the timeline we were going to have to follow, and then showed us how to self-administer the Follicle Stimulating Hormone injections. This hormone stimulates the ovaries to produce more eggs than usual. The more eggs they can harvest, the more eggs there'll be for you to fertilise, and the greater your chance of becoming pregnant.

After giving Marcus such a tough time about how it was me who would be doing all the hard work to fall pregnant,

Marcus was the one who ended up giving me my injections every day. We got ourselves a practice cushion so he could get used to stabbing the needle in, and by the end he was pretty good at it. I had to take the drugs for two weeks. We did the injections at 10 pm every night, and then during the day we'd go to our various appointments—having blood tests to measure my hormone levels, internal ultrasounds to measure the size and number of my ovarian follicles—and then the rest of the time we watched DVDs at home, walked to cafés, and generally hung out together. It was like we were spies, agents on a special mission. It was exciting, and we felt like we were a team. It was a good time.

I also went to see an acupuncturist who'd been recommended to me. Her name is Lily Liu and they call her the baby maker—fertility acupuncture is her speciality. Although my closest friends knew what we were doing, I certainly wasn't broadcasting to the world that we were doing IVF, so when I walked into the waiting room one day and saw a PR girl I knew there (I didn't know her well, but we were acquainted) I was mortified.

'So you're trying to have a baby then?' she said.

'Oh no, no no no,' I said, 'I'm actually here for some acupuncture in my neck.' I went through this elaborate performance of showing her how my neck was stiff and sore, and she just looked at me and said, 'Ohhh, right.' The two of us were sitting underneath a huge poster with pictures on it of all the babies Lily Liu had helped bring into the world. It's practically all Lily does. I wasn't fooling anybody. The girl just smiled at me.

◆ ◆ ◆

Luckily for me, I didn't really experience any of those unpleasant side effects some women have. The hormones made me feel bloated, but otherwise I felt good, and let myself eat whatever I wanted; I chilled out, and hoped that it would all work out.

When the tests showed I had a good number and size of follicles, it was time for egg collection. That meant another injection of hCG (human chorionic gonadotropin) in the evening to trigger ovulation, then I'd have to go back to the clinic about 36 hours later so they could perform the egg retrieval operation.

The morning of the egg retrieval, the two of us went to the clinic feeling excited, nervous, and very emotional. This was the first big step in the process, and we were desperate to know how many eggs I'd managed to produce. While I was waiting for them to start the procedure, I couldn't stop crying. There we were in a medical suite, Marcus and I, Dr Bowman, the nurse, the lab technician. It all seemed so scientific, and so very public. It wasn't exactly a romantic situation! But, on the other hand, I also felt so grateful that there were all these people doing their best to help us have a baby and make our dreams come true.

To our relief, the egg retrieval went well, producing eight eggs. Marcus was sent away to produce a sperm sample in a little cubicle—yet another not-at-all-romantic twist to this whole weird situation—and then they took both eggs and sperm away so they could work their magic in the laboratory.

In ICSI (intracytoplasmic sperm injection), the embryologist examines the sperm under a microscope and then chooses the best individuals for insemination. A single sperm is then injected into each egg. After that, each egg and sperm are put into an individual incubator and kept at 37 degrees Centigrade to mimic the temperature of the human body.

The clinic called us regularly to keep us updated on our progress. From an initial eight eggs, we ended up with five good fertilised eggs, which was a fantastic result. Five days after the egg retrieval, I went back to the clinic for the embryo transfer. They had a massive screen on the wall so Marcus and I could watch while the embryo was being placed inside my uterus. It felt very strange to think that after all those years of trying, we might actually be watching the moment when I got pregnant. After they'd finished the transfer and let me get up I was busting to go to the loo, but I was almost too frightened to go—in case I peed the baby out!

◆ ◆ ◆

Then there was nothing to do but wait and see whether our embryo had decided to stick around. My next appointment was for a blood test two weeks after the transfer, which would let us know whether we were pregnant or not. The nurse had warned us that there was no point getting a pregnancy test kit from the chemist and trying to find out for ourselves, because all the hormones I'd taken were still floating around in my system and might produce a false reading. There was nothing to do but cross our fingers and hope.

About a week and a half after the transfer, I began to feel that I might be pregnant. It was strange, and I couldn't put my finger on anything definite. I just felt . . . pregnant.

But I hardly dared to hope.

◆ ◆ ◆

By this time my holidays had come to an end. I was due to have my blood test on a Friday. I decided I'd go to the clinic early, have the blood test, then have a quiet day at work easing back into things, checking my emails, touching base with my contacts, getting things in order for the new year, while I waited for the nurse to call with the results that afternoon.

But, of course, that's not how it worked out—at all. My first day back, a big story broke in Hollywood: Charlie Sheen had been rushed to hospital with abdominal pains after a night of hardcore partying, forcing the producers of his show, *Two and a Half Men*, to halt production temporarily, sending shockwaves through the media industry. Charlie Sheen was famous for his hard-partying ways—two months later, he would be sacked from the show, sparking a media frenzy and some memorably crazy sound-bites—and even though it wasn't surprising, it was still a hot story and we had to cover it.

As I explained with the Sophie Monk/Shapewear segment, same-day stories are a nightmare. When something like that happens, you have to find out the details, get the vision (by vision I mean any kind of material that's relevant to the story: news footage of the incident, interviews *with* the celebrity, interviews *about* the celebrity, clips of the celebrity doing whatever it is that made them famous, that kind of thing) sent over from wherever it is—in this case, Hollywood—then you interview local talent for their views, write your piece, film it, get it subbed (journalism jargon for having your story checked and approved), then send it to the editor to put it together for that night's broadcast. I was making a million phone calls, writing, filming, rushing around, trying to get everything done before deadline, and everyone was hassling me about where the story was and whether I was going to pull it together in time.

In the middle of all this, Dr Bowman's nurse, Mary, called from the clinic, but I missed the call, and she didn't leave any details in her message. Of course, I called her back, but this time I got their voicemail. I left a message, asking her to call me back, and tried to focus on my story. I was working like a lunatic, everyone was on my case, and I didn't give a damn about Charlie Sheen—all I wanted to know was whether I was pregnant or not, and no-one from the clinic was calling me back! Then when the clinic *did* ring back, I missed the call again. Eventually I just gave up until I'd got the story locked down and handed over to the editors. At about 3.30 that afternoon, I called the clinic and managed, finally, to speak to Mary.

'How do you feel?' she asked.

'I feel good,' I said. I paused. 'I feel pregnant.'

Then she paused, for what felt like an eternity, before she said, 'You feel pregnant because you *are* pregnant.'

I was completely speechless. Happy, elated. But stunned. The nurse's voice on the phone sounded so excited and happy for me that I started to tear up at my desk. I was so touched that this woman who didn't really know me was so genuinely happy for me—I could hear and feel her excitement and joy.

I ran off to the office kitchen and called Marcus. 'I'm pregnant!' I whispered. I didn't want anyone to overhear me.

'Are you lying?'

'I'm serious.'

We were both stunned. Absolutely blown away. After trying for so long, and going through so much angst and disappointment, we'd finally done it. It was amazing.

I felt so incredibly lucky. All my life, I've believed that nothing ever falls into my lap, everything I've ever done has taken a huge effort. But not this. We'd managed to fall pregnant with just one cycle. I was, and am, so incredibly grateful.

And because we knew we had another four embryos ready to go, I remember thinking, *I might just sneak in four kids after all! Okay, maybe not four, but I could* definitely *go three*.

I went back to my desk and for the next two hours sat there grinning like an idiot while discussing Charlie Sheen, but after a while I knew I was going to burst if I didn't tell someone the good news. Lucie's desk is near mine and I could see her frantically organising Monday's shoot, but I just *had* to tell her. I caught her eye and gestured for her to sneak into the office of Matt White (the then host of *Today Tonight*), which was just behind my desk. She followed me in and I shut the door. 'I'm pregnant!' I said, and started crying. Lucie was absolutely thrilled. We'd had many long discussions, many heart to hearts about the challenges of trying to have it all before the clock ran out. She knew how excited I was, how nervous I was and how much this meant to me. I ended up bawling my eyes out with happiness until it was time to go home.

I just couldn't believe it had finally happened. I felt unique. I know people get pregnant every day, but to me, it felt as if the universe had entrusted me with this special task. And for the first time, my job paled into insignificance. This thing I was about to do was so important and so extraordinary that it didn't matter how many celebrity interviews I'd done, or what I'd achieved in my career. This was bigger than any of them.

That night, Marcus and I sat on the couch and looked at each other in utter incredulity. We didn't go out to celebrate—instead, we celebrated in true Obermeder style, with Thai home delivery, high-fiving each other over a Massamun curry.

Sally's parents

Ever since Sally was born, everything we did and wanted was for her and her only. We loved her and wanted her to be happy, and did the only thing we knew to do—love her with all our hearts.

There was one thing we wanted for ourselves and that was for her to have kids. So, as soon as Sally and Marcus got married, I suggested she have a baby right away, but Sally (unfortunately for me, but fortunately for her) is a career-minded person. She didn't want to have babies until she found a job she loved.

It was fine to want a career, we understood that, but I wondered what she meant by 'Now's not the right time for kids.' I wondered when exactly the right time would be. As a mum I knew there was never a right time. She would say, 'I am not ready' to which I would reply, 'But I am ready! Actually I have been ready from the day you were born!' I have always wanted to become a grandma but I realised that I would have to wait. After Sally got married, my husband was asking me every second day, 'Is Sally pregnant?' and when the answer was 'No, she doesn't want babies right now,' he was very sad and worried too.

Finally Sally and Marcus decided to start a family. Of course we were very excited. I felt like my heart was dancing inside me. A couple of times I asked 'Well, are you?' Her reply would be 'No, I am not' so I stopped asking because I didn't want to pressure her, I didn't want her to feel bad and I didn't want to be disappointed by her answer.

Time passed and our worries grew. My husband had a colleague from work who had tried for many years to have a baby, and was unsuccessful, resulting in enormous heartache. Hearing that caused my little heart to stop dancing and it sank in sadness.

After six years of trying Sally told us that she had decided to try IVF. I didn't really know what that entailed. All I knew about IVF was what I had read in magazines and newspapers. None of my friends, their daughters or daughters-in-law had gone through IVF.

I thought about our roles and what it would mean for us. What would Sally go through and what could we do? The answer was simple: love and support, and we were determined to give her and Marcus lots of it.

I remember at that time how Sally had hope and that hope came so naturally to her. She is a very positive person, a quality it turned out she would need later with the challenges that were to come.

As the IVF procedures started, I could see the happiness in Sally's and Marcus's eyes, but I also could sense the fear, the fear of not being able to have the baby that they so desperately wanted. But I think Sally's desire to be a mum was bigger and stronger than her fear.

Sally has many close, amazing girlfriends in her life and they were also a great source of support. Marcus is a caring, compassionate husband and their love for each other helped a lot during that time.

Sally managed the IVF process quite well. I think she was fortunate to have minimal side effects and any that she did experience she didn't care too much about because she was just so happy to be doing something proactive towards her dream of having a baby.

Through the IVF process Sally and I talked about what she was going through and I told her that I thought everything would be alright and that in my heart I believed she would be a mum soon. Her answer was always, 'Really, Mum? I think so too.'

While Sally was going through IVF, I found out that some of my friends' daughters and daughters-in-law had also been through IVF, but they kept it a secret. I didn't understand why. They later told me that in some cases they or their daughters thought it was embarrassing that they hadn't been able to conceive naturally. When they found out that Sally was having IVF treatment, they started to talk about it openly. They felt that some of the stigma had been lifted. They no longer felt like they needed to hide.

For many women it takes quite a few IVF cycles to fall pregnant, but Sally was so lucky to fall pregnant the first time. Thanks to her amazing doctor, Dr Mark Bowman, Sally's experience was not only successful but also made easier by the support and empathy of the staff at the Genea clinic. To top it all off, Sally's ever-positive attitude was always reflected on her face. She was always so smiley and happy, so both my husband and I kept thinking positively as well, and were excited in anticipation of good news.

We were overjoyed the day Sally told us that she was pregnant. My husband and I walked around grinning excitedly like little kids at Luna Park.

When I reflect on that period of my life, I always think of other people who are experiencing the same thing. I say to them, please do not despair and always think positively. Even if it doesn't work the first or second or even third time there is always hope and if you can, try to talk with family and friends about what you're going through. You may be surprised to find you are not the only one in this boat. There is nothing to be embarrassed about. No matter what things look like on the outside, everyone is going through their own battle.

It may have been a long six-year journey for Sally and Marcus to have a baby but the day that our incredible granddaughter Annabelle Grace was born, our lives all changed. With her birth and Sally's diagnosis it reaffirmed Sally's favourite saying 'All that matters is to love and be loved'.

Pregnant
and loving it

With that one phone call, a new phase of my life began. The doubt, anxiety and stress of trying to get pregnant was finally gone. I was really, truly pregnant, and it had been so ridiculously easy—that is, as easy as an IVF pregnancy can be.

Once I knew I was pregnant, I could feel myself beginning to change. While from the outside I don't think I seemed very different, on the inside, I could feel my perspective shift. The pressure I'd felt to do more, to work harder, to keep proving myself, eased. The need to prove myself, both professionally and as a woman who was ready to become a mother, had driven me to more and more extreme lengths. But now that I was finally pregnant, that source of anxiety was gone and I didn't feel the same desire to overcompensate by throwing myself into my work. At the age of 37, it felt like things were coming together for me: my work was in a good place, and I'd finally achieved the thing I'd wanted for so long. I was pregnant, we were starting a family, the next phase of our married life. For the first time in years, I felt like I could actually relax and enjoy myself. And that's exactly what I did.

◆ ◆ ◆

After telling Marcus and Lucie the good news, I told Maha. Her workplace is right next to our Channel 7 studio in Martin Place and we would often go to work and travel home together since she also lived down the road from us. That afternoon, I waited for her on the benches in Martin Place and before she could even sit down I blurted, 'I'm pregnant.' We sat there crying and hugging.

I called Camilla, Lizzie and Sarah and they were all ecstatic. I waited till I got home to call my parents because Marcus wanted us to do a conference call with his parents at the same time, so that all the grandparents found out at once. That was a noisy phone call with lots of cheering and squealing and crying.

I know you're supposed to keep it a secret until the first trimester's over in case something goes wrong. But I've always believed that when important things happen, good or bad, it's better to share them with the people you are closest to.

After all, my family and friends had been with me through all the years of trying, all the failed attempts. Now that it had finally worked, I wanted them to share the joy from the beginning.

Of course, that didn't include telling everyone at work. I have a number of close girlfriends I work with and, naturally, I told them, swearing them to secrecy. I didn't want to have to make it official until I absolutely had to.

My first full week back at work was busy, with lots of events to attend. I went, but always left after the first hour. What had happened to us was so wonderful and so huge I didn't feel like standing around chatting to people. I wanted to be home with my husband, sitting on the couch and letting the wonder of it sink in. Not even the best party could compare with that.

Like so many pregnant women, I spent those early weeks in fear of being caught out. For me, there were two dead give-aways: the first was my ongoing rejection of blue cheese and sashimi at parties. The other giveaway was the size of my breasts.

At around eleven weeks I was booked to do a magazine shoot and then to host a *Home and Away* fan signing. I was excited about the shoot, but nervous about what to wear. My breasts were growing at such a rapid rate that all my pre-pregnancy outfits looked slightly R-rated—not the image I was going for. To make it worse, my stomach was still quite bloated and swollen from the IVF. I decided to go for a bright red top for the shoot and hope that the colour and detail would distract anyone from noticing what was happening underneath. The shoot went well until the photographer decided my top was too flowy and that we needed to clip it back and make it look more fitted. Oh no! I did my best stomach suck-in, until I actually started to feel ill, and began to remember why modelling is such a tough job. But it was worth it. The shots were fantastic. I had a lovely time imagining showing the photos to my bubba and telling him or her that they'd been right there inside me when those photos were taken.

My next event was the fan signing, and by then nothing I owned fitted. In a matter of days my breasts had grown even bigger—I couldn't believe that was possible—but I managed to stuff myself into a Spanx slip which bound my breasts just enough for me to squeeze into an orange A-line dress which accentuated my legs. I prayed my legs and Summer Bay's young sexy male actors would be enough to distract everyone from my ever-growing mid-section.

My breasts wouldn't stop growing. I saw Maha one day and she took one look at me and said, 'Dolly Parton called, she wants her boobs back.'

◆ ◆ ◆

Quite early on in my pregnancy, I had to make a decision which would turn out to be one of the most important of my life: choosing an obstetrician. Naturally, I turned to my girlfriends for help. They all recommended someone different, but I noticed one unifying theme: they all *loved* their doctors. Everyone swore hers was the best. I had four recommendations, and decided to do an initial visit and see who I clicked with. Two had retired since my girlfriends had their babies, which left me with two.

The first one I went to see seemed annoyed by my questions and told me not to interrupt him with 'meaningless baby questions like some rude mothers' until he'd finished giving his new baby speech. Eventually when I felt brave enough to ask a few questions, he told me, 'Some babies die. That's life.' Rightio. One more doctor scratched off my list.

Camilla recommended Dr Stephen Morris, and the minute

we started talking, I knew what my girlfriends had meant. I'd found my doctor and I *loved* him. He was compassionate, understanding, and factual, with a great (albeit slightly quirky) sense of humour. Looking back I know how fortunate I was. Without the exceptional care he gave me, my life might have turned out very, very differently.

◆ ◆ ◆

Most people have their first ultrasound at around 12 weeks, but because we were having our baby through IVF we went a little earlier, at around eight weeks. I wasn't feeling any symptoms—I experienced none of the morning sickness or mood swings some of my friends had warned me about—and was starting to get a little worried I wasn't actually pregnant. I was looking forward to seeing physical proof. Being a novice, I didn't expect to see anything of note—when my friends had shown me their ultrasound printouts they'd kind of looked like grey staticky blobs—and Marcus and I were floored when the sonographer showed us our baby, clearly visible on the screen. Usually I'm the Wendy Waterworks, but this time it was Marcus's turn to be a bit teary. I just felt a deep sense of calm, as though I was finally where I was supposed to be.

We decided we wouldn't find out the sex of our baby. Marcus wanted to know but I didn't, and he gave in and let me keep it a surprise. Of course, that didn't stop us looking for clues. Was that a penis? No. Yes! No. We couldn't tell and had asked the sonographer not to let on. So we left still not knowing.

Camilla Crotty

Sally's best and oldest friend

Sally and I met over twenty years ago at university and although graduation was a goal, it wasn't the biggest achievement at uni—that was meeting my best friend Sally.

At university, we were like two peas in a pod: we liked all the same things (except Bon Jovi) and began what would become a lifelong friendship. We planned our goals together and celebrated milestones. Today, following a friendship that has spanned over two decades, I am uniquely qualified to say that if Sally sets a goal, she always achieves it.

When Sally called in January 2011 to say she was pregnant I burst into tears of joy. This was not an overnight journey. She was in her tenth year of marriage, and had spent six long years trying to conceive. In the beginning, it was assumed after a few nights of loving and sweet nothings, one plus one would equal three. A few months passed, and then a few more. Sally would always say 'Practice makes perfect, right?' and although Marcus agreed, things didn't seem to go to plan. Her maternal clock was ticking and the frustration and angst of not falling pregnant was growing by the day. Sally desired a baby so much she would often convince herself, and me, she was pregnant. She would say 'I can feel my body changing. This month is different, I know I'm pregnant.' Unfortunately it wasn't the case.

Sally felt incredibly grateful she had a loving husband, family and friends and a job she enjoyed, which I think in turn, made her feel guilty for wanting more—to be a mum. It's hard seeing someone you love dearly want something so much, and you are helpless to control or change the situation. All you can do is be there for them, share the pain and help keep their hope alive. Motherhood isn't for everyone and most of us are never ready, but Sally was meant to be a mother and she was ready.

Most people would feel despondent after six unsuccessful years of trying to fall pregnant but not Sally—she is made of tougher stuff and never gives up until the result is achieved. She realised it was time to ask for help. Doing IVF was a difficult decision for her. Not everyone feels the same, but Sally felt inadequate that she couldn't conceive naturally. Thankfully she stayed focused on her goal and after one attempt at IVF, she hit the jackpot.

As new life stirred inside her, Sally exuded a beautiful glow. In true Sally style, she still sported her six-inch stilettos, fashionable outfits and gorgeous long Rapunzel-like tresses. Sally decided upfront, no matter what challenges pregnancy would throw her way, whether it be morning sickness, acne, tiredness or swollen legs, she would do it all with a smile. She wanted never to take for granted the opportunity she was given to be a mum. True to her word, she was the happiest and most energetic pregnant woman I've ever known. She just loved life and being pregnant.

Pregnancy brought one challenge for Sally, how to keep her beloved job. Some working pregnant women don't want to be at work and have mentally checked out, but not Sally. She was a late starter in the TV industry and wanted to make up for lost time.

I remember the day when at age 29, Sally told me she wanted to leave finance and become a personal trainer and undertake a TV presenting course. All I could say was 'Are you crazy?' I couldn't understand why she wanted to leave security and everything she knew to head into unknown territory. All I could put it down to was she was suffering from Excel spreadsheet overload. She spent all day at work creating Excel data spreadsheets then more at night for her personal life. Everything was in a spreadsheet, including recipes, outfit combinations, home improvement ideas, shopping lists, to-do lists and calendars. Everything in the house was labelled, including shoe boxes, herb and spice containers, her pantry and even her linen cupboards. She definitely needed another outlet—the opportunity to use the right side of her brain before it disappeared. Ironically, she set herself some goals, listed them in a spreadsheet, of course, and was off on a mission to realise her dreams.

After finishing a few presenting courses she worked at a community TV station for a couple of years for free. She then did work experience with Channel 7 as a researcher, again without pay. To earn a living she studied personal training and worked hard building up her clientele and her business. She would take personal training clients from 5 am till 8 am, do a full day's work, and then train more clients from 7 pm to 10 pm. The clients loved her because she gave them healthy recipes typed in Excel and would chart their weight loss in spreadsheets. She was obviously having withdrawals from her finance job. I had such admiration for Sally as this gruelling schedule continued for nearly three years. Most people would have surrendered many years earlier. While absolutely exhausted, she refused to give up. Finally she got the opportunity to present on Sydney Weekender and earn an income. Her courage, belief and perseverance certainly paid off and the rest is history.

When you've risked everything to pursue and achieve your dream, it's scary thinking you could lose it. As far as Sally was concerned, women could do it all but that didn't mean not feeling nervous about it. The last thing she wanted was to finally fall pregnant after six years of trying, have all the stars align and then endure the hardship of losing her job. Little did she know what was about to come. Sally's job was secure, she felt incredibly blessed, loved life and looked forward to a happy future with her new baby.

Sally Obermeder

Sally's long journey to fall pregnant taught me two valuable life lessons. The first was the realisation that on the surface someone may seem to have the world and be fulfilled, but you don't really know what's happening on the inside. Pregnancy is one of the things in life that can't be controlled or purchased, and is therefore an emotional roller-coaster. The second, which sums up Sally to me, is believe your future can be whatever you dream it to be. Never give up, because you never know what beautiful experiences you could be blessed with.

Sally, I love you with all my heart. You taught me to never stop believing.

Zara HQ

At the three-month mark I'd managed to convince myself I still wasn't really showing, and decided I'd keep my secret at work just a little bit longer. That week was busy in the office, and then after-hours I had a photography exhibition to attend and the *Prix de Marie Claire* awards. The *Marie Claire* awards are always an amazing evening and I wanted to look my best; the only problem was, the dresses that had fitted last week didn't fit this week. When I went in to see Brooke Martinez, a good friend and our wardrobe stylist on the show, she gazed at my body inquisitively and looked suitably perplexed. I could tell she knew I'd put on weight—or perhaps my enormous breasts had tipped her off about the real state of affairs—but I could also tell she didn't know how to broach it with me. (Has she put on weight, had a boob job, I think she has put on weight . . . wow how much weight has she put on? I could just see the thought bubble above her head!) I attempted to deflect it by mumbling something incoherent about missing the gym, praying she wouldn't ask me directly. She found me a dress the next size up and I then decided the best course of action was to wear more scarves to draw attention away from my mid-section . . . and avoid the Wardrobe department for the next few weeks!

I was working really hard on one of the biggest stories of the year in Australian fashion: the long-awaited opening of Australia's first Zara store. Anyone who cares about fashion was incredibly excited and all the major TV shows like *A Current Affair, Sunrise, The Today Show,* and the news outlets were all desperate to get an exclusive. Zara's team was offering one lucky show an amazing story: the opportunity to go to Spain—where Zara has their headquarters—and do a big behind-the-scenes story, meeting their design team, going to the factory, seeing the packing and shipping and fabrics warehouse, meeting the management team, and getting an insight into what they'd be offering the fashion-obsessed of Australia. As a die-hard Zara tragic, I was beyond excited. I *had* to get that story.

The Zara management team came to Sydney on the quiet, and not many people even knew they were in town, but Lucie and I had been working all angles to secure this story. I was liaising with the Australian PR companies who were working with Zara, Lucie was liaising with the Zara team in Spain. We were desperate to ensure that we didn't miss out and were doing our best to fly below the radar. It was like some kind of CIA operation and we were covert operatives. We didn't want any of our competitors to know who we were talking to. We didn't discuss it with anyone. The only person who knew what we were up to was our Executive Producer, Craig McPherson. (I highly doubt whether he would equate getting a Zara story with a CIA mission. But we did.)

We arranged a meeting with the Zara management team where I pitched myself and the show, giving an extensive and in-depth presentation, and tried to convince them to give the story to us, rather than any other reporters, shows or networks. And they grilled me. For over an hour I had to discuss the show's ratings, the network's ratings, explain what stories I'd done, talk about what coverage they would get, explain the story angles and run through my plans.

Some stories fell into my lap. Some I spent a few weeks on. Most I spent months on. And then, a handful—like this Zara one—I spent over a year working on. And when we got it, I breathed the deepest sigh of relief because the thousands of emails, the hundreds of phone calls and all the long-distance-middle-of-the-night conference calls weren't a waste of time.

When I found out we'd got it I was absolutely thrilled. By this stage I was more than three months pregnant, but I couldn't bring myself to tell Craig until after I returned from Spain. I think I was a little bit afraid he might suggest I shouldn't go. After all that work there was no way I was missing the opportunity to see this amazing story through.

My trip was top secret. No-one in the office, apart from Craig and Lucie, knew about it. I left the office on Monday afternoon and went to the airport without telling a soul. The reason for the secrecy was that Channel 9 thought they were still in the running, and we didn't want them to know they'd missed out on the story.

I know it sounds ridiculous, and when I explain it to my non-TV friends they shake their heads. They can't believe the hoo-ha over a story about what is, at the end of the day, a shop. But it's more than that. Getting these exclusives helps win viewers, and viewers equals ratings, and ratings means advertising. When you're the number one show it means that you get momentum. It helps you secure future stories. Being number two in a two-horse race isn't good for morale.

We were terrified that Channel 9 might get wind of what had happened and run some kind of spoiler. (In TV terms, a spoiler is what you run when you don't have the exclusive, so you just pull together a story to make it *look* like you do. For example, if *TT* has an exclusive Hugh Jackman interview for a new movie he is promoting, and *A Current Affair* doesn't, *ACA* might pull out some old footage of Hugh Jackman, put it together with some bits of the new movie trailer and then get a movie expert in to talk about it. It looks like they've got a brand new story on Hugh Jackman, even though they don't actually have Hugh Jackman, which 'spoils' the sense of exclusivity and excitement around the *TT* story.) It sounds ridiculous, but you never really know you've got an exclusive until you get the story on the air. I've turned up to film events that we thought we had exclusive rights to, only to find film crews from other shows and other networks there. It drives me crazy, but it happens a lot. The media industry is quite small. The Sydney media industry is even smaller. You only have to tell one person a secret and the next day it's in 'Sydney Confidential'. And that's why we kept the Zara story a secret. No-one told Channel 9 it was no longer in the running until the day before our story was to go to air. I felt bad for them—I know what that feels like. It sucks. But after a ten-year love affair with Zara fashion, and having spent a small fortune on their stuff, I felt like I deserved the scoop.

The Zara trip was fantastic, beyond full-on, and totally worth all the hard work we'd put in. It started in Madrid where I landed at 8 am and hit the ground running. I teamed up with a local cameraman and sound guy and we spent all day filming at Zara's massive packing and distribution warehouse. When I say 'massive', I don't really think the word does it justice. To clarify, most fashion retailers offer 2000 new products a year but by comparison Zara produces 14,000 new products, which means their factories make 800 million items a year. So you can see how they've earned the title of 'retail powerhouse'.

After a huge day of shooting the logistics centre, we caught a 10 pm flight to La Coruna, in the north of Spain. La Coruna is where Armencia Ortega started Zara and opened their first store in 1975. He originally began by making dressing gowns then moved into fashion, where he was quickly successful. His retail stores spread through Spain, Europe then America.

We didn't arrive in La Coruna till 2 am and had to be up at 7 am to start filming. I loved standing outside the original store. I bought myself a Zara scarf (of course, what else?) as a memento of how one man's dream produced an extraordinary global empire.

Then we went to Zara HQ, which houses the design and manufacturing teams and is the size of fifty-seven football fields. That's 400,000 square metres! Truthfully my heart was beating so fast the whole time I was there. I was stupidly excited. Before I left, the Spanish Zara team bought me a box of baby clothes. They'd guessed I was pregnant; I suppose when you're working with three mums, one of them is sure to guess. And they did—less than a day into my trip. They were incredibly warm, kind and generous to someone they'd only just met. Since they'd guessed, I felt safe confirming it, because I was on the other side of the world. I thought my secret would probably be safe—and, of course, I wanted some advice on where to find the best European maternity fashion. Armed with their advice, I spent the last few hours before flying home shopping up a storm. I went crazy at Zara, H+M and Topshop—all of which have maternity lines in Europe. I bought dresses, jeans, jackets, and bags, scarves and shoes (because no matter how big I got I knew they'd always fit!)

Two things happened while I was in Spain. I felt the baby fluttering around. It was incredibly exciting. I talked to the baby constantly on the flights and told it about the adventures we were having. Even though I was travelling solo without my usual Channel 7 crew, I didn't feel alone. It was strange but nice to be sharing it with my bubba in my belly. I got home exhausted but thrilled to have had such a unique and memorable experience.

The other thing was my stomach popped out. Almost overnight, my waist completely disappeared. There was no chance of squeezing into any of my old clothes now. I knew all the tricks celebrities used for hiding their bumps before they're ready to go public—big scarves, big coats, really big handbags (it worked for Grace Kelly—that's how the Hermès Kelly bag got its name). I'd decided that when I reached four months I would come clean, but in the meantime I was just going to get crafty with the way I dressed.

When I returned from Spain it was autumn. I accessorised with some of the fab new scarves I'd bought while I was away, and thought I was doing okay. Attending an event for *Women's*

Health magazine, I wore my own navy jumpsuit (I was still avoiding Brooke in Wardrobe), and sucked my stomach in all night. No-one said a word. I was chuffed, thinking this hiding-your-pregnancy scam is easy!

Then my Zara piece went to air. It went really well, and the next day *The Morning Show* asked me to come and have a chat about my trip with the hosts, Larry Emdur and Kylie Gillies. I chose my favourite new red Zara dress, and with the help of Spanx and a little breathing in, went down to make-up to get ready for the show, convinced that no-one was on to me.

Kylie was there getting made up when I arrived. The two of us are quite good friends, and we chatted away, then we went upstairs and did the show. But as soon as Kylie was finished on the set she went to see her boss, Sarah Stinson, the Executive Producer of *The Morning Show*. Sarah used to be Chief of Staff of *TT* and is also one of my best friends. Kylie walked straight into Sarah's office and said, 'Sally's pregnant.'

Sarah already knew, but she'd promised not to say anything. 'No she's not,' Sarah stalled. 'Why would you think that?'

Kylie wasn't fooled and any attempt Sarah made was quickly rebuked. It was clear my secret was out. Sarah swore Kylie to secrecy, then frantically rang me and said, 'Kylie knows.'

And I thought I'd been doing such a good job of hiding it!

I went straight down to Wardrobe where Kylie was getting changed. The moment I saw her I groaned and threw my hands up in the air.

Kylie just laughed. 'Please. The second I looked at you, I saw your waist had disappeared—and I knew you were pregnant.'

'Is that a thing?' I asked.

'Everyone who's had a baby knows the waist is the first thing to go,' she said, adding, 'And that whole scarf situation didn't fool me for a second.'

Nothing gets past these mums.

Damn! If Kylie had noticed, that meant other people had probably noticed as well. And if it was getting *that* obvious, I really had to tell my boss.

Craig McPherson was my boss and the man who had hired me. As National Executive Producer of *Today Tonight*, he was extremely busy, managing a top-rating prime-time show that airs nationally. He would get up at 4 am every day and had almost 100 staff around the country. I knew he was under immense pressure and idle chit chat was not high on his daily agenda. If you had something to tell him, you went in there, you told him, then you got out. Now, this was not a conversation I desperately wanted to have, but I knew I had to. It was Friday afternoon, and I went in and asked, 'Can we have a chat?' But he was busy and didn't have time, so he said, 'Let's talk on Monday.'

I spent the whole weekend stressing about what he was going to say, with Marcus trying to reassure me that it was all going to be fine.

On Monday I went to work knowing I had to tell Craig, but I wouldn't get a chance to talk to him until late in the afternoon, when all the stories had been done and Craig had finished writing the overnight promos. Each night we promote a few stories for the following day. Craig has to decide which stories they are and how to promote them—what angle to take, how to entice the viewer to tune in. He does this every afternoon and a lot of thought goes into it. Unless the building is on fire, Craig shouldn't be interrupted when he's working on the overnight promos. I spent the whole day pacing and stressing, and when I get stressed I get sweaty armpits, so I had sweaty armpits all day. Nice. From about lunchtime on, I was looking for my opportunity. I kept walking past his office, pretending I was going to the bathroom so I could peek in. I tried to pick the perfect moment: Is now a good time? Does he look like he's in a good mood? Did we win the ratings last night? Should I go in?

This went on for a few hours, but I couldn't keep putting it off. I just knocked and said, 'Can we have that chat?'

'What chat?'

'Remember: I was here on Friday and wanted to talk to you?'

'Yeah, okay.'

I went in and shut the door, and said, 'Look, I don't know how to say this,' then started mumbling, 'I don't know how this happened and I love my job and I'm so sorry.' And, as so often happens, I started to cry. (I have no idea why I said I don't know how this happened, since I did know how it happened—IVF!)

Craig's accustomed to me crying in his office by now. I usually do it twice a year, at the beginning and end of every year, when I go in to have a chat about strategy, goals and all the things I want to achieve for *TT*. I always, inevitably, end up teary and saying, 'I love my job!' over and over again. It's unprofessional, I know, and every time I do it I promise myself I won't let it happen again but I cry because I can't believe how lucky I am to do what I love. I might be tough and strong and driven, but I'm also emotional and soft at my core. If it's something I care about, I cry. Craig just rolls his eyes, shakes his head, and passes me the tissues.

This time he didn't have any idea what was going on. 'What's the matter, Sal?' he asked, looking confused and a bit irritated.

I think, given that I kept apologising and crying, he thought I'd come to resign.

Somehow I managed to blurt out, 'I didn't mean for this to happen, but I'm pregnant.'

Craig, of course, was lovely about it. He congratulated me and asked, 'Why on earth are you crying? This is great news!'

'I don't know,' I sobbed. 'Because I love my job.'

'I've never had anyone cry so much over a job they like. Most people cry because they hate it,' he said. 'Don't worry, everything is fine. Go, have the baby. Come back when you want to come back.'

I was so thrilled and so relieved, I shed a few more tears and wished I could blame wild pregnancy hormones.

Once I'd told Craig, and he'd promised me I could come back, I felt like I could breathe a little easier—and not just because I could retire the Spanx and stop sucking my stomach in. I could stop worrying and make whatever choices were right for Marcus and me and the baby, knowing my job would be safe. I could have the baby and spend time with bubba, and, when the time was right, I could come back a few days a week, and have the best of both worlds: be a mum and work.

News travelled fast once I made it official. Brooke from Wardrobe was thrilled to hear I didn't have a doughnut addiction—just a bun in the oven. It was a relief to be able to let my bump show. I went to the Zara launch party and officially announced my pregnancy to my work colleagues, acquaintances and industry friends. I was a bit shocked that people were so pleased for me and I was touched by everyone's kindness. I never expected that sharing the news with people beyond my immediate circle would be so enjoyable and heart-warming.

The news is out

While people were genuinely delighted for me, my pregnancy stirred up my old anxieties about my job. I'd go home to Marcus and share my concerns.

'Why are you letting it upset you?' Marcus kept saying. 'You've worked really hard, you've built up a great reputation, you've got a great job, you're obviously going to be able to go back. Craig appreciates and respects you, there's no drama.'

I couldn't help it. Even then, it was still hard for me to feel like I'd made it. It didn't matter how many times Marcus told me I'd worked really hard and achieved a lot. Instead of beating up on myself all the time, I should've been saying to myself: job well done, good on you. But I let fear get the better of me. That little voice in my head kept telling me I hadn't done enough.

The thing is, when people come to me and say, 'I really would love a job like yours,' I don't feel offended. I understand, because that was me once.

I didn't have a problem with the idea of training someone up. I'm not the kind of person who wants to pull the ladder up behind me to prevent anyone else from getting into the industry. For one thing, I don't have that power, but for another, I'm so grateful to all the people who gave me a chance when I was starting out that I want to be able to return the favour whenever I can. Sometimes Lucie would get people coming in to do work experience with us, and if it turned out they were interested in entertainment or fashion, I'd be excited that I'd found a kindred spirit, I'd work closely with them, using my contacts in the industry to help them find a job. I love nurturing new talent, it's great being around people who are keen to learn. If they're prepared to work hard, then I'm prepared to show and tell them everything I know. It's the big sister in me. I would have loved to have had a mentor like that when I was starting out. It feels really good to be able to give back and help other people get their start.

I just hoped the right person was going to appear before my labour started.

◆ ◆ ◆

My second trimester had begun and I was still feeling fantastic. I had a huge amount of energy. Being pregnant didn't slow me down at all. I'd modified my exercise routine, giving up jogging to switch to a more pregnancy-friendly gym regime of light weights, swimming, Pilates and yoga.

The only pregnancy symptom I had was really intense food cravings.

From the first trimester onwards, all I wanted was watermelon and tomatoes. I started eating a watermelon every day: half for breakfast and half for dinner, no exceptions. It wasn't in season and I was being charged an extortionate amount, but I didn't care—I *had* to have it. Tomatoes had never featured heavily in my diet before, apart from toasted cheese sandwiches, but now I was obsessed. Tomato juice, cherry tomatoes, roma tomatoes, green tomatoes on bruschetta—hold the bread.

I loved everything about being pregnant. I wasn't worried about my weight going up. I didn't feel fat. In fact, I felt gorgeous and feminine, like I could finally enjoy my body without having to worry about dropping those last five kilos. I loved the feeling that I'd been entrusted with this baby and was helping it to grow. It was a wonderful new step in the evolution of my relationship with my body, an even more amazing transformation than the one I'd experienced when I became really fit and strong. It was as if my body was saying, 'You thought that was cool? Check this out: I'm making a baby! From scratch!'

Marcus, too, loved the way I looked, and he was just blown away by all the changes, especially towards the end when the baby was really big. We'd sit on the couch together at night and watch my bump moving around. It really is the most amazing thing: if we gently rubbed, the baby would turn over inside me. It seems so far-fetched, like something from a science fiction movie: you're growing a human in your stomach. It's crazy. But such fun.

Everybody stares at you when you're pregnant, but people are so excited that you don't mind. Although I'm quite a touchy-feely person, before I got pregnant I thought I might object to having strangers touching my belly, but I didn't. I actually loved it. Some people would ask first, some wouldn't. Either way it didn't bother me. I loved showing off my growing bump. I was mesmerised by actually having a bump, and seeing their smiling faces made *me* smile even more.

Plus I loved getting people to guess the sex of my baby. Although I was the one who hadn't wanted to know, I was desperate to find out, and asked everybody for an opinion. Most people thought I was having a boy; only a handful thought I was having a girl. Rebecca Gibney, star of *Packed to the Rafters*, and Jackie O, host of 2Day FM's *Breakfast with the Stars*, thought it was a girl. Napoleon Perdis, creator of Napoleon make-up, told me, 'Oh, I've had three girls. That's a girl, I know that's a girl.' I told him everyone else thought I was having a boy and he just waved his hand dismissively and said, 'Oh, they're idiots, that's a girl, I can tell.'

But I didn't just ask celebrities, I asked everyone I met: the cab driver, the woman at the fruit shop, the guy at the newsagent, everyone.

Early in the pregnancy I became convinced I was having a boy. I kept noticing things I never would have looked at twice before: I'd see a fancy motorbike and think, *Hey that's a* really *nice motorbike* . . . I felt like I was looking at things with a newly male perspective, which could *only* mean I was having a boy. Marcus was pretty excited about that idea—he really wanted a boy. But as the months progressed, I began to change my mind.

'Actually,' I'd tell him, 'I don't think it's a boy anymore.'

'Really?'

'You'd better prepare yourself, I think it's a girl.'

'What happened to my boy?'

I think he had a fantasy about introducing his little boy to football and cricket.

I had my heart set on having a girl. I think it's because Maha and I are super-close. I love my sister so much, and I had this fantasy that I'd have a girl, and then I'd have another girl, and then they'd be sisters, just like my sister and I, and they could be besties, just like us.

Maha did the ring test on my belly. You put your wedding ring on a string and see which way it swings. If the ring goes in circles, you're having a boy. If it goes from side to side, you're having a girl. The ring said I was having a boy.

The uncertainty was driving me crazy. Of course the only person I didn't ask was my obstetrician, who could have put me out of my misery and told me once and for all.

◆ ◆ ◆

Meanwhile, the pressure was building at work for me to choose my replacement. I knew we needed to give my replacement time to settle in.

There was a lot at stake, and it wasn't just about finding someone who'd do a good job, I also had to find someone I could trust to take care of my contacts. It was important for the show that we find someone who was able to keep up the momentum, lock down the stories we already had in the pipeline, as well as securing more great stories in the future to help keep our show at number one. We needed someone who could take the lead on the entertainment and fashion stories our viewers love, and someone like that isn't easy to find.

On our show, I was the first point of contact for all entertainment, fashion and lifestyle stories. If a story came in, it would be referred to me. I liaised with the PR music/movie companies. That way I always knew where we were with all the stories in my area, and there was no possibility of miscommunication or confusion. It wasn't about control, it was all about making sure the process was seamless, professional, and organised. And it was because the onus was on me. If we missed stories, or if opportunities fell through, I had to answer to Craig and Lucie, so it was my responsibility to ensure I was across everything. We'd worked this system out through trial and error, it was working well, and we were keen to maintain it.

◆ ◆ ◆

Some of the most exciting events on my work calendar came during my second trimester: the Logies and Fashion Week. I covered the Logies red carpet and after-party and worked until 2 am. Brooke and I had picked out what I was to wear weeks before. It was a pink one-shoulder Charlie Brown dress that was made especially for me, and when I came to the final fittings, I loved it. On the Logies night I felt as though I didn't do the dress justice. I hadn't yet worked out how to do the bump evening style. Months later I saw Beyoncé wearing almost the exact same style dress—one-shouldered satin with sheer fabric— to announce her pregnancy at the Video Music Awards (VMAs). Brooke and I laughed: it confirmed what Brooke always told me, she was miles ahead in the style stakes.

The week after the Logies was Fashion Week. There are parades, events, stories, early mornings, late nights. I'm always running, literally running, the whole time. Running from where the models' hair and make-up is done, in a tent out the back, to the dress rehearsal—to try and get some vision—then it's back to interview someone, before heading behind the scenes to see the designers. Whenever I ask the crew if they want to do Fashion Week with me, everyone flees because they know they're going to spend the whole day running from one tent to another. It's always a big headache.

I braced myself for the whirlwind that is Fashion Week. I love it and always look forward to it, but this year felt like I was being tortured. Not because of the long days, but because I knew I couldn't wear any of the amazing trends on the runway. By the time spring came I knew I'd be nine months pregnant. I felt very despondent until a girlfriend pointed out that if I lost all the baby weight within a few weeks of giving birth, I'd fit into everything by summer. Perfect! Done! Then I remembered that I am not an Amazonian supermodel with the BMI of a six-year-old boy. Chances of that happening were zero. Back to feeling despondent.

But I was cheered up by my mate Napoleon Perdis, who sweetly regaled me with tales of how amazing life is with children. I met Napoleon early on in my time at *Today Tonight*. We were doing a story about beauty trends, but I really wanted to go a bit deeper and do more of a story about Napoleon himself and how he managed to build such a successful empire, and, more importantly, why make-up? When you meet Napoleon you are immediately struck by his warmth. We clicked instantly. He was the son of migrant parents who worked hard to support him and his siblings and who passed their work ethic on to him. He'd been fascinated by make-up from a young age when he watched his mum applying it. The transformation was what enthralled him. His skill, hard work and personality have enabled his business to grow from one

Sydney store to hundreds across the globe. In the process he's transformed the faces of more Hollywood A-listers than I have time to name.

I wondered if he had a 'pinch-me' moment when working on the face of his first big American star. 'No,' he said. 'I was amazed the first time a woman allowed me to do her make-up here.'

'Really?' I asked.

'Yeah,' he continued. 'When I finally got to that first celebrity, it was like, oh yeah, she's just another chick. Let's just slap it on a little bit and make her look good.'

It still makes me laugh so much. You can take the boy out of Australia . . .

I loved talking to Napoleon that day because he's such a devoted dad. Some people harp on the bad points of parenthood (sleepless nights, you'll never go out again) but he made family life sound so enjoyable, I couldn't wait to get started.

LA with Enrique

About a month later I was off to LA to interview Enrique Iglesias. I know not everyone is a fan of LA but I love everything about it—the people, the weather, the food, the palm trees, the shopping . . . and the caramel-covered marshmallows. My ritual as soon as I get off the plane is to go straight to Joan's on Third and buy a box of caramel-coated marshmallows. Joan's is a trendy café with amazing coffee and the hugest array of salads and gourmet treats. It's a celebrity hangout and everyone there looks like they've stepped out of a magazine—except for me with my big bump and my caramel marshmallows. On this trip I put my watermelon craving temporarily on hold while I satisfied my marshmallow addiction—and ate the whole box. I justified it by telling myself I couldn't get them at home and it wasn't like I was in LA every day . . . plus I decided it was the baby that wanted it, not me. Yeah sure.

It was a super-quick trip: one day of travel each way and one day on the ground to do the interview. I had no time to waste and was grateful the shops stayed open till 10 pm . . . that's my kind of city! I was lucky enough to be staying at the Beverly Wilshire—the hotel from *Pretty Woman*—usually you stay in normal hotels, but every once in a while you hit the jackpot and get a night somewhere amazing. I intended to shop up a storm like Julia Roberts' character . . . except mine would be maternity wear and it wouldn't be from Chanel.

I got chatting to the concierge. He said, 'We've got a test in Mexico to tell if you're having a boy or a girl.'

'Oh yeah, what is it?'

'Turn around.'

'What for?' I said, a little bit surprised.

'I have to check your bottom.'

'What?'

'Yeah, if your bottom has grown then you're having a boy.'

'But you didn't know my bottom before, so how would you know?'

He just laughed and said, 'Let me just check anyway.'

I turned around, he had a look and said, 'No, no, no, you're having a girl.'

I really hoped he was right. Not just because I hoped I was having a girl but because I didn't want anyone thinking my bottom had grown.

The interview with Enrique was heaps of fun, he's charming, as you'd expect, but *waaaay* funnier than I gave him credit for, and best of all he didn't take himself seriously. It was one of the interviews I've had the most fun doing and at the end, totally unprompted by me (I swear!), he told me he thought I was having a girl. As soon as we wrapped the interview, I raced to the shops. I bought quite a few things for myself but even more for the baby. With the dollar so strong and the big price difference, I justified it as saving not spending.

The one thing I did splurge on was a Bugaboo pram. It was about a thousand dollars cheaper than at home, so I snapped it up and used the money I saved to buy more things for me. Win win, I say.

You can't help but have a preconceived notion of actors and musicians before you meet them. Magazines and TV are saturated with celebrity news and gossip so you often think you know what you're in for. When you get the unexpected—that's what I love about my job. Because if, with my Wikipedia-filled brain of celebrity news, I can manage to be surprised, then chances are the viewer will be too and that makes for a much better story than just a rehash of old news.

As the son of famous Spanish crooner Julio Iglesias, I expected the ladies' man cliché. It was well documented that women, young and old, would swoon at Julio's good looks and smooth voice. Blessed with both of those from his dad, with Enrique I predicted the typical good-looking, everything-has-fallen-into-my-lap pop star.

Nothing could be further from the truth. Enrique had started out his career under an alias to prove that he didn't need the family reputation. At just 19, he scored his first album deal under the false surname of Martinez.

I couldn't have liked him more. His work ethic was strong and he was completely unpretentious. 'Sally, if you want to be successful it's not going to be given to you, you're going to have to work hard.' Amen, brother. It wasn't just some line, he believed it. He'd written a song, 'I Like It', which he felt passionate about but his record company at the time didn't feel the same way. For two years they fought over it. So how did he get them to change their mind? I asked. He didn't. He changed record companies. Some songs, he explained you love, and others you would kill for. This was the latter and he was prepared to stake it all and back himself. Of course the song went to number 1 on the charts in a gazillion countries.

◆ ◆ ◆

After I returned from LA, Marcus and I decided to give ourselves a holiday. That was quite an event for us, because we hardly ever take holidays—we are always too busy working, or we decide to be sensible and save our money for something important. But we realised that this might be our last chance for quite a while to have a proper holiday as a couple.

We took off to sunny Byron Bay for ten days to relax and enjoy our last big hoorah. I had been flying so much for work that I welcomed the opportunity for a road trip. I loved taking our time driving up and stopping in small country towns, exploring and lunching at places we'd usually miss. We decided to splash out on amazing accommodation, and splurged on Rae's on Watego's—it had been on my bucket list for years and I was so excited to be staying there. When we finally got there, the sun was shining and the hotel manager told us we'd stumbled on the first week of sunshine in over a month. Yippee! It was so sunny, I managed a solid five or six hours of bikini time every day. We ate, sunbaked, ate, swam and ate a little more. The food at Rae's was too good, and for the first time in my life I wasn't sucking in my belly while I was wearing a bikini.

But what made it really special was the chance to spend some time together as a couple, really slow down and unwind. I know Marcus had hoped that once I got pregnant, I might take it easier, start to wind down a bit, get used to the different pace of life I'd have as a mother, and just be home more. We both had extremely demanding jobs—while I was pregnant, Marcus had made the decision to wind up his own financial services business and take a wealth advisor role at a large finance firm. Between his job and my job, we didn't often spend much time together, especially during the week. Marcus thought I'd been driving myself even harder through my pregnancy, trying to cram in as much work as I possibly could before the baby came.

As I gradually got into the relaxed holiday vibe, I realised just how frenetic my life had been over the past few months. I told Marcus, 'If I get really frantic and busy like that again, just remind me of this moment and tell me to slow down.' He promised that he would. You get such a wonderful sense of clarity and tranquillity on holiday. Such a pity it doesn't tend to last more than a few days after you get back to work.

That holiday—actually it was a babymoon—was almost like a second honeymoon. Just the two of us, staying in a beautiful place, going for walks, talking all day and staying up late. We're very different people and we're interested in very different things, but when we're together, especially when we're on holiday, we never run out of things to talk about. And because we were on holiday, there was never that need to be sensible because we had to work in the morning. We could stay up and keep talking for as long as we wanted to.

It was a happy, peaceful, beautiful time.

◆ ◆ ◆

After we returned to Sydney, I tried to keep my promise and stay in relaxation mode, but it didn't last all that long. Soon I was back to my usual cracking pace. While my bump kept getting bigger and bigger, I was working harder than ever, doing my usual long work days, and then attending three or four evening events a week. Marcus worried I was doing too much, but I couldn't see it. For me, it was just a really happy, fabulous time.

My bump was out and proud—it looked like a little basketball, all at the front and nice and high. Every time I caught a glimpse of it in the mirror I'd do a double-take. I'd decided it was worth investing in a good maternity wardrobe—I'm a big believer that how you look on the outside affects how you feel on the inside, and vice versa—so I stocked up on ruched jersey dresses, Paige Denim maternity jeans (worth the expense because they were so comfortable and made my legs look skinny—upon reflection, my legs looked skinny simply in contrast to my big belly), maternity leggings for weekend lounging, plus a good selection of cocktail and evening dresses. With so many events on, including a black tie charity dinner and a wedding, I couldn't do without evening wear, and found some glamorous options that made me feel fabulous.

And everyone kept saying within seconds of seeing me: 'Oh my God, you're still in high heels!' I've always worn at least six-inch stilettos and being pregnant didn't change that. If anything I tend to trip over when I'm in flat shoes! I didn't think it was that big a deal but everyone mentioned it. It became a running joke with my crew . . . at every shoot we went to it was mentioned, usually within the first three minutes. After a while the boys created the stiletto countdown: if no-one said anything within the three-minute mark I had to buy them lunch. I never had to cough up!

As I moved towards the third trimester, I started to make plans about finishing work and starting the new chapter of my life: motherhood.

I finally set a date to leave: I would work up until 39 weeks, leaving myself a week off before my due date, and I'd be gone for six months. (I told myself that a lot of that would be non-ratings period, so it was almost like I wouldn't be away!) Lucie and I had found my replacement: a good friend of mine, Adene Cassidy. It was such a relief to have that sorted. She was also a reporter on *TT*, and, as well as being a lovely person, she's smart, capable and organised. With her on the job, I knew the fashion and entertainment beat was in very capable hands.

I was now feeling more content about myself and my future, and all my friends were commenting on the new, more relaxed me. They'd been expecting me to bring the old Sally to the pregnancy: nursery finished by six weeks, baby essentials bought, labelled, and organised, a spreadsheet for everything. But I was not my usual fastidious self about a lot of those details. I'd bought the Bugaboo already, and a tonne of adorable baby clothes. But as for the rest? Not so much. I was happy to enjoy being pregnant and hadn't put too much pressure on myself to get organised. As time passed, however, I realised I was actually beyond relaxed and bordering on unprepared.

Maha was super-excited about becoming an aunty. It was so

sweet to see and I loved how keen she was to know everything that was happening. In the same way that I was reading pregnancy books, she also wanted some books that catered just for aunties. I told her I'd never seen anything like that and she'd just have to wing it, but she wasn't satisfied with that. She Googled her way to a bunch of books, and 48 hours later was immersed in Aunty 101. Twenty-four hours after that and she'd shopped up a storm for bubba's nursery—books, toys and onesies—and she wanted to know what time I was conducting the nappy demonstration and when we were doing Pram Prac. I broke into a sweat. I was disorganised and in disarray. It was a lot of pressure keeping up with the aunty!

Marcus and Maha get along really well; over twelve years they've become brother and sister. Both enjoy having a laugh at my expense. Together they're a fierce combination, taking the piss out of me, and I don't stand a chance. It makes me laugh so much and always ends with me in hysterics crying, begging them to stop.

I'm fiercely protective of Maha, and it's my job as her proud big sister to be just that—her big sister. I'm supposed to be the strong one and to look after her. I think that's why I found it so tough when I was sick. I wanted to protect her from how bad it was, but I couldn't and she never expected me to. She did what she'd always done—she held my hand, she guided and encouraged me, and I realised then that all along it was Maha who was the big sister.

Marcus and I decided to head into a baby store to get everything we needed. We started by shopping for a second pram for Mum and Dad, but there were so many makes and models we both were completely overwhelmed and after a couple of hours, left despondent and empty handed. 'That was harder than choosing a car,' Marcus said, as we walked out of the store, pramless.

We decided to brave the baby shopping again after a girl-friend recommended Baby Kingdom. We were nervous, but encouraged by the good things we'd heard, and from the minute we walked in we were looked after beyond our wildest dreams. The staff helped us with everything, and best of all they answered our 4000 questions, including all my ridiculous ones. (Do you think the baby will like the Elton John or the Abba melodies CD better?) They guided us through the list of essentials, showing us what we really needed and helping us to separate it from the other stuff that's nice to have but not critical.

They also told me how many of each item we would need. When I said I needed 20 blankets and Marcus said, 'Ah, I doubt you'll need that many,' Pauline, the store manager, gently agreed with him and said that perhaps three or four would be sufficient. I appreciated her honesty because even though everything in the store was gorgeous and I wanted it all, the last thing I needed was to develop an even bigger shopping addiction than the one I had already!

Before arriving, we'd agreed to just choose a pram, cot and change table and then get the hell out of there, but they were so informative, patient and enthusiastic, and we were having so much fun, we decided to make an afternoon of it, and stayed until we'd crossed everything off the list. Three hours later we were smiling from ear to ear, and had everything we needed to make bubba's nursery a little piece of heaven.

When the furniture was delivered on Saturday morning,

I was like a kid on Christmas Day, up at 6 am ready to play with my new toys. I tried to get Marcus up but he lived for his weekend sleep-ins, and, since I knew they would soon be coming to an end, I took pity on him and let him sleep.

When everything was finally put together that was when I launched into typical super-organised Sally mode—washing, cleaning, sorting, and labelling like a woman possessed. I didn't stop until one o'clock on Monday morning, and collapsed into bed dead tired, knowing I had to be up for work in five hours but ridiculously happy and unable to stop smiling. It was full-blown nesting and I loved it.

◆ ◆ ◆

Most baby books suggest that you write a birth plan. Anyone who's actually *had* a baby usually laughs at that idea. Despite usually being very big on plans, I found I brought my new, more relaxed attitude to the birth. I knew what I wanted, broadly speaking—a natural birth, as drug-free as possible—but I was willing to let whatever happened happen. I certainly didn't issue instructions, which is so unlike me.

Of course I'd looked into all the options while I was doing my research, and I'd decided I wanted to try to incorporate Calmbirth methods. Calmbirth was created by a man called Peter Jackson (not the director of *Lord of the Rings*, the *other* Peter Jackson). It's all about breathing, and you have meditation CDs to listen to before the birth, and you take them with you when you go into labour to help you stay calm and focused. It's all about helping you let go of your fears so you can relax and stay calm and have a nice birth experience. I began listening to the CDs at night before bed. They helped me relax and I hoped they'd help on the big day. As the weeks progressed and I kept listening to the CDs, I actually found myself looking forward to the birth. I wondered if I'd look back on that and laugh at my naivety.

Peter teaches you how to practise Calmbirth at a two-day workshop, and you go along with a whole lot of other couples so he can show you what to do. I think Marcus liked the idea of it, and he thought the CDs were a good idea, but when it came to the actual workshop he was not so keen. We were in a room together with complete strangers, and the teacher was saying, 'Make sure you hug your partner a lot and stroke her hair.' So the women sat on the floor together and breathed and made noises while our partners held our hands and stroked our hair. Marcus was not into it.

'This is so weird,' he muttered. 'Why are we in this room with all these people, stroking each other?'

'It releases endorphins!' the instructor said.

'It releases endorphins!' I told Marcus.

I liked it and watching Marcus squirm made me laugh!

After the workshop was over we realised it *had* been worthwhile. It had helped us really think about the birth, so we could talk about how we'd manage it and what I thought I'd need Marcus to do to help me through it (massage, massage, massage!). I knew we'd be fine when we got into the delivery room. We were a team, we were going to a great hospital, the Mater, and I had an excellent obstetrician, so we were in safe hands.

◆ ◆ ◆

Towards the end, Marcus really began to worry I was doing too much.

The pace at which I was working was pretty full-on, and I never slowed down. If anything, I think I actually revved things up. In the back of my mind, I had the idea that this was my last window of opportunity to go full-throttle, my last chance to throw everything I had into work before I had to change gears and start being a mum.

Marcus would tell me, 'I think you should slow down. I think you need to rest more.'

I'd get mad at him and say, 'Don't tell me what to do,' and, 'I don't need to rest,' and 'I'm not tired.' Because I felt fine.

Nonetheless Marcus was concerned. He could see I was working at a blistering pace, and was more than a little worried, because he felt that what goes up must come down. I'd been on such a high, working so hard and burning so much energy for so long, he was concerned that when I finally stopped and had the baby, I might be at risk of post-natal depression. I didn't have a history of depression, but we knew from all our reading about pregnancy and birth that it was often high-achieving women who found it hardest to adjust to the radical change in their lifestyle that comes with a baby.

I think Marcus hoped that I might take the foot off the pedal so that we could spend some quiet time together as a couple, getting into a more relaxed frame of mind and preparing for this new stage we were about to enter, our life together as a family. But there was none of that. I worked almost up until the last possible moment. I couldn't see any reason not to: I felt great, I was enjoying life.

And even though people said I needed to rest *before* the birth because I wouldn't have the chance afterwards, I couldn't really see the point of that. Why rest when I didn't feel tired? I was feeling the fittest and healthiest I ever had and I couldn't see why that was going to change.

♦ ♦ ♦

Meanwhile, the parties kept coming. First, my baby shower. Maha and Camilla organised it for me, but being a bit of a control freak, I chose the venue, the menu and the invitations and insisted on having a baby-free baby shower: no baby games, baby balloons or baby ornaments, nothing with babies and nothing that referenced babies. 'So, it's basically a cocktail party by day?' Maha said. Exactly! And they happily complied. I chose the amazing Gazebo Wine Garden for the location—they do the best food and the courtyard is such a pretty girly spot that it made for the perfect setting. I loved having my closest friends together, and I could feel the love and excitement and felt very emotional. I realised how blessed I was to have such amazing girlfriends, and found myself hoping that my bubba would be just as blessed with equally beautiful girlfriends (or if I believed the ring test . . . great mates).

I finished up at work on 30 September 2011 at 39 weeks. The next week I was officially on leave, but I had a few things to finish off, so I had to pop back into the office for a few days. My last day in the office was 7 October 2011. On my last Friday at work I was 39 weeks pregnant and was still at my desk at 8 pm. My workmates had to pretty much force me out the door. At my farewell party, Gavin, our Supervising Producer, prepared a special poem to send me off. He covered my love of shoes, spreadsheets and Jon Bon Jovi, as well as my excitement about becoming a mum. It was just perfect, so funny and touching. All the people I worked with were there to wish me well and give me presents and a special gift for bubba—a Gucci Onesie. I was kind of jealous. Of course, I was teary. I'd been determined that I wouldn't cry, but I did. Everyone had been so supportive and kind that I found it very hard letting go—even though I knew I'd be back in what would probably feel like the blink of an eye.

Baby prep

Once work was over, it was time to prepare for the birth.

I packed my bag for the hospital, and put in things like lavender candles and scented oils and my iPod with a playlist of all my favourite Bon Jovi songs on it. I don't think the playlist ever got played in the end. I'd also put together a huge pregnancy folder that was itemised and categorised into sections. It was full of information and spreadsheets I'd made, on things like bath time, feeding and sleeping. That went into the bag, too. I'd bought the most beautiful gown—it wasn't just chic, it was also very practical—to wear instead of the standard issue hospital gown. My girlfriends told me it didn't matter what I wore and that it would end up covered in gunk, but I stubbornly refused to let the fashionista within die at the hospital doors.

Now it was just a matter of sitting back, enjoying my last few precious days of me-time, and waiting for bubba to come.

◆ ◆ ◆

In those last few days before the birth, I felt as if my life was finally in a good place. I'd left work on a high after a really good year; I'd pulled together some great segments—like the Zara story—met some amazing people, and I was finally beginning to feel comfortable with the progress I'd made within my career. I was leaving work knowing I had a few exciting, fun things lined up—magazine features and a series of 'Celebrity Mum' TV segments.

And I was hopeful that I was moving towards a more balanced perspective on my life. It's funny to think I sometimes teased my sister about her work–life balance when I was just as much of a workaholic. As I looked forward to the birth, I felt good about the idea that the balance of my life was about to change—I was sure—for the better. Although I loved my job, I never wanted to make my career the be-all and end-all. I didn't want all my happiness to be riding on this week's ratings or whether I landed that celebrity interview. I wanted a life where work was a part of my life, not my whole life.

If I'm honest, I was a bit nervous about how I would cope with not having my job to go to. I'd spent so long validating myself through work, I was a little bit afraid that once I stopped I'd collapse in a heap. I knew I'd be starting a new, even more satisfying job—I'd be a mum, the one thing I'd wanted for such a long time. But even when it was about to come to fruition, I couldn't be completely sure how I'd feel about it. I was certain I'd love my baby—I *already* loved my baby and I hadn't even met him or her yet. But I wasn't exactly sure how I'd feel about *me*. I think that was the source of all the tears and anxiety over telling Craig I was pregnant, and choosing a successor, and weeping at my farewell party. It wasn't because I was afraid of getting replaced. It was because I'd built so much of my identity and sense of self-worth into my job I wasn't sure who I was without it. Once all the noise and the bustle and the work stopped, what would I do? Who was I?

In spite of those lurking fears, I felt alive and full of hope and optimism. I really wanted to be a good mum. If I can pull that off, I thought, that will be my greatest achievement.

◆ ◆ ◆

Marcus and I had agreed that I was going to have six months off work to spend with the baby. Then when I went back to work, I'd go back three days a week, and the baby would be looked after by my mum and dad during the day. The rest of the week, the baby would be with me. We thought after the baby turned one we'd put her or him into daycare for two days a week, for some social interaction, and spend the third day with my mum and dad.

The conversations Marcus and I had about the childhood we wanted for our baby got me thinking about my own childhood, my parents, and the kind of mum I wanted to be.

Looking back, I could see I'd sometimes been harder on my parents than they deserved. When I was younger I'd been upset about things I felt they hadn't given me: material things—toys, travel, music tuition. I also used to criticise them for not being supportive enough of my dreams and ambitions, for nudging me towards safe choices instead of encouraging me to follow my passion.

Now, I see how hard it is as a parent: on the one hand you want the best for your child, you want them to be safe and secure and protected. But on the other, you've got a responsibility to allow them to be who they are and find their own path. How do you walk the line between protecting them and holding them back, supporting them and letting them fail?

And it became really clear to me that my parents gave me the one thing that really matters to a child: so much love. That was the best thing they could have done for me. They loved me and let me feel loved, and I would much rather have that than a life full of fancy holidays and toys, where there was something missing at the very core. If you grow up without that feeling of being loved, you can never go back and get it later. So I knew that was the one thing I wanted my baby to feel, above all else.

That love my parents gave me and their sense of optimism about life is their greatest gift to me. I think it's the thing that's truly shaped me and made me who I am. And, because they gave me so much love, I feel like they've given me more than I could ever use, so I'm happy to share it around. All my relationships are centred on love—I don't know how to do a half-hearted friendship. When I like someone, I'm all in.

So these are the gifts I wanted to give my baby: all that love my parents had given me, and all the courage and bravery Marcus had shown me and helped me to find in myself. I wanted my baby to grow up with the courage to be bold, to take chances and follow dreams, knowing that whatever they do and whoever they are, their parents will still love them to bits.

Sucker punch

I was 41 weeks pregnant when I was told I had stage-three breast cancer.

'You've got a large tumour in your breast,' the doctor at the Sydney Breast Clinic told me. 'It's difficult to assess exactly how big it is because of your pregnancy, but we estimate it's over five centimetres. You'll need to see an oncologist and go through it all in more detail, and you'll need to start treatment within the week. We've already called your obstetrician. He's going to induce you, so you'll have your baby tomorrow. He's waiting to see you now.'

Marcus and I sat there in the doctor's office, stunned, staring at the doctor. I felt Marcus reach out and take my hand. I honestly felt like I'd had a collision with a semitrailer. Cancer? How could I have cancer?

'What does this mean?' I asked. 'Am I going to die?'

'I can't really advise you on that,' she said. 'Your oncologist will be able to tell you more. You'll need to have more tests to find out exactly what we're dealing with.'

We were both completely floored. How were we supposed to process something like that? They'd told me I had breast cancer and that it was stage three, but what did that actually mean? Did I have six months to live? Could I die tomorrow? Or was this totally treatable? The doctor wasn't saying—I'd have to wait to get the answers from my oncologist—and I didn't even *have* an oncologist.

I could see the worry, concern and the sadness in her eyes. That look made it clear that something terrible was happening to me, and I was so frightened I couldn't stop crying.

'I'm so sorry.' She said again. 'You need to go and see your obstetrician now.'

So we left the doctor's office, went to the front desk and paid the bill. It had cost me about $2000 to learn I had cancer. I reckon if you go and there's nothing wrong you should pay, but if you've got cancer, they should just say it's on the house. You've got bigger issues. The bill's on us.

We found a cab and went across town to see Stephen Morris, my obstetrician. I'd stopped crying, but was utterly dumb-founded. I couldn't speak. When we got there the waiting room was full of people, but Lex, the nurse, came over immediately, looking so full of concern I started howling again. She whisked me away to a quiet room so I could sob in private and not freak out all the other pregnant ladies.

Then she took me in to see Stephen. He said, 'Let's focus on what's important. Let's focus on getting the baby out. Tomorrow we'll induce you and we'll make sure that the baby's safe. Together with the hospital we've found an oncologist for you—she'll come and see you and we can get the ball rolling. But for now, try and focus on the baby.'

He told us to go home and try to get some sleep, so I'd have the energy I was going to need to get through labour.

'I can't do it,' I said. 'I can't give birth now, I just can't. Can't I just have a caesarean?'

From the beginning I'd been very focused on having a natural birth. But now all that went out the window. There was no way I was going to be able to go home and get some sleep and have enough energy to do this massive thing. I just didn't have it in me. I wanted to curl up in a dark room and cry.

'I'm sorry, Sally, but you can't have a caesarean. You need to go into chemo as soon as possible, and one of the things chemo does is prevent your body from recovering from surgery. Now, more than ever, we need you to have a natural birth. Of course if things do go wrong, we will give you a Caesar, but we really need to work together as much as we can to have this baby naturally, so you can get treatment for this other thing as soon as possible. Okay?'

I didn't know what to do. It was all so overwhelming. I couldn't think. I couldn't process any of it. And it seemed like all the decisions had been taken out of my hands anyway—I was in the care of the doctors now. I just said, 'Okay, okay, sure.'

I was sobbing as we went back to the car. 'What do we do now?' I said. 'I don't know what to do.'

I realised I was going to have to tell my parents and my sister, and that's when I really began to howl. I kept thinking, *Oh my God, how will I tell my mum? She's going to fall apart.*

We drove across the Sydney Harbour Bridge, heading for my parents' house. Marcus and I were struggling to come to grips with the news, and what made it so terrifying was the fact that they'd given us so little to go on. Yes, we knew there were tumours, and they were big. But there was so much we didn't know, the kinds of things you're desperate to know: what are my chances? What can we do to fix this? What's going to happen? We didn't have answers to any of those questions, and it would be days before we did. And in the absence of that information, our fears multiplied.

It's strange the way I reacted to the news: I swung from worrying about my mortality, to worrying about the silliest, most trivial things. One minute I was thinking that I'm going to die and how terrible that's going to be, and then I'd try and pull myself together and think, no, it's going to be okay. And that's when I'd start to cry about all these other ridiculous things like, losing my hair, and I'm going to be ugly, and I'll lose my eyebrows and my job, and no one will be friends with me.

And then I'd swing back to, Oh my God, my mum, how will I tell her? And then I've worked so hard, and how did this happen? Do you think I got cancer because I once made a mean joke about someone? And then I'd think, why now? Why did I get it? I don't understand, did I do something? Is the universe punishing me?

And then I'd go wildly back to, Oh my God, I might die. And I can't bear to think about that. So it's on to worrying about my job. Then I'd swing back to thinking about my unborn baby, and what's going to happen to us—and that really is just sickeningly unbearable—so I'd turn back to worrying about losing my hair. It's like my brain was a wildly spinning top, and I couldn't keep up. I'd focus, briefly, on the trivial things because the huge stuff was too hard to face.

And the warning that Christine, my naturopath, had given me all those years ago kept ringing in my mind: 'Don't have IVF—you'll get breast cancer.' Had she been right after all?

◆ ◆ ◆

I'd arranged to do these five little segments on *The Morning Show* called 'Celebrity Mum'. I had already shot one, on pregnancy fashion, and we were going to do some others on exercising post-pregnancy, baby sleep routines, that kind of thing. I'd been so excited about having this little project to do while on maternity leave. Now I was crying about that too. 'What about my "Celebrity Mum" segment? No-one wants a celebrity who has no hair.' And then I thought about it some more. 'No hair and no boobs!'

Marcus kept trying to reassure me as my mind skipped from one anxiety to another, but I knew he was absolutely devastated. Later, he told me that mentally he'd gone straight to the worst-case scenario. He was really afraid that on the eve of what should have been the most joyful time of our lives, we'd just been handed a death sentence.

In the end we didn't go to Mum and Dad's straight away. We went and sat in a park and tried to come to terms with what had happened. It's not the kind of thing anyone can come to terms with in two hours, but we tried.

Marcus was trying to be positive, telling me they do great stuff with breast cancer. His mum had breast cancer, and she hadn't needed chemo, she'd survived and is fine now. He kept insisting, they can do good things for breast cancer, you'll be okay . . . He was doing his best to stay calm and help me not fall apart.

Then we went to see Mum and Dad. They'd known I was having tests that day, but I'd told them it was nothing to worry about, so they weren't expecting bad news.

I still remember walking into their house. It was one of those heart-stopping moments, because Mum just looked at us and said 'What's wrong?'

She must have seen it in our faces.

I said to Marcus, 'You say it.'

So he told them.

◆ ◆ ◆

In the beginning, I couldn't actually say the words 'I have cancer', because if I said them, it was real. I just couldn't believe I had cancer.

I'd been so worried about Mum and Dad and how they were going to react. I couldn't bear to see my parents in any pain. And I knew if they fell apart, then I'd have to be the strong one, saying, 'Don't worry, it's going to be fine.' But they were both amazing. Mum was so strong and so positive. She told me all the things I needed to hear: 'You're going to get through this. You're going to be okay. Lots of people have cancer and they get through it. You'll be fine and we'll stick together, and whatever you need we're here for you.'

I think if she'd fallen apart, I would have been really scared. That would have made it real: Oh God, Mum's crying her eyes out, this is serious. Maybe I *am* going to die! But when we finally left their place, I didn't feel quite so bad. I'd broken the news to someone, and they hadn't reacted like it was the end of the world, they'd really made me feel it was all going to be okay. I started to think, *Maybe it's not actually so bad. Maybe they'll just take the tumour out and I'll be fine. This isn't going to be so terrible after all.*

This is why they're such wonderful parents. What could be more devastating than to have your child, who you love so much, tell you that she has cancer? I can't even imagine how I'd feel if something like that happened to my own child. I'd be gutted. But because you love your child so much, you have to be strong enough to give them *your* strength. And that's what my parents did for me that night. They helped me believe that whatever lay ahead, I could get through it, because they loved me and they were going to be there to support me. I know there were plenty of times when my mother cried over what happened, but not in front of me. For me, she was as strong as I needed her to be. I'm so grateful to her for that.

Then we went to see my sister.

Maha and I had made plans to meet for lunch that day, but when the tests dragged on, I'd had to cancel. At lunchtime I'd texted her to say I'd let her know what was happening as soon as I got the results—and then I'd gone completely silent. Since then she'd sent me about a hundred messages and I hadn't replied to any of them. She knew something was wrong.

When we arrived at my sister's house she had a mate over for coffee. I kept sending psychic messages to this guy saying, *Please leave, why are you still here, please leave, please leave.* But I didn't want to make a scene in front of him and I certainly couldn't say it with him there. Eventually, he left, and I was able to tell my sister what had happened. And she completely fell apart.

Maha has always looked up to me—she adores me, and I adore her. We've always been close, super-close, we talk to each other twenty times a day, and throughout my life she's been my partner in crime. We live near each other, we work near each other, we drive to work together. Our lives are entwined and we love each other to bits. So for her to hear that something so terrible and so frightening had happened to someone who loomed so large in her life was just devastating. Later she told me that I'd always been the strongest person she knew, and the thought that I *wasn't* going to be the strongest person she knew any more was just too much. 'You can't abandon me,' she said, and she was sobbing and sobbing and sobbing. It was heart-breaking. In that moment I wasn't worried for me, I was worried about her. It's awful to see someone you love in so much pain. I kept reassuring her over and over, 'It's going to be okay. No, really. I'm going to be okay.'

I wasn't sure if I believed it or not, but I knew Maha needed to believe it, so I repeated it until it seemed to sink in.

Finally we left Maha's place and went home at around 10 pm. It's shocking to walk in the front door and think that in less than one day, everything has changed. It's the same apartment, but everything feels so different.

Just this morning I was happy and hopeful and I was about to embark on something magical, but now I'm back and everything has changed. The future looked bleak, and terrifying.

I did what Stephen Morris had told me to do. I went to bed and tried to get some sleep, but my brain was churning—deep sleep was impossible. I kept thinking and thinking and sobbing. And I'd fall asleep, but then I'd wake up and remember and start sobbing again.

Marcus tried to comfort me, but I could hear him crying in the dark, too. He didn't want me to know—and that was heartbreaking too. Here he was, finally about to become a dad—his lifelong dream—and now his wife and the mother of his baby might be about to die.

The night before I gave birth was the worst of my life. There was so much we didn't know about what was to come, it was terrifying. The urgency with which they were rushing me into hospital left us fearing the worst—were they rushing because they needed to get me into treatment, or because they wanted to get the baby out before I died? I was in fear of my life, and my baby's life. It was horrifying. And no-one had said anything reassuring, like 'It's just a bit of keyhole surgery and you're going to be alright.' They'd told me nothing. But I'd seen the look of panic on their faces, and that made *me* panic.

I've had bad nights since then. But I still think that night was the worst. Being told you've got cancer really is a game-changer. Your happy pre-cancer life comes to an end, and your new life begins, your life with cancer, and that's a very different prospect.

Welcome to the world, Annabelle

The next morning we went to the Mater Hospital, and it was the first of many times I felt a horrible sense of irony. Not long ago we'd been in the same hospital, going up in the same lift to go to our pre-natal classes. I remembered telling Marcus, 'The next time I come back here I'll be in labour! I'll be holding my stomach and I'll be having contractions and we'll be having our baby!' I'd been giddy with excitement about this wonderful thing that was about to happen to us.

But now that I was here and it was finally happening to us, there was no joy, no excitement. I was filled with dread and the fear of death. It felt so wrong that I should be coming here to give birth feeling like I was under a death sentence.

Marcus held my hand as we walked into the maternity ward. I was bawling my eyes out. A nurse came up to us and asked, 'Are you being induced?'

I nodded and cried, and she gave me a sort of sympathetic look and said, 'It's really not that bad, you know.'

She thought I was just being a drama queen. Later she came back in and apologised. Somebody had obviously told her about my situation. That would happen to me a lot in the months ahead.

They gave me the drugs to induce me at about midday, and then we just had to settle in and wait for it all to start. I'd promised to let my best friends know when I finally went into labour, but now I didn't want to tell anyone. When you're about to drop, everyone's so excited and they keep sending you messages: How are you? Where are you at? Any news? Have you had the baby? I knew if I told them all I was in the hospital the number of messages would be off the charts. How could I tell them some of it without going into all of it? How could I explain why I was being induced when I'd told everyone I wanted a natural birth? I couldn't face having to deal with everybody being happy and upbeat and excited, when I had something terrible hanging over me. Something I couldn't even say out loud, let alone broadcast to all my friends.

I told a few people but not the people you'd imagine you'd call in a crisis. It's actually harder to tell your friends because you love them so much. So I avoided it. It felt too big, too hard, too painful. So I opted for the practical measures. I called Jane, my agent, and she was as floored by the terrible news as I'd been. I also sent Craig an email that morning, asking him to call, but he didn't. So while I waited for the contractions to start, I got on my Blackberry and sent a few emails to Craig and the Melbourne *Today Tonight* office, who were going to be doing the Sarah Jessica Parker interview.

Marcus, watching me, said, 'What are you doing?' He couldn't believe I was thinking about work at a time like this. It seems ridiculous that, with everything that was going on, I could care about a celebrity interview. But I was trying to believe it would be alright, and I desperately needed the distraction. Still Craig didn't call me. I called Naomi Shivaramen, a good friend of mine; she was filling in as our Chief of Staff, because Lucie was on holiday in the States with Sarah. I wanted to find out what was going on.

'Oh, Craig's not in the office. Did you need to speak to him about something?'

'Naomi, I've worked there for four years and I've never asked him to call me about anything, so if I've asked him to ring me, I thought it'd be obvious it's important, and it's urgent.'

'Oh. Okay.' Pause. 'Are you resigning?'

'No. I'm not resigning. Just please get him to call me.'

At last, Craig did call me. 'Sorry I didn't ring you. I thought you wanted to talk about Sarah Jessica Parker, but then I saw your email about it and assumed it was all sorted.'

'Craig, I'm in the hospital.' I started. I took a deep breath and continued. 'I've got cancer.'

'And I'll be honest,' I added, 'I'm really quite worried about my job.' Then I started to cry.

Craig was shocked by the news, but he said what he always says: 'Don't worry about your job. It will be here whenever you come back. Just focus on getting through this.'

I look back now and think, *What idiot worries about their job when they might not actually survive?* But it's just too painful to think that you might not. Especially when you're about to give birth, which ought to be the best thing that's ever happened to you. The idea that I might not be around for the baby I've just brought into the world is too cruel, so I reverted to these other more mundane issues, like Sarah Jessica Parker, and my job.

Mum and Dad and Maha came in to visit, and that was good. We talked about normal stuff, and everything seemed alright, and there were a few little moments where I could forget about everything.

But only a few moments, because while I was waiting for my labour to start, a flurry of doctors and nurses were coming in to perform more biopsies and tests, and saying, 'Hi, I'm your surgeon.' 'Hi, you're going to have this oncologist.' 'Hi, we're going to do blood tests, we're going to do bone scans . . .' And the whole thing was driving me crazy because I was thinking, *None of you people should be here. I haven't even unpacked my lavender candles yet, what are you all doing in here?! I've been trying for so long to get to this point, and I'm finally here and now everyone's in my space, and all I want is to be alone with my husband and have my baby in peace.* But I could see the worry in their faces, and the sadness and the pity for the poor pregnant girl with cancer. And I couldn't escape the frightening feeling that if they were all rushing around like this, doing a million tests, introducing me to a bunch of doctors, it all had to be really serious.

At about 6 pm, after six hours of waiting and having tests done, the drugs kicked in. I was experiencing serious contractions, and was in quite a lot of pain. My family left and the cancer people left and it was just Marcus and I and the two midwives. Finally, I could shut everything out, and focus on the baby. All I could think was I want to meet this baby. I'd been so freaked out by the diagnosis that I wasn't completely sure I was going to make it through the next 24 hours—if I was *that* ravaged and riddled with cancer how long was I going to last? But I knew I wanted to meet and hold my baby. That's all I wanted. For the next six or seven hours I pushed through the labour. I had a bath, and I resisted the drugs for as long as possible. By midnight, however, it was all getting too painful. My contractions were relentless, like a barrage and coming every three minutes, lasting a minute each. I was so tired, I felt delirious. My teeth were chattering uncontrollably and I was in excruciating pain. (Now I know that chemo is much worse but at the time it was the most intense pain I'd ever felt.) It was time for an epidural.

When we'd first talked about the birth, I'd warned Marcus not to keep asking me if I wanted an epidural. 'I'll tell you when I want it, but don't ask me.' And he'd said, 'Okay, fine.'

'Are you sure?' he asked now.

'I said I want an epidural!'

'Well, you said don't ask me.'

'You're not asking, I'm telling!'

I got my epidural. Putting it in was tough, because you're in the middle of contractions and your whole body wants to convulse and they're telling you 'Don't move.' But once it kicked in, it was bliss. We both got a couple of hours' precious sleep, me on the bed, Marcus on a fold-out bed in the delivery suite.

The epidural started to wear off down one side, and the pain was so severe, I was yelling for more drugs. By this stage it was about two in the morning. Stephen came in then and said, 'No, no more drugs, it's time to push as the baby is starting to crown. It's time to get this baby out.' He then left me with Marcus and the midwife as I started the pushing, for the next couple of hours. When the baby's head still hadn't progressed, Stephen came back in.

When my obstetrician first turned up he looked all schmick, like he'd just stepped off the golf course. He was in his polo shirt and chinos and his designer shoes, and then he got changed and put on a pair of Wellingtons, and I thought, *Oh, what's happening that you need those?* And then I found out: it's messy and disgusting, there's blood, and worse, everywhere. And I thought, *Oh, it's so good that I'm up the top and can't see what's happening down there.*

Stephen told me to push, and I tried to push, but because the epidural hadn't worn off fully I couldn't.

'You're pushing in the wrong spot,' Stephen said.

'What spot? I can't feel anything, I don't know!'

By this stage I had already been pushing for a few hours. And it was so hard, and I was so tired, and we weren't really getting anywhere. But we tried, all four of us. Before I had the baby I used to think, *What do obstetricians really do? They come in at the end and catch the baby and say, 'Well done, it's a girl. Where's my big fat cheque?'* But Stephen was right in there, he had his knee up and he was pulling and pulling, his muscles were straining and I thought, *Oh wow, you're really earning your money.* I had Marcus on one side of me holding one leg, a midwife on the other side holding my other leg as I pushed through each contraction. I pushed and pushed—4 am, 5 am—but progress was slow and I just couldn't get that baby out. I'd tried my best but I was exhausted. At 5.45, Stephen told me he was going to try suction. He attached the suction cap to the baby's head and started pulling like he was trying to remove a stuck cork from a wine bottle. And there was a lot of grunting, and a lot more pushing. I felt like I had no push left.

Finally, at 6.32 am on Saturday 15th October 2011, my baby was born.

'It's a girl!' Stephen announced, and placed her on my chest.

Such an overwhelming moment, in so many ways: my first sight of my tiny little beautiful baby. The feel of her skin on my skin, still slick from the birth. The relief that the pain and struggle of bringing her into the world is over. The sheer love I felt for her the instant I saw her. After everything that had happened to me over the last 24 hours, I'd been so frightened she'd be sick or harmed or that something would be wrong with her, so it was an immense relief to know that she was whole, healthy and perfect.

And I'd given birth to a little girl, just as I'd wished. It felt like a lovely bonus, a gift from the universe: Hey sorry about the whole cancer thing, here, I'll throw you a girl to make it up to you.

I couldn't get over how small she was. I felt fiercely protective of her, filled with joy at the thought that we were finally going to be a family. But, at the same time, I felt a crushing sadness at the possibility this might be the only moment we had together. I thought, *What if this is it?* The tears flowed as Marcus and I held each other and our baby for the first time.

I looked down at her, trying to see whether she looked like me or like Marcus, and then she grunted. She was pink, and all scrunched up, and she was grunting. Marcus looked at me and said, 'She looks like a little piglet.'

I laughed so hard. It was true. She did. She looked like a perfect pink piglet, and she was ours. I thought my heart would burst with happiness—and sadness.

◆ ◆ ◆

After the baby had been checked and weighed and washed, I got up and had a shower, then we were moved from the delivery suite to the maternity ward.

Only a few weeks earlier I'd been joking with Maha about the maternity ward at the Mater. I'd heard there was one room in the maternity unit which was bigger than the others. It was a corner suite, unofficially called the Packer and Murdoch Suite because it was supposedly where all the famous people go to have their babies.

'I would love to get that suite,' I said to my sister.

'What can we do to make sure you get it?' she asked.

We started imagining ridiculous schemes together and rolled around laughing, trying to think up different ways we could wrangle that suite.

'I could ring up and pretend to be the paparazzi and just make out someone really exciting is coming, and it's you, and then maybe you'll get it,' my sister said.

'That won't work,' I said. 'When they see it's just me, they'll be disappointed and take the room off me.'

Guess which room they moved me into?

It's funny how life turns out: there were all these things I'd really wanted—but not under those conditions. I'd really wanted the corner suite and I'd really wanted Marcus to be able to stay with me in my room (something they don't usually allow at the Mater), but not under these conditions. And in the months that followed, it kept happening to me. I wanted to write a book, but not about having cancer. I love Kyle and Jackie O and have always wished I could go on their show. When do I get to go? When I have cancer. It's like the old saying: be careful what you wish for.

Now, when we're wishing for things, we're always really specific. Sometimes Maha will say something like, I wish I had more time to spend with you and the baby, and then she'll quickly add, not that I want to lose my job. We know better than to tempt fate.

◆ ◆ ◆

We spent those first few precious hours after the birth having a quiet morning as a family with our new baby. The first thing we had to do was decide on a name. We had a shortlist picked out: three girl's names—Annabelle, Alyssa and Lucie—but no boy's names. Every time I suggested a boy's name, Marcus would say, 'Nah. I went to school with a Lachlan/Xavier/Sebastian/Terence, and he was a dickhead.' Every name I loved had been tainted by someone Marcus knew. All the names he wanted were things from Greek and Roman history, and I vetoed his choices. So it was lucky for all of us that we had a girl, otherwise he might still be nameless.

After much careful consideration, and a lot of gazing adoringly at her to see what name suited her best, we decided on Annabelle Grace Obermeder.

My parents came in to see us, and Marcus's parents and sister came from Canberra, and they were all thrilled to meet Annabelle. For my parents she was their first grandchild, and for Marcus's parents she was the first girl. It was a happy, magical time. Everyone wanted to hold her and have their picture taken with her. We were briefly like any family with a newborn. There was cooing and excitement and love and laughter as we all stared at this miracle. It was a brief reprieve.

And now, looking back, I'm so grateful to Stephen because he made sure I had the birth I wanted. He said to me, 'So much is going to happen to you after this that you won't have any control over, I want to make sure that you get the birth you want.' I had a natural birth, and it all went really well, and even if I can't have another baby, I won't die wondering what it's like, because I know that I've done it.

Marcus Obermeder

Sally's husband

My wife is everything to me. She doesn't always know it, and like a lot of husbands, I don't often say it, but it's true. I married her because I knew she was the one . . . the one to share my life with, the one to have a family with. I could never even imagine a future without her and to conceive a child was for me the ultimate blessing of our union. So how could it be, on the eve of what should have been the happiest day of our lives, that I should receive that fateful call asking me to come down to the breast cancer clinic to pick up my wife.

Instantly I knew that it was bad news—they don't call you in for anything else— yet when I got there Sal seemed strangely detached from reality. My heart was instantly crushed by the cruelty of the situation . . . Sal sitting there as innocent as our unborn child in her belly, trying to keep her mind busy on work matters in a subconscious attempt to hold back the walls of her life, which were caving in all around her. I thought, 'You don't deserve to die and I can't live without you.'

I sat down and held Sal as the staff at the cancer clinic looked directly at her with as much mercy as they could muster, and delivered the death blow, 'Sally, you have cancer.' This time I could see the poison arrow shatter her veneer and the truth now struck her in the heart. I became very angry as there was nothing I could do to save Sally from this painful new reality. I paced about hyperventilating and became extremely agitated. I just needed to get out of there, grab Sal and save her from everything, but of course there was no escape. This was just the beginning of a relentless, exhausting nightmare that would last many, many months, the outcome of which was very uncertain. At that time things looked grim at best.

Never Stop Believing

Twenty-four hours later, I watched my wife bravely and instinctively conquer that miracle of miracles that is childbirth. At that point in my life it was both the most awesome and the most shocking thing I had ever witnessed. Regardless of how tired I was during that 18-hour ordeal, I was so proud and inspired by my wife who endured ten thousand times more. This would be the first of many times over the next year that I would feel this way as I witnessed the strength of her spirit and the way the love of humanity can help anyone rise to defeat insurmountable odds.

I wasn't sure what to do throughout this devastating period in our lives, so I did the same as other men I knew in very similar situations: I prepared for the worst and then got busy doing everything in my power I could to help Sal beat this illness. But in truth this amounted to very little as it was a journey that in its darkest hours Sal would have to face alone.

I continued to go to work and do my best, so that there was still some sense of stability and normality to everyday life. I wanted to quit and look after Sal but as great testament to her conviction that she would beat this, she urged me to do well at work so that when we came out the other side we would at least have some financial stability.

On the flipside to such positivity were Sal's darkest moments. As I was there trying to support her emotionally, we often cried together into the small hours of the morning. In reality people face the prospect of death alone. Almost selfishly I would beg her not to give up on Annabelle and I, but I could see how difficult it really was. In the end, to say Sal dug deep is a gross understatement, yet with the grace of God and the love and support of all our family, friends and thousands of other people she has never even met, she eventually triumphed.

My wife Sally is the most beautiful, courageous and inspirational person I have ever met and I continue to love her and our gorgeous daughter Annabelle with all my heart and soul. To everyone who supported us, I humbly thank you.

The honeymoon
is over

But by lunchtime our honeymoon was over. It was back to our new reality. Back to the sea of doctors flooding in, saying, 'Okay, baby's out, now let's get back to it.'

It was totally overwhelming. It had been 18 hours since I was induced, I was in a daze and had barely slept in two days. Like every new mum, my hormones were going crazy, but instead of spending those first few days resting, recovering and getting to know my baby, I was thrust straight into full-on cancer treatment. I had no idea what was happening or where I needed to be. I had a nurse, Caroline, who looked after me, and she'd come in and tell me where I was going and what I was doing. I was like a befuddled starlet being wheeled from interview to interview by her PR person, only in my case it was, 'Okay, I'm going to take you downstairs now. You've got to have a bone scan.' 'I'm taking you downstairs, you're going to have a cat scan.' 'At 2 pm this doctor's coming, this person's coming. Someone's coming to take swabs, tests.'

I was also trying to get to grips with all the stuff I needed to know as a new mother. I'd never changed a nappy before. I wanted to be with the other new mums, popping off to the bathing talk and the breastfeeding class, but I was too busy having medical tests.

I'd been very clear before all this happened that I wanted to breastfeed, and when the doctors told me that wouldn't be possible, I was devastated. I was going to be starting chemo shortly, so if I did feed, it would only be for a couple of days. Obviously, there'd be no feeding off the breast that had the cancer in it, so I'd only be able to breastfeed from one side. Given those restrictions, some of my doctors couldn't see any point in trying.

The point was, I had always thought I *would* breastfeed, so I was very upset that the choice was being taken away from me. I wanted to put my head in the sand about my condition and walk out of the hospital with my baby and say to hell with you all. But I couldn't. I had to do the right thing. Then Dr Kylie Snook, my breast surgeon, intervened. She has small children of her own, so she understood how I felt, and she suggested that I could try to breastfeed, even if it was only for a day or two, so that at least Annabelle and I would have had the experience. I was so grateful to her for stepping in and giving me the choice, even if it was only for a very short time.

Annabelle had two colostrum feeds. It was painful, but I endured it. I wanted to make good. I knew this was the start of tough times for all three of us, and I wanted to be sure she got whatever I could give her. I was desperate to ensure she didn't suffer or lose out. I felt so terribly guilty I couldn't feed her. Rationally I understood why I couldn't, but in my heart I felt guilty. Breastfeeding seemed so special, so personal, a gift of love, a connection and bond that you give your child. Knowing that there are plenty of other ways to bond with your baby, and to feed her, didn't diminish the sadness I felt. It was one more loss among so many losses. After those two feeds I started taking the pills to stop the milk. It was like all of these important decisions are made for you. But at least we had the chance to try, albeit briefly.

While all this was going on, my friends were ringing to find out if we'd had the baby. At first I hadn't known what to tell everybody. I didn't want to send out a general text message saying, 'We've had the baby. Yay! By the way, I've got cancer.' I didn't want something as joyous as Annabelle's birth to be overshadowed by this terrible news. I wanted to protect her from having her first moments on earth tarnished by what had happened to me. She'd finally arrived and I wanted her to feel special. She deserved her own welcome. So we sent out a note announcing the birth and left it at that. But then, of course, my friends kept ringing and wanting to come to visit—and I didn't want to see anyone. I didn't want to have to tell them. Every time the phone rang, I'd hand it to Marcus and say, 'You tell them.' Poor Marcus. He had to tell my best friends. He had to tell everyone. I just couldn't speak to anyone.

The same thing happened whenever we had a conversation

with my doctors. I'd been really lucky with the doctors I got. Stephen Morris had helped put me in touch with them, and later people told me how lucky I'd been, because Fran Boyle, my oncologist, and Kylie Snook, my surgeon, are two of the top people in their fields. Both of them came in to see me in those early days and explained what was going to happen. I had a million questions, but when I was face to face with my doctors I couldn't ask them. The doctors would talk and I'd zone out. I'd try to listen and stay focused, but then I'd drift off and start thinking, *Wow, she has really nice shoes.* It was too much for me to hear, too much for me to take in. Marcus had to do all the listening and ask all the crucial questions.

The questions I really wanted answered were: What are my chances? How likely is it that this is going to work? How much time have I got? But we could never really get answers to those questions. Until the results of all my tests came in, no-one knew what we were facing. We were in limbo, waiting.

◆ ◆ ◆

My room was right at the end of the corridor, so whenever I was coming and going from my appointments I'd walk past all the other rooms, and there'd be nothing but laughter and happiness. That's the maternity ward, that's why people love to work there, it's a place of joy, until you reached my room. In my room, it was a sea of doctors, with me always crying my eyes out. The contrast between how it should have been, and how it actually was, was extreme.

Every few hours there was another test. A cat-scan, blood tests, bone tests, more mammograms, more biopsies. One day I had to have a full body scan, which meant drinking this radioactive substance, so for the next 12 hours there was no skin-on-skin contact with my baby. I couldn't hold her; I couldn't be near her. She was only two days old, and I couldn't pick her up. I know twelve hours isn't forever, but it felt so wrong.

So much of the news we were getting was bad, we celebrated every little piece of good news we could get. When I was first diagnosed, my tumours were so big and so aggressive they were worried that they'd spread to other parts of my body as well. A lot of my tests were to find out whether I had any more tumours in my bones, brain, all the rest of me. When those results came back clear it was a huge relief. One of my besties, Lizzie, had brought around cheese and bickies, so with Marcus we had celebratory cheese and bickies in my suite. Yay! I only have breast cancer! This is great news. We were on a high that day.

The next day, of course, I was crying again. Stephen Morris came in to see me and noticed that my eyes were puffy.

'What's wrong with you?' It was as if he was irritated with me.

'Why do you think I'm crying?' I thought to myself. 'Because I got the fish instead of the chicken at lunch?' but instead I just said, 'Hello? Cancer? Remember?'

'Oh, but it's only in the breast,' he said in an attempt to cheer me up.

Oh, I thought, *only breast cancer. Good! Why the fuss then?*

I laughed to myself and still laugh about it now.

On reflection, I feel sure that everyone we saw at the hospital in those first few days was convinced that the tumours in my breast wouldn't be the only ones. I think they imagined I was riddled with them, and once the results of the tests came back, we'd know that I was a goner. Nobody said so, of course, but we could sense it from the way they looked at us.

When the tests showed that there weren't any other tumours, the mood shifted a little. Things were still grim, but the fact that they hadn't spread, meant that there was just a little ray of hope, whereas before they'd thought there was none.

◆ ◆ ◆

I may never know what it's like for other mothers to be spending those first few days in the strange little enclosed world that is a maternity ward. My friends have talked about the swooping emotions, the hormonal highs and the blues that come when your milk comes in. I missed out on all that. I spent those days with my emotions swinging dizzyingly between fear for my life, to celebrating any good news, to grieving for all the things Marcus and Annabelle and I should have been experiencing together in our first days as a family. But in the midst of it all— the tests, the visits from the oncologist, the terror—there was this little baby, so tiny and so precious. My baby, the baby I'd longed for. Whenever I could, I'd hold her, and breathe in the smell of her, and feel her softness and her fragility and her strength. It felt miraculous to think that even though death was hovering, my baby was full of powerful, wonderful life. All I could think about was how much I wanted to love and nurture and protect her, for as long as I possibly could.

Before my diagnosis I'd thought a lot about the importance of my baby and the gift of love; but now it seemed more urgent than ever. If there was even the chance that I might not live to see my baby grow up, it was more crucial than ever that I made sure she knew how much she was loved. That was my mission:

to let my child know, with every means I had at my disposal—my words and my touch, my gaze, my presence in the room, even through the power of my thoughts—that she was loved. I told myself that if the worst happened, and she had to grow up without me, at the very least I could leave an impression upon her heart that would let her know that at the profoundest level, she had been deeply loved.

◆ ◆ ◆

A week after the birth they finally let us go home.

It was bliss to walk into our apartment again. After the constant bustle of the hospital it seemed wonderfully peaceful and quiet. And it felt like the culmination of a dream to be introducing Annabelle to the home that we'd created for her.

The first day, we put Annabelle in the pram and walked around the block. We did ordinary stuff—we went to the shop, we bought bread and milk—and I thought, *This feels so nice. We've got our baby and she's so beautiful. Life's good.* It felt like we were back in our normal lives.

That feeling was short-lived, of course. On the way home we ran into our neighbours Mike and Dominique, and they'd heard the news. I started crying and they started crying. It was never possible to keep the unhappiness at bay for long. But we tried.

Of course everybody wanted to come round and meet the baby. Marcus had told a few people the news, but many people still weren't aware. They'd come round to see us, and they'd bring presents and it was lovely. We'd talk about the baby, and then I'd have to say, 'Look, there's something I have to tell you. I've got cancer.' And there'd be silence. They'd be floored, and we'd be sitting there staring at each other, and I'd be crying. It happened over and over again. It was such a sad way to have to introduce my baby to the world.

Sarah and Lucie, my darling friends from work, had both been on holiday in the States when all this happened. I had called them to tell them and they were desperate to come and see me. They got off the plane and came straight to the hospital. I cried as soon as I saw them. Then when I thought things couldn't get any worse, they said, 'have you heard? Giuliana Rancic's been diagnosed with breast cancer.' A minute before I didn't think I could possibly be any sadder. Then my heart broke a bit more.

As the host of *E! News*, Giuliana Rancic has the dream version of my job. It used to be a running joke between Lucie and me that I should run away to LA and become besties with Giuliana. There were so many parallels in our lives: the job, the struggle to have a baby. We even share the same birthday. But it's cancer that finally brought us together. She gave me a lot of support through my own battle—both publicly and personally. I'm eternally grateful to Sarah and Kyle and Jackie O for putting us in touch. Guiliana has become a great friend. She's a beacon of strength and positivity—her fight and her will are inspiring. We've joked that hopefully Annabelle will grow up to be a 'cougar' and hook up with Guiliana and Bill's younger son Duke. I just wish neither of us had had to get cancer to become besties!

◆ ◆ ◆

It's hard to describe what a huge adjustment it was, having two massive changes in our lives at once.

First, there was the change all new parents experience: we had to learn what it meant when Annabelle cried, how often she needed to feed and the best way to do it, how to change her and comfort her and cuddle her and amuse her. We started adjusting to sleepless nights and the endless worry that you're looking after your new baby properly. Is she okay? Why is she crying? Is it serious? Am I holding her right? Should I take her out for a walk or should I try and put her to bed? Suddenly you need a whole new skill set, and you're in charge 24 hours a day. It's wonderful, of course, because she's your baby and you love her. But it's full-on.

And then on top of that, we'd entered this other world, the world of cancer, which brought its own set of fears, and its own organisational challenges: doctors' appointments, hospital visits, and the treatment itself. We were still feeling shell-shocked by the pace at which everything had happened: the diagnosis, the induction, the birth, the flurry of tests. Everything was flung at us so fast it felt like we barely had time to catch our breath. I'd been looking forward to some quiet, peaceful new-mum time with Annabelle, but that clearly was not going to happen. My diary was already filling with appointments—and not happy ones either.

I was facing the gruelling slog of cancer treatment when all I wanted to do was spend some proper time with this new little person who'd come into my life. I just wanted to sit around and gaze at her and show her off to people because she's so amazing and fascinating and beautiful.

And every time I looked at Annabelle I thought about how lucky I was to have this precious baby. What if I hadn't agreed to IVF? What if that cycle hadn't worked? What if we hadn't fallen pregnant on the very first go? I'm not lucky to have cancer, but if it had to happen, I'm so lucky that it happened when it did. Because I got to have Annabelle first.

Lucie McGeoch

Chief of Staff, Today Tonight, *and one of Sally's best friends*

It was one of the more bizarre assignments: to interview Michelle 'Bombshell' McGee, the tattooed stripper accused of destroying one of the more unlikely Hollywood marriages. Whoever told America's sweetheart, Sandra Bullock, she could change motorcycle rebel, Jesse James, must have convinced Katy Perry of the same about Russell Brand. Jesse's affair with the 'Bombshell', as she liked to be called, was revealed soon after Sandra won the Academy Award for the aptly named movie, The Blind Side. *Sally and I were to fly to the US for a world exclusive 'tell-all' interview with the mistress who ruined the fairytale.*

Thankfully we had some help from an LA-based entertainment reporter, Henry Meller. He had Fleet-Street smarts and an impressive Hollywood contact book, but even Henry was a tad nervous about Bombshell's reliability. Bombshell did promise exclusivity but somehow we weren't sure if her word was as solid as the ink all over her body.

The great thing about being Sally's producer was that celebrity gossip was right in her comfort zone. With her encyclopaedic knowledge of Hollywood lives, Sally could challenge the editor of People *magazine and the writer of* Fantale *trivia to a celebrity trivia contest.*

We were 'team USA' en route to bag the Bombshell. Anyone who overheard us preparing questions in the back row of that economy flight must have had a giggle. We knew we weren't about to interrogate Warren Buffet on the fiscal cliff but we were determined to deliver a good interview.

Sal and I arrived on Bombshell's doorstep at her small suburban home in San Diego, California. We were greeted by her posse of not-so-soft porn film producer friends. Her entourage was very friendly and Bombshell wasn't the hardcore man-eater we'd envisaged. She was surprisingly well spoken, quite matter of fact. I can't say she was oozing with empathy for Sandra Bullock, but she knew Sandra was going to be fine, which was more than she could say for herself. As a 32-year-old single mother who stripped for a living, she was only too aware that this was her fifteen minutes of fame. She was going to milk it for all it was worth.

It's never a problem to get the best out of talent with Sally. Her genuine and friendly nature makes people want to tell her their life stories. The fact that Sally doesn't fit the mould of a typical current affairs reporter has helped her in countless interviews because she has no trace of cynicism. Whether it's a celebrity mistress or a nice guy like Hugh Jackman, interviewees always seem to give Sally a little bit more of themselves.

Bombshell was prepared to share several intimate details that weren't appropriate for the 6.30 pm TV timeslot. During the interview she attempted to apologise to Sandra, but in her eyes the only villain in this story was Sandra's unfaithful husband.

Eventually we wrapped, said goodbye, and, as always, it was a mad rush back to the Seven Los Angeles bureau to put the story together and get it to air on time. Surrounded by empty cans of Diet Coke, Sal and I spent the next day and night transcribing, scripting and feeding the material back to Sydney. It wasn't perfect but we'd done the job we set out to do.

In a show that thrives on variety like Today Tonight, *the entertainment and fashion stories are a necessary part of the formula. While some may cast it off as 'fluff', Sally takes great pride in her work and gives those stories as much attention as other reporters do the harder-hitting material. Sally has gradually built a contact book from scratch, made friends with many of those contacts, who now trust her and grant her exclusive interviews.*

Reflecting on Sally's arrival at Today Tonight, *she didn't resemble any current affairs journalists I had ever met. Wearing a short black dress and the highest pair of platform stilettos I had seen outside a catwalk, she made heads turn as she walked into the office. Of course Sally is more attractive than most of the population but was she at the wrong place? Maybe she'd missed the turn-off to* Australia's Next Top Model *host auditions. I did overhear someone asking what the hell this girl was here for. What would* **she** *know about current affairs? It didn't worry me at all. I knew that if I was producing her, she would look great on camera, which never hurts.*

I also had a lot of faith in my close friend Sarah Stinson, then Chief of Staff at Today Tonight, *and her recruiting skills. Sarah is an excellent judge of character and chose Sally because she was clearly a hard worker with a good heart who really, really wanted the job. The more experience I have behind me, the more I realise that dedication and hard work count for everything. You can be the most experienced and naturally talented person in the world, but you will eventually be out-run by those who are consistently dedicated.*

Next stop for team USA was New York City to interview Oprah Winfrey's unauthorised biographer Kitty Kelley. Feared by any celebrity with a secret, Kitty Kelley is infamous for her controversial biographies of Elizabeth Taylor, Frank Sinatra and the British royal family. Let's face it, who else would be game enough to face 'the big O' and her highly paid defamation lawyers? Kitty arrived and she was a blonde pocket-rocket, happy to take on the highest-paid female entertainer in the world. Kitty's airtime was somewhat limited by the fact that Barbara Walters and Larry King refused to welcome her on their shows so as not to offend their close friend Oprah.

As every former Oprah employee had signed a confidentiality agreement, I can't say the information was explosive, but Kitty certainly did her best to piece together insights into Oprah's early life, her partner Gayle Stedman and Oprah's constant weight battles.

We had booked a huge suite in the New York Hilton for the interview. It would have been the best place for a party, so it was a pity we spent the whole night writing the script and feeding our material back home. Jason Hinsch and Dean Casciato were our talented camera crew for this assignment. We called them our 'work husbands', and joked that they had all the disadvantages of marriage and absolutely no benefits to speak of. Jason, who helped produce the New York shoots, is very creative and a true pro who demonstrated that a good cameraman can make or break a television story.

My one regret about this trip is that we didn't enjoy it to the full. The whole time, Sally and I were fretting about whether the stories would be good enough and whether our boss thought we were hopeless frauds or bludgers.

The reality is the Executive Producer, Craig McPherson, was far too busy running the show and looking at the bigger picture to worry about what we were up to. Craig and Sarah were always very supportive of hard workers, so we shouldn't have worried and yet we did, constantly.

When I consider what would happen to Sal just over a year later, when she would be staring down the barrel of her own mortality, I wish we'd stopped for a moment. I wish we'd clinked a few glasses of wine and celebrated how lucky we were to be doing the job we loved in New York City.

We all strive so hard towards the next goal, reaching for the point when we can call ourselves big-time reporters, executive producers, partners, managing directors and CEOs, or when our boss finally *pats us on the back for a job well done. For ambitious people the praise and the title aren't enough; there will always be another hoop to jump through. Sometimes ambition is a curse that blinds us to the joy right in front of us.*

The real achievement on that American adventure was making a lifelong friend. I thought I had a kind nature until I befriended Sally. She is a really good person with a generous spirit and an open mind. What I've learned about Sally since then is she also has a huge capacity for strength, resilience and bravery, and an unwavering self-belief.

When the perceived glitz of television is taken away, the clothes, the cameras, the spotlights, when your work identity is stripped back completely, when even the hair on your head has fallen out, what are you really left with? When all of that is taken away, do you like the soul staring back at you in the mirror?

Despite all the hardship, suffering and debilitating cancer treatment, I think Sally learned that she has more than she ever realised: true friends, a loving family, husband and a beautiful daughter.

I'm not sure Sally is really aware of the enormity of all that she has achieved. By overcoming her illness in the public eye she has shown others you don't have to hide at home because you have cancer, you're still a human being who people want to help and see come out the other side. Sal, because of you, people who fall ill will be less afraid; you've taken away some of that fear and given them hope.

Survivor: chemo

On the third day after the birth, while I was still in hospital, Fran Boyle, my oncologist, came to introduce herself, to tell us more about the kind of cancer I had, and to discuss treatment options. After the horrible uncertainty of the previous few days, it was a relief to finally get some information about what we were facing, although it wasn't a happy encounter.

Fran told me I had two tumours, and the main one, a high-grade triple negative invasive ductal carcinoma, was quite large. Triple negative cancer is one of the least common types of breast cancer and derives its name from being negative to the three main hormones usually associated with breast cancer: oestrogen, progesterone, HER2. Between 15 per cent and 20 per cent of new diagnoses are in the triple negative group, and there are several subtypes within that. Some grow fast and are difficult to treat, others are less serious. Mine, unfortunately, was the fast-growing type.

One of the first questions I asked was, 'Did the IVF cause this cancer?'

Fran assured me that it didn't. If there is a connection between IVF and breast cancer, it's because IVF allows women to have babies later in life, when there's a greater risk of getting breast cancer—and, after your early 30s, the risk of breast cancer is a bit higher in the year around a pregnancy. Getting pregnant later in life is the problem, rather than IVF.

It was a great weight off my mind to know that the IVF wasn't to blame.

Fran then began talking about my treatment options. We would begin with chemo. If the main tumour shrank enough, I might be a candidate for a lumpectomy rather than a full mastectomy. Chemo would give my breasts time to return to normal after my pregnancy, which would allow them to get a more accurate image of the disease in my breast. This, in turn, would give them a chance to see how well the disease was responding to treatment and help make a better decision about surgery.

Marcus and I wanted to know what the prognosis was: Can I get better? If I can't, how long have I got? But Fran wouldn't discuss a prognosis, she still didn't have all the information she'd need. There was a strong chance the cancer was in my lymph nodes, but they wouldn't be able to tell until they'd done surgery, and that had to wait until I'd finished chemo. Fran wouldn't

221

make predictions, but she did mention that pregnancy-associated breast cancer, triple negative breast cancer and large breast cancer were all adverse prognostic features, which was worrying. However, the fact that initial and subsequent scans to other parts of my body had come up clear was more positive. Things were very serious. But, she told me, they were doing a lot of good work in this area, and were developing better and more effective treatments all the time.

When I first heard the seriousness of my cancer diagnosis from Fran Boyle, my mind turned to the movie, *Dying Young*, which I had seen years before. If you haven't seen it, it stars Julia Roberts, whose character begins work as a private nurse for a young man dying of blood cancer (Campbell Scott). I thought to myself, 'Oh no, cancer doesn't end well. I mean, the title is *Dying Young*. Surely that says it all?' It was a shocking and terrifying realisation.

After she'd taken me through the sobering details, she asked how long I was planning to take off work.

'I'm on maternity leave for six months,' I said.

'Well, if I were you I'd probably flag with your boss that you won't be back for at least 12 months.'

I was appalled.

Until that point I'd been trying to look on the bright side, thinking, *Oh well, better to be sick now during maternity leave and knock them both off at once. I'll do my chemo, have that finished by December, and in January I'll have surgery, and then I'll be finished in March. I'll have a couple of months off, and be back in July. It's only a couple of months after I was going to be back. That's not a big deal.*

I was so desperate to get my life back—not just my job, my *life*. I wanted this to be something small and minor, not a really big deal. But when she said 12 months I knew it *was* going to be a big deal, and I started to cry.

'But I'm supposed to interview Kim Kardashian!' I wailed.

Fran just looked at me. I knew she was thinking, *You're weird. I'm talking to you about saving your life and you're crying about Kim Kardashian?*

Then she started talking about the side effects I could expect. The chemo would make me lose my hair.

'But I've got new hair extensions!'

And now I was going to lose them all. I started crying even harder.

Even *that* wasn't the worst. I'd been hoping there might be just one little ray of sunshine in all this misery—if I was doing chemo, maybe I'd lose weight. I thought it was going to be like Bali Belly—I could shed some of that baby weight, save myself having to go to the gym, maybe I'd actually end up really slim.

No.

'I'll let you know now,' Fran said, 'chemo makes you fat.'

'What? No. How?'

She told me that chemo slows your metabolism plus the extreme nausea means you eat substantially more—I could expect to put on between seven and ten kilos. No no no, I don't want that, chemo, I'm interested in the *other* kind of chemo. Have you got any kinds that make you skinny?

Fran looked *totally* unimpressed. After about an hour of me crying about my job and my hair and my weight and the Kardashians, she looked at her watch, said, 'I have to go home. I need to give the kids dinner,' and walked away, mid me bawling my eyes out.

Afterwards I said to Marcus, 'I don't like her. She doesn't understand me. She thinks I'm just some person who doesn't have anything to go back to. I'm a high achiever!' I want to curl up with embarrassment and shame every time I think about it. Here I was talking about being a high achiever to a doctor. An oncologist. A woman who was at the top of her field. Um . . . I think *she's* the high achiever.

I have no idea what was wrong with me. I blame the pregnancy hormones and the stress of the situation. At first Fran and I had a real disconnect. I remember complaining about her to my breast-care nurses—Alice and Claire, whose job it was to guide me through the cancer treatment at the Mater—and telling them, 'I don't like Fran, I want to get another oncologist.'

They said she was tough on everyone at the first meeting, to ensure they understood the gravity of the situation and they gently reminded me that she was the best in her field. They thought I should meet her a few more times and then if I still felt that I wanted someone else, they'd help me find someone.

I realised they were right—what did it matter if we didn't become best friends? If she's the best, why am I complaining?

I did seek a second opinion, not because I doubted Fran but because it seemed like the right thing to do. We went to see Professor Martin Tattersall at Royal Prince Alfred Hospital. He is renowned for being the grandfather of cancer research in Australia, and he confirmed everything that Fran said, and agreed with her on the appropriate course of action. Which isn't surprising given she is the foremost authority on breast cancer research in the country. That made me feel a lot better.

I loved Kylie Snook, my breast surgeon, from the minute I met her. She really understood how I felt as a new mum. She was warm and compassionate and understanding. I felt Kylie got me, in a way that Fran didn't.

Later, I discovered Marcus had a slightly different take on Fran's manner. In our early dealings with her, she was very business-like, very factual, and a bit impersonal. After my third round of chemo, Marcus saw a change in her—she loosened up and became more friendly and jokey. He saw these signs of friendliness from Fran as hope. The odds were tipping in my favour. I don't know if she'd agree with that, but that was how he read it.

When you have cancer, you become hyper-attuned to what people *aren't* saying. They won't give you answers about what you can expect, they don't want to give you false hope, or frighten you more than you already are frightened—and besides there are so many variables it's difficult to give the kind of concrete answers you want. So you end up trying to glean every bit of information you possibly can from their expression, their body language, their choice of words, even though they're always very cautious. You're like a fortune teller, trying to read the future in your oncologist's expression.

One of the things Fran warned us about was the internet. She told us that ten years ago, they didn't know how to treat the kind of cancer I had, so if we went online and looked for information about treatments and outcomes, we were going to get a whole lot of very bad news. The information online was likely to be old and out of date. In the last two or three years they've made real progress on this form of cancer and discovered treatments that are a lot more effective, but, because they're relatively new they don't have much data yet.

Marcus kept pushing for numbers and statistics, but Fran

wouldn't give them to us. She said it didn't work like that and that there were a series of hurdles, and with each one you get over, your chances of survival improve. You just have to keep jumping those hurdles until you're back to where everyone else is. But with cancer, even if you beat it, it can always come back. And that's the big unknown.

◆ ◆ ◆

This is the course of treatment Fran recommended.

I would start by having three cycles of an aggressive kind of chemotherapy. That would take about three months. They'd check to see whether the tumour was shrinking, and then I'd probably have three more cycles of chemo. Then I'd have a lumpectomy or possibly a mastectomy, radiation, and, if I wanted it, breast reconstruction.

I was booked in for my first course of chemo on 3 November 2011, a week and a half after leaving the maternity ward.

Walking into the chemo room for the first time was a shocking experience. Up until then, even through all the tests, cancer treatment had been an abstract idea for me. Now I was forced to confront what it was actually going to be like. The chemo room was full of people with no hair, no eyebrows and terribly grey skin. They looked *sick*. It was gut-wrenching. I couldn't believe that's what was going to happen to me—I was going to look like them.

Marcus and Maha came with me, and were just as horrified as I was. None of us really had any idea what to expect, and the reality was shocking. The fear was too much for me—I started to cry. Marcus was crying too, and so was Maha. It was terrible seeing them cry; it made it all more real—and frightening.

As well as feeling terribly afraid of what lay ahead, I felt sad and guilty that I'd left my eighteen-day-old baby girl at home so I could come to hospital to have this awful thing done to me. She was beautiful and fresh and new, and I was coming here to be poisoned, literally poisoned. I knew when I left the room that day, I would be so totally toxic I wouldn't be able to kiss those I loved so deeply. That's a shocking thing for any person to have to come to terms with, and for a new mother, it's heart-breaking.

The treatment, called FEC, consists of three bags of fluid— F (fluorouracil, or 5FU), E (epirubicin) and C (cyclophospha-mide)—which were pumped one by one into my body through a drip. E is bright red, and thick, like soup. And because it's thick it feels as if it doesn't belong in your veins. It's like trying to suck Irish stew through a straw—for what feels like hours on end. It's just disgusting. And it feels like your veins are burning.

C is pure poison. I'd been warned that it was the most toxic of the three drugs, and it caused the strongest side effects—nausea, hair loss. I remember watching the nurse put the drip in, and she was wearing these massive industrial-strength gloves. Marcus asked her why she was wearing them. She told us she had to make sure there was no transference, so when she was finished with the gloves they couldn't be put in a normal bin, they had to be sent to a special incinerator because the stuff's so toxic. And I looked up at the drip bag she was attaching to my arm, and it was like a whole two-litre bag of the stuff. I thought, *Really? You're worried about what might be on the gloves and yet you're pouring all that into my body?*

I hadn't been prepared for how much it would hurt. And the tears flowed again, from the pain, and the knowledge that I was going to have to keep coming back for more of this—again and again.

I am a huge *Survivor* fan. *Survivor Borneo, Survivor Philippines, Australian Survivor, Celebrity Survivor*—you name it, I've watched it. Over the years I've often said to Marcus, 'I want to be on *Survivor.*' Once chemo started I thought, 'You know what? This is just like *Survivor.*' You have to outlast your competitors. I had to outlast the chemo. I was on my own version of *Survivor. Survivor: Chemo.*

This chemo combination made my wee bright red, and it's so bad for you that they warn you, when you go to the bathroom, make sure you put the lid down first and then flush, and then flush again because they don't want any little bit of it getting into the air or getting onto anyone else. You can't kiss anyone either. So for the first week after I'd had it, I couldn't kiss Marcus. I had to get into the habit of giving him my cheek to kiss instead of giving him a proper kiss whenever one of us was leaving. I still do it now, even months after the chemo is over. He has to remind me we're allowed to kiss now. It's devastating.

But, even worse, I had to be super-careful around Annabelle. She wanted to put everything in her mouth; when I'd hold her, she'd get my hand and put it in her mouth or she'd open up her mouth and start sucking on my neck. And I'd have to stop her—because the poison could filter through my skin. It made me feel like I was an infection. Not just sick—an infection, as if I'd become the poison.

Marcus and Maha could see how much I was suffering, and they did their best to stay strong and help me through it. When we were getting ready for that first day at chemo, I'd asked Maha to buy some cards so I could get on with sending thank-yous for all the gifts we'd been sent after Annabelle's birth. (Typical me, I'd sent Maha out with strict instructions about exactly what the cards were allowed to look like—nothing pink, nothing fluffy, they needed to be simple and chic, thanks very much.) So Maha got busy writing the thankyous, and together we made a bit of a dent in my to-do list. I don't know how I would have got through that first day without them. They were just as shell-shocked and frightened as I was, but they did their best to stay strong and managed to find ways to make me laugh even if we were in a chemo ward. And it really helped me. I think being able to make me laugh helped them, too.

That first day, it wasn't just chemo I had to contend with. I'd also elected to have cold cap therapy, a groundbreaking treatment that stops some people from losing their hair. It's basically an ice helmet that you wear for six and a half hours while you're having your chemo.

Imagine a huge icepack that's come straight out of an industrial freezer strapped very tightly to your head and under your chin, and every 20 minutes they change the icepacks over so that your head stays ice cold. The concept is based on the principle that hair cells are fast growing—like cancer cells. And because chemo kills any fast-growing cells, it also kills hair cells. The idea is the cold cap freezes hair follicles so that the chemo doesn't affect them. I was young and healthy and my hair was in good condition, they told me there was a chance this treatment would work for me. I jumped at it. The nurses warned me it would be incredibly painful but I didn't care. I'd do anything to save my hair.

To give you some idea of how cold it is, your freezer at home is minus 15 degrees Celsius. This is minus 35 degrees. The pain is unlike anything you can imagine. Perhaps the closest thing you can come to experiencing it is to stick your head in the snow for a few hours, then see how you feel. Almost immediately a headache started. This was no ice-cream headache, no brain freeze thanks to a cold slurpee. It was the most intense, searing pain, and it started at my head and went all the way to my bones. Within minutes I was shivering. The nurses wrapped me in hot blankets, and Marcus brought me cups of tea to try to warm me up. But nothing worked. I was in agony, and knew I'd have to endure the cold and the shaking for six and a half hours—and if it worked, then I was going to have to do it fourteen more times, for every chemo session. That was almost 90 hours in total. I still believed it was worth it but it was excruciating.

For a long time after the treatment, whenever I would open the freezer at home, the cold rush I felt would cause me to break down in uncontrollable tremor and tears as my body recalled the trauma of the ice cap treatment. Whenever I needed anything from the freezer I'd ask Marcus to get it.

With me wrapped in blankets and wearing my weird cap, shivering and shaking and my teeth chattering, I must have looked totally bizarre. At one point Marcus looked me up and down, and said, 'Where's your camel?' And in spite of everything I started to giggle. And so did Maha. I *did* look like one of those guys who hung out in the desert. And then we were all laughing, even though it wasn't really that funny. It's a bit like being at a funeral—when things are really intense and your emotions are running so high, you need to laugh at something just to relieve the tension.

We were still laughing when Mum and Dad came in.

We'd had a few hours to adjust to the shocking reality of the chemo room by then, but for Mum and Dad it was all brand new. I saw them experience all the feelings that washed over us when we walked in—the shock, the fear, the grief. And then they looked at me and saw me in my cold cap and blankets, hooked up to a drip and shaking. Poor Mum just started to cry.

From the day I'd been diagnosed, Mum had gone straight into super-positive motivational mode. She never cried in front of me, she refused to fall apart, she was always full of optimism and positive affirmation. Talking to her was like talking to Anthony Robbins: 'You're a winner, Sal! Winners don't quit! You can fight this thing and you can beat it! Come on, you can do it!' I half-expected her to turn up to chemo holding a banner, chanting, 'Go, Sally, go!' But I guess this was too overwhelming even for her.

It broke my heart to see my mum cry. I thought of my little baby at home and the incredible love I felt for her and how I'd feel if I saw her strapped up to chemo tubes. I knew that was how Mum felt. It killed me, so all I wanted was to desperately make it less painful, even if it was just a teeny tiny bit.

'Hey, Anthony Robbins,' I teased her. 'Don't cry!'

Though I was really struggling with my own pain and grief, I knew I had to give her a bit of my own strength, just to help us all get through this. In the days to come, I would discover how important that process is: you have to give strength, love, smiles and support to the people around you, because their heart is breaking. It's not just your heart.

◆ ◆ ◆

When we'd finished for the day and it was time to go home the nurses took the cold cap off and warned me to be super-careful with my hair. I couldn't brush it, wash it or even touch it—it was so fragile. All I could do was hope and wait—for two weeks and three days. After that, I'd either shed a little bit, or, if it hadn't worked, it'd start to come out in clumps. They sent me away assuring me there was a good chance it would work.

I was desperately clinging on to the hope that I'd keep my hair. But I think, deep down, I knew that wasn't going to happen. There wasn't going to be any celebrity treatment here. Cancer doesn't discriminate. It's not going to say, yeah, most people lose their hair, but guess what, you're on TV! *You* won't lose yours. *Please*, that's for everyone else.

It doesn't know I'm on TV. It doesn't care. It's cancer.

I had a feeling that whatever the reason was for me having cancer, I was supposed to experience it fully. No cutting corners, no getting away with anything. In the same way that other cancer patients lose their hair, I would too.

Those tresses

Long before I ever worked in television, I went to the hairdresser like other people go to the corner store. My mum loves to go to the hairdresser and she taught us the importance of good grooming. First and foremost on the list was a wash and blow dry. While I rejected some things mum tried to instil in me, this was definitely not something I ignored!

From the age of 18 I would treat myself to a wash and blow-dry at least once a week, more if I could afford it. Everyone assumes that if you work in television, you get your hair and make-up done for you every day. The truth is, only the hosts of shows get their hair and make-up done. The rest of us just do our best on our own. When I was starting out on *Sydney Weekender* I did my own hair and make-up—sometimes in the most absurd locations—in a shed, on a farm, in a pit-stop toilet on the highway or in the back of a chocolate factory.

When I finally got my job on *Today Tonight*, I rationalised that getting my hair done properly was no longer a luxury—it was a professional necessity. So began my expensive habit. Three times a week at the crack of dawn, Josh, my favourite hairdresser, would turn my wayward hair into Beyoncé curls, or the Nicole Richie boho look, or whatever my latest obsession was. I would turn up with pictures ripped out of the tabloids and say, 'Let's do this.' It was fun and I loved every minute of it.

It was a running joke among my family that Josh would shortly be rich enough to purchase a harbourside mansion in Vaucluse, one of Sydney's most expensive suburbs with cash. Thanks to me and my hair.

Not long after I started work at *TT*, Kim, one of the hair and make-up artists, tried to talk me into cutting my hair. Actually, she insisted. She felt it was too long and not in keeping with the network look for journalists. I tried to explain that I was different. I wasn't a newsreader or a political reporter or a foreign correspondent. My job was fashion, entertainment, beauty—basically, what I call, fluff. And fluff reporters don't need a proper-looking bob. I should keep my long locks, I explained, because that would allow me to change my look and keep up with the trends. I told her it was essential for my 'fashion journalism credibility'.

I've never been a short hair girl, not since I was six and a lady at the local fete mistook me for a boy. I cried, blamed my mum and vowed never again to let anyone cut my hair. Thirty-three years later and I've stood strong, never cutting my hair. In fact, I'm scared to even trim it.

Kim wouldn't hear of it. She told me I had to cut my hair. So I did what any self-respecting professional would do—I hid from her. For weeks she called me and I refused to answer. Sometimes I would pick up the phone and even though I was at my desk just one floor up, I'd lie and say I was out on the road covering an urgent groundbreaking story. (That should have been a dead giveaway. What's groundbreaking in fashion or beauty?)

Sometimes she'd corner me in the hallway and I'd make an appointment for a haircut, knowing full well I had every intention of cancelling. It was a stalling method; I hoped she'd eventually tire of me and forget the whole thing. She didn't. She even rang Lucie to complain that I was dodging my haircut. I felt like I was a fugitive being hounded but still I refused to give in. This game of cat and mouse went on for months.

'Why don't you compromise and let her trim it?' Marcus would say. 'What's the big deal?'

'What's the big deal? Are you joking? I'll be on my deathbed before I let anyone cut my hair!'

It's funny how the things you say can come back to haunt you.

◆ ◆ ◆

When I was first diagnosed with cancer, I didn't want anyone to know what had happened. I wanted to go away by myself somewhere, be sick, get better and come back as if nothing had ever happened. I didn't want to be Cancer Sally. I didn't want cancer to become the only thing people remembered me for. I didn't want to be overshadowed by my disease. And that's one of the reasons I was so afraid of losing my hair: once it's gone, everyone can see what's happened to you. It's horribly visible.

Of course it ran deeper than that. For any woman, I think, the thought of losing your hair, your lashes, your eyebrows, of having your physical appearance changed so much, is very difficult to cope with. For me, it was particularly difficult because it stirred up a lot of old demons: my childhood feelings of inadequacy and difference, my fear of being rejected for the way I looked. And in my job, appearances are everything. Whatever we were shooting, we'd always tweak the visuals— through props, lighting—to make the pictures look as good as they possibly could. When you work in a visual medium, you do become very concerned (some might say obsessed) with appearances. Naturally my own appearance was a part of that. For me, *looking* good was an essential part of *feeling* good about myself. I didn't know how I was going to feel if that was suddenly taken away.

During my pregnancy I'd done a story with *OK!* Magazine, talking about how hard it had been to fall pregnant , the joy I was experiencing and the excitement of preparing to be a first-time mum. I was committed to do a follow-up story, announcing the birth of the baby. The classic 'It's a boy!'/'It's a girl!' magazine feature. Obviously I'd agreed to do it before I'd been diagnosed and now I wasn't sure what to do. I had to decide if I wanted to say anything publicly about the cancer. Marcus and I talked at length about it. Part of me wanted to hide. The other, stronger part said 'No! Why hide? By hiding you're acting as if it's something to be embarrassed about, even ashamed of. There is no shame.' Also, how do you not tell people? I mean, this isn't a minor illness, this is *cancer*. It's big. It's not going to slide under the radar. I decided I wanted to tell it like it was, tell the truth. But I didn't know how to do it.

Should I make the cancer announcement public at the same time as the baby announcement? I didn't want to include it in Annabelle's story. But I didn't quite see how I could *not* mention it either.

I went to Craig for advice about how I should handle all this. He talked to Peter Meakin, our then Director of News and Current Affairs, about what I should do. They suggested I announce 'It's a girl!' with *OK!* magazine and let that be the lovely, happy story it deserved to be. Then a week later I could do a separate story with *New Idea* and *Today Tonight*, about the diagnosis.

As soon as they proposed it, I knew it was a much better arrangement—it meant the announcement of Annabelle's birth wouldn't be tainted by cancer. She could have her first little moment in the spotlight all to herself. We could talk about cancer later.

Normally I look forward to any excuse to get styled from head to toe. Josh came to do my hair at home, and was so excited to see me. It was the first time I'd seen him since having Annabelle, and he'd missed our almost daily banter. I broke the news to him, and I cried, and he looked almost as devastated as I was. Having my hair done had once been a commonplace occurrence and nothing special, but on that day it felt like something to treasure. I knew it might be the last time I had my hair done for some time. I guess for Josh, the Vaucluse harbourside home would have to wait.

The *OK!* magazine shoot turned out to be a lovely experience—it felt like a connection to my old life, my life before cancer. The same reporter, Kelli Armstrong, who is the sweetest, loveliest reporter, had done the first story about my pregnancy and now she was meeting Annabelle. I loved that sense that we were coming full circle. I stayed strong and was really happy all day, and then, just before she left, Kelli said, 'Sal, I'm so incredibly sorry about what's happened.' I could see the heartache in her eyes. I couldn't help it—I broke down. It still didn't seem quite real: not a month before we'd both been sitting together at the Myer spring/summer parades, and, now, here I was, sitting in my dining room, crying about cancer. How could this be happening?

The *New Idea* story was not the same happy experience. Introducing Annabelle to the world had been a joy, but talking about cancer was much harder. It was still so new, so raw and shocking, I hadn't really fully grasped it—which made it hard to explain to anyone else. But Jenni Brown, the sensitive and kind journalist from *New Idea* made it as easy as she could. Her compassion and warmth made a huge difference.

The *TT* story was harder still. This time I was talking with people I knew well. We shot it at our apartment with a crew I've worked with a hundred times over the last four years. We've shot food stories, fashion stories, interviews in my lounge room. And now here we were again, but the mood was so different. It felt heavy, sad. I don't know why it's worse when you're talking to people who know the old you, but it is.

The night the story went to air, I watched my dear friend, and the then host of *TT*, Matt White introducing the segment, struggling not to cry, and that made me cry even more. You don't realise how much your friends love you until something like this happens.

In the end, though, I was glad that I'd agreed to do the story. It felt good to come clean and say, 'This is what's happened.' And once the story went public, I realised it was important for other people to hear cancer stories, because the response I got was absolutely astonishing.

When somebody famous is diagnosed with cancer, it makes the news—household names like Kylie Minogue, Delta Goodrem, Giuliana Rancic, Kerri-Anne Kennerley. Their cancer stories touch us because they're important to us.

I'm not famous in that way. Occasionally someone will stop me and say, 'Hey, I think I know you from TV,' but that's about it. Who cares if I get cancer?

I think my story struck a chord with people because what had happened to me was so awful: I was young, healthy, I'd been diagnosed just as I was about to have a baby. It was such a shocking thing to happen to anyone, whether I was on TV or not.

After the story came out, the response was immediate. The network received thousands of emails, letters and phone calls. My Facebook page was flooded. People sent gifts and cards by the thousands. Every day, the doorstep outside our apartment would be covered in gifts and packages, fruit and flowers. I never expected anything like that, and I was amazed and touched by how generous and kind people are, how much they want to help when they hear of someone in trouble.

Now, I realise there was more to it than that. It was bigger than me. Cancer is such a huge and terrible thing and it affects so many people in so many different ways. The public wanted to reach out and share what they'd experienced. People wrote to me about so many different things: the shame they'd felt about having cancer, the pain they went through when their loved ones died. I heard from women who'd also been diagnosed when they had young children, and who wanted to share their stories, experiences and advice. Even though they'd survived, hearing my story had brought back all their grief and pain. I also heard from men who'd lost their wives. Some of those stories were very hard to read.

But there was good news too: I had people emailing me to say that because of me, they'd gone and got themselves checked, some of them were clear, but five told me they'd been diagnosed. And even though that isn't good news in itself, it was great that they'd caught it at an early stage. Awareness is everything. Early detection is everything. Sometimes you need to read about it in a magazine before you go out and do what needs to be done.

Naomi Shivaramen is a producer at *Today Tonight* and a friend of mine. She's sweet and petite with a heart of gold. You know the saying, 'She wouldn't harm a fly'? That's a description that's made for Naomi. That fly, though, well, it wouldn't survive if it landed on Naomi's keyboard. She is the loudest, most violent typist you've ever met. You can hear her banging away on her keyboard two departments away. Sluggo, nicknamed her 'Thumper' 'cos she thumps the keys so hard.

Naomi, with her heart of gold and super-fast, super-loud typing, could see that I was struggling to reply to the thousands of letters and emails. People had been so kind and so generous and I wanted to reply to everyone, at least once. I wasn't always able to write back and forth, but definitely once. So Naomi offered to help me, as of course did Maha. So after I'd put Annabelle to bed, the three of us would set up laptops all in a row in my dining room and I would dictate replies to them both while I also typed. We would do as many hours as we could until I would get too weak and too weary to do any more.

The emails would often pile in quicker than we could reply. Whenever we felt like we'd gotten on top of them, more would come, and never once did Na say it was too much trouble or a hassle. All she would say is 'Tell me when you feel up to doing more and I'm here for you.'

In those early days, I couldn't really understand why some of these people were writing and telling me how ashamed they felt to have been diagnosed with cancer. I had emails congratulating me for my bravery in admitting I had cancer, saying, 'I couldn't tell my friends I had cancer. But you're willing to just say it so simply—to just come out and say I have cancer.' I thought why are these people ashamed? Why do they feel bad, as if they've murdered someone? Why do people feel like it's their fault?

Later, I would experience that shame for myself. But that was still some months away.

One of the reasons some people feel it's their fault is because other people unconsciously blame you for getting sick. It was the same situation as when I was having tremendous trouble conceiving: people told me, 'You probably got cancer because you're really stressed.' 'You probably got cancer because you did IVF.' 'You probably weren't eating really healthily.' 'You probably weren't exercising.' 'You've probably got a family history'. 'You probably didn't get enough sleep and you're quite an anxious person.' People need to find a reason because they're trying to make sense of it all.

But sometimes there *is* no reason, and that's the hardest thing of all to accept. It's like unexplained infertility—a mystery. And that was something I really struggled with in those early days. How had this happened to me? How could I have got sick when I felt so well? There was no cause and effect. It wasn't as if I had gone on safari in Africa, been bitten by a mosquito and contracted malaria. It's not as if I tripped over and fell and bumped my head. I was really healthy, I got pregnant, I felt amazing. How could I have cancer and feel amazing?

I'd ask Fran, 'Did I cause this? Is it something about me, is it something I did?' She'd say, 'No, it has nothing to do with your mental state, this is just something physical that went wrong with your body.' But then other people would say your mental state can definitely bring on cancer—and affect the outcome too. Everyone's got an opinion but there's no definitive answer. I decided I wouldn't beat myself up about it.

◆ ◆ ◆

For two weeks and three days after my first chemo cycle I checked my hair in the mirror each day, thinking, *It still looks okay, maybe it worked, it's going to be alright.* And then bang, just like they said, I woke up one morning and my pillow was covered with hair. We live in a small apartment—and my hair was everywhere. I'd walk from the bedroom to the kitchen and it would fall, like leaves. The cold cap treatment hadn't worked. And once it started, it fell out quickly, really, really quickly.

I couldn't let go of it. I'd touch it and a whole chunk of hair would come out, and then I started to keep it all in a zip-lock bag. I didn't know what to do, it was clearly not on my head but I also couldn't bear to let it go. I was clinging to my old life, to my old self, but clearly I had no control.

I cried and cried: for my hair, for my old self and the carefree life I'd left behind. But I was also crying out of fear of the future, because my falling hair felt like a warning, a sign that death was approaching. I did my best to stay positive and keep those dark thoughts at bay. But sometimes those thoughts, that fear, overwhelmed me.

Marcus tried to comfort me. 'It doesn't matter. You'll look hot with no hair. I love you for more than your hair.'

It didn't matter. I was inconsolable.

My hair fell out to the point where I looked like I had a bald man's comb-over. I knew it was time for the inevitable.

◆ ◆ ◆

Belinda Jeffrey, one of my best friends, has been my colourist for years. She has her own fabulous salon in Sydney's Double Bay. We met originally when she worked at a salon called Synergy. I followed her there. As with most things, after I started going I told Maha she absolutely had to go there too. In fact, I send all of my girlfriends there, not just because Belinda does amazing hair, but also because she's amazing to be around. Then when she opened her own salon she mentioned to Maha that she was thinking of getting a personal trainer. In those days I was still trying to build my client list as a trainer, and Maha said, 'Well, you know, Sal is a personal trainer. She's *very* busy, but I think she might *possibly* be able to squeeze you in . . .' Belinda was my colourist then, became my client, and then one of my best friends.

Since the diagnosis she'd been doing everything she could to help, and once my hair started to fall out, I asked her if she'd let me shave my head at her salon. It's not exactly the look of the season and not what she's renowned for but I didn't feel brave enough to just walk into the local barbers and ask for a number two. As always with Belinda, she went one better. She organised for me to have my hair shaved at the private home salon of celebrity hairdresser Kenneth Stoddart. There would be no-one there but Belinda and me, and Maha, who was coming to hold my hand and wipe away my tears.

When I told Marcus, he chuckled about it. 'Of course, you get cancer and then you want to have your hair cut by the celebrity hairdresser who does *Vogue*.' It made me smile.

I was so grateful to Bel for arranging it. They made it special for me: put music on, we gossiped, and they reassured me I'd look gorgeous, making me feel as comfortable as possible in such hideous circumstances.

Kenneth gave me a number three. When it was all gone, I felt strangely relieved—lighter, better than desperately clinging onto dead hair. I left smiling and feeling healthier than I had felt in days.

My poise lasted all of 45 minutes before I found myself sobbing on the floor of a Witchery dressing room in Westfield. Maha and I had gone to the shops so I could treat myself to some new clothes. It probably wasn't the best idea since I'd given birth only a few weeks ago and was hardly going to be at my fashionable best. And when you add a hairless head into the mix, tears are a certainty. I felt I was less of a woman, like my femininity had gone. I didn't know who I was without my hair.

When I went home to Marcus that day he was so lovely. He kissed me, and kissed my head, and told me it was beautiful and I was beautiful, that he still loved me and I needn't worry. It was exactly what I wanted to hear, because even though I know he loves me, and he'll stand by me no matter what, suffering a drastic physical change like that struck at the heart of how I felt about myself, and I worried that it might have an effect on our relationship too. What if he didn't find me attractive anymore? What if he didn't want to be married to me anymore? But Marcus reassured me, that day and many more times afterwards, that I was still beautiful, and for him I always would be.

Falling apart

Once your hair is gone, you have to make a choice. Do you get a wig or a scarf? Or just bare all?

When you break your arm you don't cover it up. There's no shame in a broken arm, so why attempt to disguise a bald head? I decided to bare all, to be out and proud. I kept reminding myself over and over of something D-man, my original *TT* producer, liked to say: 'It is what it is.' I found a strange kind of relief in that idea and it was one of many sayings that would help me through my dark moments.

My resolve broke down the first time I had to do some publicity with no hair. I was off to chat with Kyle and Jackie O on their radio show, and once I was forced to be seen beyond the four walls of my apartment, suddenly I didn't feel so brave —not so out and proud. I opted for a scarf and hat and big fake diamond earrings. I kidded myself I was channelling the JLo Miami look. But I didn't feel really comfortable about it. I knew I was hiding, and I felt caught between two wishes. On the one hand, I didn't want to look sick, but on the other I wanted to say there's no shame in having cancer, why hide it? Both Kyle and Jackie O were, as they've been from day one, kind, supportive, encouraging, loving and always ready for a laugh. They made me feel so cocooned with love and at the same time, completely normal. They told me I looked great, even though I didn't feel like myself at all.

While I was sick I often told people that I was still the same old me, that I didn't want to be defined by the cancer. I remember Giuliana Rancic saying the same thing after she was diagnosed too. It felt important to remind people that I was still the same girl who loved fashion, who loved make-up and skincare, who loved celebrity gossip, who still kept up with all of the magazines. I was still me.

It was especially important because my own external identity had been stripped back so much from the treatment. The grey skin and hollow eyes didn't mean that I wasn't still alive and full of hope and optimism on the inside. And it didn't mean that I wasn't interested in buying a lipstick to make myself feel better.

I got to thinking about a blog. Given my experience at Seven and all that I was going through with the cancer, it seemed like a natural next step—an extension of what I loved in my day job at Seven. It was a chance to connect with other women and to share with them all of the tips and tricks I have learned along the way.

That's how swiish.com.au was born. It's a how-to guide for women but the difference is that it's about living a fabulous life affordably. Even before the many bills and expenses related to cancer treatment, Marcus and I had dealt with plenty of financial constraints. I always looked for bargains, shopped frugally and tried to look my best on a budget. I wanted to share that passion for affordable style with other women.

Swiish stands for stylish women inspiring inner strength, health and happiness. The response to the blog has been nothing short of amazing. Every time I get an email from someone telling me that they loved something on the site, I am so happy and excited. It's exactly what I hoped it would be.

Maha and I did some research on the internet to work out what celebrities with cancer did. We downloaded pictures of Kylie Minogue when she was having treatment, and looked up different ways to tie scarves. I wished I was one of those women who can rock a gorgeous scarf, but after a lot of experimenting I realised every scarf I tried made me look like a pirate. I used to joke, 'All I need is a parrot and a patch.' Matt White told me he almost bought me a parrot once, but then his wife told him I might find it offensive. I wouldn't have, I would have found it hilarious, but I guess you can't be too careful when it comes to the funny side of cancer.

My two close friends and colleagues Andy and Jason rallied around me brilliantly. We'd spent so much time working together over the previous few years and we'd had some fun times at work, some stressful times too, but mostly the stressful times are pretty fun with the benefit of hindsight and the distance of time. When I got sick they dropped everything to spend time with me. They took days off work and we'd do long lunches while Annabelle slept in the pram beside us. I tried to keep things normal in my life, so that meant that my odd jobs around the house (mostly involving my passion for organising) continued. I decided that there was too much clutter in our small apartment so it was clear that floor-to-ceiling shelves were needed in the garage. Andy didn't hesitate when I told him. He said he would make them and Jason also volunteered in a second. They took the day off work and spent the morning chopping wood and building shelves.

As they worked we talked and gossiped like the old days. Andy excitedly shared with us that he'd just bought a car. He'd splashed out and treated himself to a second-hand convertible. As he described the joy of driving the new car, he explained, 'There's just nothing like the feeling of driving with the wind blowing through your hair.' As he said this he looked at me. The second it was out of his mouth he realised. Shit. Sal has no hair. Big mistake. I saw him frantically look across at Jason and say, 'You know what I mean . . .' That was also a big mistake as Jason has no hair either. Andy looked at us awkwardly.

'Um, that's bit insensitive, Andy, just gloating like that in front of a bald man and a woman who's lost her hair to cancer,' I said jokingly. He turned red and Jason and I started laughing. He desperately tried to backtrack but we didn't care, it was funny. You could see that he was worried his innocent comment had somehow hurt my feelings, but it hadn't. It was actually cause for a great deal of laughter.

There's no right or wrong answer to the question of what to do about losing your hair—whether you cover up with wigs, hats or scarves, or just go out bald. You have to do what's right for you, and that might very well change from day to day, depending on how strong you feel.

The day after Kyle and Jackie O's interview was one of the

first times I actually went out in public with no hair. I ventured out with Matt White. Matt is the kindest, most decent human being you could have the pleasure of knowing. My desk at *TT* was outside Matt's office so over the years we've become great friends. Our afternoon coffee was a daily ritual, and Matt promised that we'd still do regular coffee catch-ups when I was on maternity leave. He never let me down. Being sick didn't change our plans, it just meant I walked much slower to the café.

When I was diagnosed, I hadn't been able to tell Matt myself— Lucie called him from the States to break the news. Matt was the first person outside my family to see me without any hair. He saw me before my girlfriends, before anyone. I think I expected him to be horrified, or disgusted, or ashamed to be seen with me, but he wasn't. He came to my house and collected me and Annabelle, and we went out for coffee. I walked down the street with no hair and no shame. Did I feel self-conscious? Totally. But somehow Matt didn't make me feel weird. He acted as if it was the most natural thing in the world.

I had a lot of friends who tried to support me in their own individual ways. Gavin Alder, the line-up producer at work, sat at the desk next to me and, over the years, we've become good friends. He knew how much my hair meant to me and how devastated I would be to lose it. In an act of camaraderie he shaved his head as well—at his 50th birthday party—just to let me know I wasn't doing it alone.

One of Maha's best friends, Shaun, also shaved his head. When Maha asked him why he was doing it, he said, 'This is my way of letting you know, that you, your sister, your family, you're in my heart and in my thoughts.' It's a big thing for someone to do, and they certainly didn't have to. I was really touched. My mum also offered to shave her head but I said, 'No way, one bald woman in the family is quite enough.' She was serious and it took quite some effort on my part to talk her out of it.

Just before Christmas, I was interviewed for a newspaper article and, for the first time, was photographed with no hair. I felt like I was doing it for all the other women out there who've lost their hair and been robbed of their crowning glory by this terrible disease. I felt happy that I was doing something to show there's no need to feel ashamed of being sick. No need to hide behind a wig, if you don't want to.

In the beginning, I felt a wig was a kind of cop-out. That it was like pretending it hadn't happened, pretending you still had hair.

But after a week or two of being hairless and being faced with people staring in the street and talking about you as if you weren't there, I suddenly understood why some women, including myself at times, would opt for a wig.

Despite my initial determination, I eventually bought one. In fact, I purchased three. Belinda put me in touch with a brilliant wig-maker and I bought a short, dark Halle Berry-ish number, a blonde bob, and a red wig. They were all totally different from the long locks I'd had before, and they were all really great, although the blonde bob was probably my favourite. Going out in them turned out to be an interesting social experiment. When you're a blonde, people do notice you more. And when I wore the red wig, people were much friendlier. Perhaps they thought I was more approachable. Who knows?

Once I had the wigs, I didn't actually wear them a huge amount, and when I did, it was often for fun, rather than because I was having a tough time.

So I understand now why you'd choose to wear a wig. Because you want to feel normal. You want to blend in. You don't want people staring at you, giving you those looks of pity as if you are just about to die.

Sometimes you need a break. You need to be able to go to the shops, get the paper and some milk and not have to make cancer small talk with the cashier. You grow so tired of having your sickness on public display. Even when I felt okay physically and the horrendous effects of the chemo had briefly dissipated, my bald head was a constant reminder, even to myself. I remember doing ordinary things around the house—walking into the bathroom, or making the bed—and I'd catch a glimpse of my hairless head and think, *Oh yeah. Cancer.*

You become tired of how other people react to you; as soon as you walk out the door, you notice people noticing you, and even if they don't stare at you, you see their shock, or the pity in their eyes. *Oh look at that poor girl with cancer!* And if I had Annabelle with me, that would make it even worse: *Oh, the poor baby! Oh, the poor mother! Oh, the poor family!* When I saw that pity in other people's eyes, it immediately stirred up all the fears I was living with every day and trying to suppress: the fear that I might not make it through, that Annabelle might be left without a mother. I'd look down at Annabelle in the pram and tell her, 'Don't you worry, Mummy's not going anywhere.' Of course it was me I was really reassuring; Annabelle was tiny, and blissfully unaware of what was going on; unaware of the cancer that robbed me of my life, of my hair and of my normality. That robbed me of me.

◆ ◆ ◆

And chemo was robbing me of enough all on its own.

At first I completed three cycles of FEC, one cycle every three weeks. With FEC, I started to feel sick pretty much straight away. I went home from the first cycle shivering, shaking, unable to eat and nauseous. And it just got worse from there.

Having chemo is like having a nuclear bomb go off inside you. There are so many side-effects, and they're all terrible.

First, you want to vomit. It's like you're seasick and your stomach is churning, but the anti-nausea medication they have now is amazing. So you never do vomit, even though you want to the whole time, for about five days. After the five-day mark, I was over the worst of it, and then it would get a bit better from there.

But each time, for those first five days, it's intense. You know what it's like when you've got the worst possible case of food poisoning? It's like that, but it never diminishes. If you've got food poisoning, once you vomit it's kind of over. But with chemo there's no relief. Even if you could vomit it wouldn't help. You've got that churning stomach constantly.

You really want to eat to fight the nausea, but you can't because your mouth fills up with ulcers—another side-effect of chemo—which makes eating quite painful.

And there's a strange taste at the back of your throat, a metallic taste that starts at your tongue. It's like you've been guzzling petrol, and you can't shake it. There's nothing you can eat or drink that will get rid of it or disguise it.

Drinking is a problem, too, because it feels like your throat's paralysed, and it's so sore, you don't want to swallow, or talk. You just don't want to do anything.

You have all these symptoms, and your body's trying to find ways to relieve them, but it can't. It's as if your body is fighting

252

itself. And that's the whole thing with chemo: it *is* actually killing your body. That's the point of it. They need it to kill the tumour, but not actually kill you. They're trying to kill you just a little bit, without *actually* killing you.

Your body starts to break down, and it breaks down everywhere. Losing your hair and eyebrows and eyelashes, that's just the surface. The damage on the inside is huge. My fingernails were starting to fall out. My toenails had fallen off. The bones in my feet felt like someone had grabbed a baseball bat and smashed them. And even now, at the time of writing, it's eight months since I finished chemo and it still hurts to walk because the bones in my feet feel like they're broken. Chemo does something to your bones, and your muscles feel as if they've disintegrated. At one stage I couldn't really even get up because the muscles in my quads felt like they'd vanished. I lost all feeling in my toes because chemo had killed the nerves. And it took six months for them to grow back again.

My body was falling apart.

And if that wasn't enough, the day after my chemo they gave me an injection to help boost my white blood cells. That injection made it feel like my bones were being ripped apart in opposite directions and someone had got a steel pipe and smashed it repeatedly down my back and down my legs until I was black and blue. And you're so sick from the chemo that you desperately want to lie down, but you can't because the pain in your bones, from the injection, is so severe you can't actually get any rest. And you're desperate to sleep, but the anti-nausea medication gives you insomnia.

I don't think you can really imagine how awful it is if you haven't experienced it. Of course they warn you that you're going to feel sick, and that your bones are going to hurt. But they don't *really* tell you, and even if they did, you couldn't grasp it. You picture yourself at your sickest, and you think, *Oh well it's probably going to be like that.* But it's beyond that. When I was giving birth and it was at its worst, it was a walk in the park compared to chemo. And I think the difference is, with labour or any kind of pain, such as when you hurt your back, it's just one part of your body, it's not *everything.* It's not your eyelids, your throat, your stomach, your toes, your bones, your muscles.

You're not thinking about getting through that day. You're just trying to get through the next five minutes. You're looking for the tiniest bit of relief. Maybe you'll eat a mouthful of something and for just one second your stomach will stop churning, and then you think, oh, that's better. And then *Bam!* it's back.

You can't take painkillers. Sure, you can have a Panadol, but that's not going to cut it. And you can't take anything stronger. Anything that helps you feel better is also helping the cancer. So all you can do is suck it up and suffer, and hope that you're just a tiny bit stronger than the cancer.

I remember one day in my third cycle, it was a Sunday in summer, and I was desperate to find some relief from the nausea. I was so nauseous, so sick, I was absolutely frantic. Nausea like that drives every other thought out of your head; you can't think or feel anything except how sick you are and how desperate you are for relief. You'd do anything, *anything* to make it go away. It was the kind of nausea that feels like it *might* go away if you could just put the right thing in your stomach, like finding an antidote to a poison. I was eating and eating in a desperate attempt to find the thing that might stop the sickness. It wasn't hunger, it wasn't appetite, it was sheer desperation.

I tried a toasted cheese sandwich, that didn't work. I had some carrots, that didn't work. I had some hummus, that didn't work. I popped a bag of microwave popcorn, and that didn't work. I wasn't eating for enjoyment. In fact, I was so full I had no room for anything else but the nausea wouldn't go away—and I still had this hope that if I could just find the right food, I could ease the sickness. I kept putting things in my mouth: chocolate, no, fruit, no.

And then I thought, *I need a pizza*. It was 10.00 am and, of course, none of the gourmet pizza places are open at that time. I rang Domino's. When the guy answered, I was overjoyed, I said, 'are you open?'

'Yeah.'

I was so relieved and desperate for a pizza, I ordered two family-sized pizzas and a garlic bread—and I ate it all. But the extreme nausea was still there.

That day I tried everything I could think of to ease the sickness and pain. I tried to lie down and rest, but that didn't work. I tried to eat, and that didn't work either. I took a Panadol, that didn't help. I tried to get fresh air, that didn't help either. I was prowling around the apartment, half out of my mind with pain, unable to sit still, unable to find any relief. *Nothing* worked, *nothing*.

In the end I had a shower, but I was in so much pain I collapsed, sobbing and sobbing and sobbing. My whole body was shaking with tears, it was ferocious. I was in there for about two hours, the warm water pouring over me, crying. It was one of my lowest points. Marcus came in holding Annabelle, and when he saw the state I was in said, 'Oh my God, babe, I'm so sorry for how much pain you're in.' He knew, we both knew, that there was nothing he could do for me. He couldn't make it better. I was trapped in this physical torture, and all I could do was endure it.

That's why cancer is so hard on the people around you. Marcus, my parents, my sister, my girlfriends could all see how sick I was, but they couldn't share it with me, they couldn't help. They could help when I was in emotional pain—I could talk and have a cry and they could listen and that helped me feel better. But with physical pain, there was nothing they could do.

◆ ◆ ◆

Many years ago the mother of one of my friends committed suicide. I used to feel so angry about that. I could only see it from my friend's perspective: how terrible it was for her that her mum wouldn't be there for her wedding, that she'd never see her children. Suicide seemed so selfish to me. But that day in the shower, for the first time, I understood the impulse. When you're in that kind of pain, and you don't see a way out, and you don't see it getting any better, you understand the desire for relief at any price.

Even at my very lowest ebb, though, I knew I had to stay alive for Annabelle's sake.

◆ ◆ ◆

Besides, I was too angry with the cancer to give up the fight.

I was angry at it for ruining my time with my child. I was angry at it for all the time it was stealing away from me. When you're sick, it's like you're watching the world go by in a movie, you're not participating. It was spring when I was diagnosed, and I love that time of year. It's warm, the jasmine's blooming, it's gorgeous—and I missed it. Then I saw summer come and go. I watched people going to barbecues and I could hear them on their balconies laughing and having drinks after work. They were living their lives, but I had no strength to go anywhere or do anything.

There's a park bench just outside our apartment block, and if I was having a good day, I would get in the lift and go downstairs, and just sit there for a little while. Even that was a mission. We live near a main road, and I'd see people walking back from the shops, carrying their groceries, or heading down to the beach. I was so jealous watching from the sidelines. Summer came and went, then autumn, and winter. A whole year was devoured by cancer.

And cancer sucked most of the joy out of our first Christmas with Annabelle. We always spend Christmas with Marcus's parents in Canberra. (We figure my parents get birthdays, Mother's Day and Father's Day, so it was only fair that we spend our Christmases with Marcus's family.) That Christmas was like a lot of other Christmases we've had over the past ten years—but it was also very different.

I'd been given an extra week's reprieve from my chemo cycle because it was Christmas, so physically I felt a bit better. But none of the usual magic was there. The fact that it was Annabelle's first Christmas just seemed to make it sad in many ways. Annabelle was only three months old, she didn't know what was going on, she couldn't unwrap the gifts we'd bought for her. I wanted to be able to share the excitement of Christmas—putting out the cookies and milk for Santa Claus, waking up and finding the presents on Christmas morning—but then, when I started thinking about that, I wondered, but what if I don't make it to next Christmas? And I was devastated. But I didn't want to spoil everyone else's Christmas, so I kept running off to the bathroom and turning the taps on so I could have a cry without anyone else being aware.

And when it came to Christmas Day, I was so conflicted—unhappy and worried about the future—the business of getting presents didn't really excite me that much. When you're worried you're going to be dead soon, material things don't have the same impact. And the fact that I wasn't that excited by my presents made me feel even sadder, because both Marcus and Maha had made a special effort to choose things I'd really love, things I'd wanted for a long time but had put off because they were too expensive—a beautiful Chanel wallet and a box of Jo Malone creams and candles. And for a materialistic person to think, *I don't really care about this stuff* is a pretty big deal. I would have traded all those lovely things in a second if it meant I could have my health back.

It was one of those days when I found myself being pulled very strongly in two different directions: I was wishing and wishing that this phase of my life, this treatment period, could be over, and I could go back to having a normal life; but I had a feeling that this might be all I got, this might be my life, so I didn't want to miss a thing. I was desperately trying to store away all the impressions and memories I could, to really immerse myself in these moments with Marcus and Annabelle, to fully experience and savour them, rather than just wishing them away.

◆ ◆ ◆

Chemo was so hard, and sometimes I felt like I couldn't get up and go back for another round—that's when I had to dig deep.

I'd talk to the cancer and say, 'It's either you or me . . . and it won't be me. That means it has to be you. Failure is not an option. I won't be beaten.' And that anger helped me find my strength.

I'm sure many before me have said the same thing and they haven't survived. If you die, it doesn't mean you didn't try hard enough.

Strong people get cancer. They undergo all the treatment yet still die. When that realisation hits, it's shattering. There is no guarantee that if you take the 'medicine', you'll live.

People ask me what did I do? How did I beat it? Why and how have I survived? I don't know the answer to that question. There is no formula; no perfect mix of a bit of this and a bit of that equals a cancer-free life.

There is no doubt in my mind that I was determined. Heartbroken, yes. Devastated, yes. Pissed off—you better believe it. How *dare* this cancer turn up uninvited? I also feel as if my life before cancer had somehow prepared me for the battle. Maybe I also got lucky. I don't know.

Pre-cancer, I thought I was super-strong and hard-working. I'd worked such long hours and pushed myself so hard to get where I wanted to be in my career. I'd take someone through a typical day in my life and they'd be blown away by how much I crammed in every single day. So I thought I was pretty tough. But what I know now is that all that stuff was easy. When you're healthy, everything's easy.

It's incredibly difficult to push yourself to keep fighting when you're very ill. I told myself, *If you're going to pride yourself on being strong, prove it. Don't just talk about how strong you are. Here's your true test. Get up, pick yourself up off the floor and keep going.*

And that's what I did. It's very difficult, because there's no break. It really is a battle to see which of you will give up first, your body or the tumour. You can't take six months off to get yourself together. The oncologist has you on a schedule that they believe will work, and you've just got to keep going.

In the beginning Fran explained what to expect from the three-week cycles. The first week is absolutely the worst; by the end of the second you're kind of okay; and then they give you one week's grace to get your strength up a bit before you go back for the next cycle. But the reality is different because over time it's so debilitating. The first cycle's terrible, the second one's worse, and it spirals rapidly down—your body is working from a lower and lower base. For the very first cycle you were at your peak health, then you become weaker and weaker as treatment goes on. It takes its toll, physically, emotionally, mentally.

When I began treatment I was told I would be doing chemo for four months. That was the plan. I was to do six cycles, each lasting around three weeks, then I'd be done with chemo and on to the next thing. It was like a kind of endurance event: I'd told myself, *Okay, it's this far, I just have to get through this, and then I'm done.* I managed to get through the four months and thought I'd come to the end of the chemo.

But the tumours hadn't shrunk sufficiently. When Fran recommended another two months, I was gutted. I could have said no; they couldn't make me do more. But they strongly recommended I carried on.

I signed up for another two months. And when that was done, the tumour still hadn't shrunk enough. I had to do yet another two months. Each time I thought I was over the finishing line, having spent all my effort trying to get there, they'd move the finishing line further away. And each time I had to dig deeper to keep coming back for more. I switched to two-weekly cycles. And by the end the cycles were weekly, and then the chemo was daily.

I've never been afraid of needles, but I reached the point where I just couldn't stand the thought of having another injection. I was going to chemo and having very regular blood tests; they had to make sure my kidneys and liver weren't on the verge of shutting down. After a while, between the chemo and the blood tests, your veins dry up. The nurses can't find a vein anymore so they're digging around to find somewhere to put the needle, slapping your hand like you're a heroin addict. And all the time, you're disrobing in front of people, and they're groping and grabbing and testing and poking. You begin to feel like you've lost ownership of your body; it belongs to a team of people trying to save your life. But sometimes you wish they'd just leave you alone.

Lizzie Pettit, Tracy Watson and Julia Bradbury

Sally's best friends from her recruitment days

After Annabelle was born, we were all desperate for news about the baby, the birth, and how Sal was doing. We were all a little surprised that after waiting so long for her chance to bring her incredibly precious baby into the world she hadn't been plastering photos of them both all over her Facebook page. So we each left several messages for Sal in the hope she'd let us come and visit them in the hospital.

None of us will ever forget reading the email that Sal sent telling us she had cancer. We were shocked and horrified by the news, and devastated that she was being robbed of that magical period of post-natal bliss that new mothers experience in the first week of a baby's life. Instead of thinking about feeding and sleeping routines, Sally was facing chemotherapy.

That Sunday, the three of us urged Sally to see us so we could meet Annabelle—even if it was just for five minutes. We were all so worried about Sal and we didn't know whether she'd really want visitors or not. But she let us come to see her, and we each had a nurse of Annabelle— she was just divine.

And then Lizzie broke the ice, by bluntly saying, 'Right, so how does everyone feel about Sally having cancer?' It made Sal laugh.

We stayed and talked and cried together for three hours. That day it felt as if we were on an emotional roller-coaster as we tried to understand what Sally was about to go through and what we could do to support her and Marcus. We felt a sense of disbelief—how could this be happening to someone we knew, especially someone like Sal? We also felt terribly helpless. We knew we wanted to help her, but at first, none of us knew what we could do to help.

◆ ◆ ◆

These are some of the things we did to support Sally through chemotherapy:

Many of Sal's friends and colleagues joined in, and we took it in turns delivering food and meals for the weeks when Sal was having chemo. Sally loves food, and so we all made sure she had lots to choose from when she was feeling tired and sick and not in the mood to cook. Sometimes she wanted to eat, other times she couldn't eat anything, it was like feast or famine.

We also continued our girls' lunches. We've been catching up for a regular girly lunch for years, and after Sal was diagnosed those lunches seemed more important than ever. We fitted them in around her chemo weeks and her endless appointments. We wanted to try to maintain some sort of normality and give her a chance to get out of the house. She'd tell us about the horrendous side effects of the treatment, and how terrible it was that they were robbing her of her time with Annabelle. But she was always so brave about everything she was going through.

We all kept calling her regularly to make sure she knew she was very loved, and we were here for her any time she needed us. She didn't always feel like talking, so we left loads of messages, to help keep her spirits up.

Sal was amazingly positive, and really brave, but her emotions were often up and down. Naturally she was extremely upset and cried at times, and we cried with her. Trying to remain strong was difficult. Worrying about losing her looks was a very big thing for Sally. She was devastated about losing her hair and potentially her breasts, and she worried that being on TV she felt no one would want her if she didn't 'look the part'. But in fact, Sally never lost one skerrick of beauty, no matter what stage of the treatment she had reached, and she was strong and brave and determined not to let the disease beat her. She worked at staying positive, and she was incredibly appreciative of anything people did to support her.

Our advice for someone who's going through the same thing? If you've been diagnosed, try and do what Sally did: manifest positive feelings, look after yourself in every way, eat healthily and exercise.

If you're trying to support someone you love, then the most important things you can do are reach out and keep on reaching out, listen, be patient, give love, kindness and generosity, suggest practical ways to support them (like bringing meals, walking their dog, taking their laundry), and pray for them with all your heart.

Thank goodness for Annabelle

Thank goodness I had my beautiful baby Annabelle to come home to.

I know if I hadn't had Annabelle, I could have just been sick, lain on the lounge for six months and focused on getting better. I could have gone to chemo, come back from chemo, gone to acupuncture, and not tried to do anything else. And I could have sat back and let people make a fuss over me.

But, really, I think it was a good thing that I had Annabelle to look after. She didn't know I was having chemo. She just knew she wanted to have her nappy changed or go to the park or see her mummy. Looking after her helped connect me to that other world, the normal, non-cancer world, that was going on everywhere else.

I've been very lucky that Annabelle is the child she is. She's feisty and determined, quite stubborn, but also very loving. And she's also been quite an easy child to have around. I don't know how we would have managed if Annabelle had been a difficult, colicky baby who cried all the time and wouldn't settle. I mentioned it to Fran once, and she said she'd never yet seen a new mum with cancer who had a difficult baby. Their babies are always easy. Maybe it's the way the universe balances things out.

Annabelle is super-cute, and she's been a joy for all of us to have around. For my parents, I think, she's been the saving grace in all of this. So much of what's happened over the year since she was born has been so unbearable that Annabelle's been a little ray of sunshine, for my parents, and, of course, for Marcus and me too. She really is like a little rockstar: more than once I've been out somewhere with her—once it happened while I was at the airport—and somebody I didn't know walked past, stopped to look and said, 'Is that Annabelle?' It's funny that I've worked like a dog for years to achieve career recognition, and all Annabelle has to do is get out of bed, and people stop to adore her.

One of the things I wanted most of all was that she shouldn't suffer. I wanted to be there for her, to look after her, to fuss over her like any other mother would. I didn't want to start thinking I can't do this and I can't do that because I'm sick. None of this was her fault. I didn't want her to be punished because of something that had happened to me. I couldn't just collapse sick into bed. I had to get up and keep doing things day after day.

She'd look at me with those big brown eyes and it was as if she was thinking, *Hi! what's happening? It's another great day, what are we doing?* Her little face made me so happy I had to keep functioning.

And life goes on, even when you have cancer. You may not be going to work any more, but you attend endless medical appointments, you go to the Medicare office and put your forms in. There were days when that felt like a big achievement. I completed all the paperwork that comes with being sick, and I shopped and did my chores and got on with things, and I carted Annabelle around with me on all my little trips, because that's what new mums do. I would've preferred it if I had been one of those yummy mummies striding up and down the foreshore at Bondi, sipping a latte or talking on the phone while their babies slept peacefully in their prams. But I made do with trips to Medicare, and Annabelle didn't seem to mind one bit.

When Annabelle was tiny and feeding at night, or awake every few hours, or unsettled and grumbly and needing to be cuddled, even though I was utterly shattered from the chemo and feeling so bad, I still enjoyed those special moments with her. I'd be feeding her on the couch in the middle of the night, thinking, *I'm so lucky to be doing this. I'm so happy that I'm here. Had I not mentioned the pain in my breast to my doctor and it had been six months later, I would've been dead.* I didn't mind being dragged out of bed because I was spending that time with her and it felt so special—even at 4 am.

People ask me sometimes why I didn't leave her to my parents to mind while I was going through the worst of it. Of course, they would have loved to have her, they adore her. But they're not her parents—Marcus and I are. I'm her mum, and I knew she needed to be with me. I wanted to make sure Annabelle was a part of it all, so she'd know she was loved and cared for. I never wanted her to feel like she'd been discarded, even if that meant being in and out of the car all the time, coming with me to my appointments. And I was surprisingly busy. People thought I had nothing to do, and asked if they could come and see me. I'd check my diary and say, 'I'm booked out Wednesday, can't do Thursday . . .' When I had a full-time job I wasn't that busy.

I kept thinking, if I don't make it, the best I can do is be here for Annabelle now, so that even if she can't remember me, hopefully I would have given her a feeling of having been loved, and maybe that would set things off on the right path.

People sometimes said to me, 'It doesn't matter who looks after her. She doesn't know who you are. As long as someone's there to give her a bottle and change her nappy, that's all she needs.' And I'd think that's a very practical way of looking at it, and on one level it's correct; but on an emotional level she's a child and she needs to feel loved and to know who the special people in her life are. And, especially now she's older, every time she sees me walk into the room her face lights up, arms outstretched as she calls 'Mama' to me, and I know how much I mean to her.

I'm sure if I'd let someone else look after her, while she wouldn't consciously remember it later on, it would still have an impact on her. And I didn't want that. It's one thing for the cancer to impact on me; I'm a big person, an adult. But it was not fine for it to have an impact on Annabelle.

I was on a mission: to make sure she felt loved and cared for. And to survive. Sometimes people would say things like,

'You're really trying to live for her,' and I'd think, *Well, yeah, for Annabelle* and—for *me.*

◆ ◆ ◆

Being diagnosed with cancer is terrible at any stage of your life. There's never going to be a good time. For me, the hardest thing to deal with was the worry about what would happen to Annabelle if I was gone. It's very hard to think about. But there were times when I did contemplate a future for Annabelle without me in it. I wondered whether I should be writing her letters or making videos for her to watch when she was grown up: advice on life. I wanted to make DVD's for different stages of her life and write letters she could open on future birthdays. I wanted to give her advice on hair and boys and career; on the importance of healthy eating and good manners. I wanted to remind her to make great friends and to cherish and love those who loved her. I wanted to tell her to follow her dreams, and to avoid crash diets and always buy napkin rings when you see them on special because they're seriously overpriced. Most of all I wanted to tell her she was my everything.

How do you actually raise a child via a letter? How do you compress everything you feel and know and everything you want to pass on in a few pages?

How do you make sure you leave your child with an imprint of you and the love you feel for them so that they don't forget, especially when they will most likely have no memory of you?

The heartbreak is unbearable. I wanted to say 'Don't forget me Annabelle, I'm your mum and I love you so much. All I wanted was for you to come into this world and even if I leave, it doesn't mean I love you any less.' But I doubted I could actually articulate it in words without ending up a sopping mess of tears. I also worried that if I said it I might be giving in, slipping and losing my fight, my will, my drive.

Then that fire in my belly would kick in and I'd say to myself, 'No. I will tell her myself when the time comes because I'll still be here.'

There were times when I realised I was trying to get all my ducks in a row, preparing for the worst. I knew Marcus would always be a wonderful father, and there was no question in my mind that he'd always be there for her. But I'd find myself reminding him where the spare nappies were kept, or where to find the extra sheets for the cot, just in case I suddenly wasn't there any more and he needed to find them.

I wasn't being melodramatic; those fears were real. Chemo destroys your immune system and makes you highly susceptible to infection. Even a little fever or infection can kill you. I got a temperature one night, and when Marcus checked, we discovered it was 39.5 degrees. They warn you in the literature that if your temperature ever goes above 38 that you need to go to the hospital—immediately. I was still saying, 'No, no I'll be alright,' as Marcus drove me to hospital. I barely got there before I was shaking and convulsing and my body started to shut down. They put me on a drip with antibiotics for 24 hours, and it was pretty serious there for a while, but I made it through.

Experiences like that remind you that you're on a knife edge. Things can go wrong very quickly and you have to be prepared.

I wanted to make sure that Annabelle was accustomed to Marcus doing things for her as well as me—bathing and nappy changing and feeding and putting her to bed—so that if anything happened, she'd still feel like she had someone she was close to. In the weeks when I'd just had chemo, I had to let Marcus do a lot anyway because I'd be so sick and weak I could barely lift her.

Marcus had started a new job while I was pregnant, and although it was a very tough, high-pressure environment where he had to work long hours, he always tried to make it home in time to help out with Annabelle. I hated the idea of him being left alone to struggle on by himself. I didn't want to contemplate how he'd feel living without me—it's too big, too heart-breaking. I compensated by reassuring myself that he knew where to find Annabelle's socks.

I also wanted to make sure that Annabelle knew my core group of close girlfriends so that if anything happened to me, she'd have good female role models in addition to my mum and sister who could be an important part of her life. Those amazing females are the women I love most in the world and I wanted them to be her quasi-aunties, so that whatever she needed, she'd always have someone she could count on. I was trying to be sensible, but can you imagine thinking about replacing yourself? It's not something you can contemplate for very long without losing it. It's better to try to focus on getting well.

◆ ◆ ◆

I remember one day I surfed the internet hoping to find a photo of myself from the day I appeared on *The Kyle and Jackie O Show*. I'd been wearing a dress someone had lent me and I wanted to send them a thankyou note along with a picture of it. I found a photo of myself on a celebrity mummy website where they'd posted an article about me that had been in the paper a few days earlier. I'd been out having lunch with Larry

Emdur and had been photographed holding Annabelle. In the comments string, someone had written: 'This baby looks clearly too small and underfed. What kind of a horrible mother is this? Obviously she's not breastfeeding and she's not looking after her child.' When I read that it was as if that person had reached out and plunged a knife into my heart. The article said I had cancer and was having chemo, so *obviously* I wasn't breastfeeding, and if the reader had even thought about it for a nanosecond, she probably wouldn't have written it. I was so upset, it fed straight into my guilt and anxieties: yes, I *should* be breast-feeding, maybe I'm *not* doing enough for Annabelle, am I a bad mother because I've chosen to do this and not that?

I tried to remind myself that I was doing the best I could under the circumstances. But those feelings of guilt and doubt are never far from the surface.

◆ ◆ ◆

When I first went public with my story I was amazed and touched by how kind and generous people could be. There was something warm and lovely about their desire to reach out and share how they felt. As time went on, however, I sometimes found it challenging to deal with some of the attention I was getting. People would say things to me that I knew weren't meant to be hurtful, but sometimes were.

When I was pregnant I'd loved all that random social contact from complete strangers who'd wanted to talk to me about my baby and my bump. But being sick, it was a different story.

People would approach me and say: 'I saw you on TV, how's it going? Are you okay?' It really was wonderful to have people telling me how well I was doing, or how good I was looking (even though I clearly wasn't!), or encouraging me to keep on fighting. Positive thoughts *do* make a difference and sometimes a kind word from a stranger can make you feel really good about the world in spite of the heartbreaking situation.

However, people sometimes shared sad stories, and that could be more difficult to take. I remember there was one day in particular when I took Annabelle to Westfield for some grocery shopping, and I must have had 20 different people stop me to tell me their terribly sad cancer stories. 'It's really bad,' they'd say. 'I don't think she's going to make it.' Then a few minutes later, someone else stopped me, 'Hey, how are you going? Keep fighting! No one in my family's made it but you can!'

Later as I was standing in the supermarket, trying to remember which size nappies to buy, a lovely woman came to me crying, telling me all about how her mum recently died of cancer. As I comforted her, I thought of my own mum and of Annabelle. Would that happen to me? Would Annabelle lose her mum? Would my mum lose her daughter? I tried to stay strong and empathise with the poor woman who was clearly still fresh with grief, while holding back my own floodgate of tears. 'Stay strong Sally, stay strong.'

I stayed strong until a woman approached me and said, 'Oh your poor baby. She really needs you. Who's going to look after her when you're gone?' All I could think was, *Are you really asking me who's going to look after my child when I'm dead?*

The floodgates opened. I called Marcus, crying, 'All these people have been telling me about their dead relatives! Everybody dies! What if I don't make it?'

Many people don't realise what an effort it is to stay strong and positive every day. You have to struggle all the time not to let the misery and fear come crashing down on you. There were days when I truthfully felt like I was holding on to the ledge of a thirty-four-storey building with my fingernails. On days like that even the most insignificant comments could tip me over the edge.

I do understand why people wanted to talk to me. They'd seen me on television and felt a kind of connection—and they wanted to share their experiences and their feelings with someone who'd been there and understood, which I did. But sometimes I'd think, *Please just share the positive stories with me? Please. Don't tell me about your aunt who died, tell me about your sister who lived and then went on to climb a mountain!*

◆ ◆ ◆

And then there are the funny moments. There's a newsagent's near my house that I've been going to for the last five years to buy my mags and newspapers. The owners saw me before I was pregnant, and they saw me pregnant too. We talked about the baby, what was happening, when it was due. I popped in right after I'd had Annabelle. I still had my hair then and they were super-excited to meet her—'Oh, you've had the baby, amazing, that's fabulous.' Then I went in a couple of weeks later, after I'd lost my hair, and they never said a thing. A few months went by, I still had no hair, and the woman asked me, 'Are you going back to work soon?'

I replied, 'Well, I was supposed to be going back next month, but obviously I can't just yet because I have cancer.'

'Cancer?!' She looked genuinely shocked. 'What? *No!*'

'Um, yeah,' I said, pointing to my bald head. 'What did you think had happened?'

'I thought you had an allergic reaction to giving birth!'

Top: With the fabulous Brian McFadden, who so kindly performed, at my fundraiser. *Bottom*: With Adene Cassidy and Sarah Stinson, whose idea it was to have the fundraiser.

Top: At the *Marie Claire* Beauty Awards, with Sam Armytage and Sarah Stinson. April 2012. *Bottom*: With 2DayFM's Kyle and Jackie O. I'm sporting my blonde wig. I could never have been blonde at any other time, so I made the most of it.

Top: The incredible Anne Geddes photo. (Copyright © Anne Geddes.) *Bottom:* With Annabelle and Anne Geddes after our amazing photo shoot. An experience that I will cherish forever.

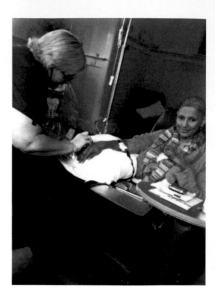

Top left: With Annabelle. *Top right:* Towards the end of chemotherapy, when it was daily. *Bottom left:* With Maha at Fashion Week 2012. *Bottom right*: At *InStyle* Women of Style awards with Kylie Gillies, Lucie McGeoch and Adene Cassidy.

Top: A pre-surgery lunch with Larry Emdur, just hours before my second mastectomy.
Bottom: Excited about launching my blog, *swiish* by Sally Obermeder.

Top: Laughter really is good for the soul. With Sarah Stinson and Lucie McGeoch at my cancer-free party. *Bottom:* With my besties, Julia Bradbury and Tracy Watson, with whom I've been friends since my recruitment days. (Photographs: Copyright © Patrick Riviere.)

Top: With Maha and Camilla at my cancer-free party. *Bottom left:* Laughing hysterically with Andy Cichanowski and Mark Wilkinson. Andy is a very close friend I met at *TT*. We have laughed so hard we've often cried, clutched each other and rocked back and forth. Now I can barely look at him without laughing. *Bottom right:* Feeling on top of the world. (Photographs: Copyright © Patrick Riviere.)

With Annabelle, 2012.
(Photograph: Peter Brew-Bevan for *WHO Magazine*)

I assumed she'd been too polite to mention it, but no. An allergic reaction to birth. I couldn't stop laughing.

A few months later I was at the supermarket on Bondi Road. By then my hair was finally starting to grow back. The cashier kept looking at my head, then glancing away, then looking at my head again, and I knew she was working up the courage to say something. Finally, she said, 'Look, I'm so sorry, but I have to ask you . . . Are you—' . . . pause . . . '—happy with your hair plugs?' I laughed so hard.

◆ ◆ ◆

I must confess I was not above using the fact that I was sick to get my own way from time to time. Not in a 'poor me' kind of way; more like a kid trying her luck to see if she can get an extra lolly.

If somebody wanted me to do something that I didn't want to do, I'd say, 'I can't, I have cancer.'

Or I'd be feeling down and my girlfriends would say, 'What can we do?'

'Lunch at China Doll might cheer me up!'

Marcus would suggest going out for dinner. 'What do you want to eat, Chinese or Italian?'

'Italian.'

'You wouldn't rather go Chinese?'

'No, Italian.'

'Really?'

'I have cancer.'

'Okay, Italian it is then!'

Or I'd say to Marcus, 'I'm so depressed about losing my hair. I need a Missoni scarf.' Marcus delivered. He bought me some beautiful Hermès and Missoni scarves. I thought, *Wow, I should ask for a BMW. With a boat.*

Every Christmas my girlfriends from my days at the recruitment agency Tracy, Julia, Lizzie and I have a tradition: we get together for dinner at my house and I organise a psychic to do a reading for us. It's loads of fun and we analyse all the predictions for the coming year over dinner. It's always an entertaining evening to end the year.

That Christmas I got a bit sidetracked with all the treatment and forgot to book a psychic. The girls told me not to worry about it, but I was determined to get hold of one. I discovered you can't book a psychic two weeks out, they're all booked up. So I called my friend Naomi at work—she seriously knows all the best psychics—and I asked her if she could help. She hesitated, then said, 'Look, I might have to . . .'

'Naomi, that's fine.'

'You don't know what I'm going to say.'

'You might have to say Sal has cancer and needs a psychic at the last minute. Yeah, go for it'.

'I didn't want you to be upset.'

'No, use it. Tell them how bad it is!'

It became a running gag with all my friends. Then my hair started to grow back and I couldn't play the sympathy card anymore. It was a great day.

One day when I was quite sick I had taken Annabelle with me to get some tests and she was at that four-month stage where she hated every single car trip. She screamed all the way there and then ten minutes later the test was over and back in the car we went. Of course, she screamed all the way home and no amount of me talking or singing or making funny noises would quieten her. Then I smelt the deadly smell of a full nappy. More screaming. I had to pull over. It was peak hour and the traffic was a nightmare but I pulled over in front of some parked cars and changed her nappy and still more screaming. I figured a feed would help. I prepared a bottle with one hand as I cuddled her with the other and started giving her the bottle. I was struggling. I could hardly support my own body weight; I felt like I needed to collapse but I couldn't because this baby needed me, so I pushed on. Then I saw a council ranger walking towards me. 'Ma'am, you're stopped in a no-parking zone.' Unbelievable. Was I sitting there reading a magazine and sipping a latte? No. I was feeding a screaming child, I had no hair, I clearly looked sick as a dog and I was barely standing. Now you want to give me a ticket? Wow. Some people really blow me away.

◆ ◆ ◆

My weirdest ever cancer moment happened to me just recently. I was in Westfield with Annabelle waiting for the lifts, and I heard a woman screaming, 'Sally, Sally, Sally!' She ran towards me and I was looking at her and thinking, *Who are you? Where do I know you from? Wait, do I even know you?* I used to have an excellent memory but chemo has messed it up and now I'm particularly hazy with faces and names. I was running her through the memory banks—work, PR person, school, uni, gym—but was coming up blank.

She ran up to me, held up her phone and said, 'Can I have a photo?'

Then I realised, no, in fact, I didn't know her. She'd come screaming up to me as if I was her long-lost sister, but all she wanted was a photo, so I said, 'Yes, sure.'

We took the photo, and she said, 'I was so excited when you walked past me.'

'Really? Why?'

'Because if I ever get cancer, then I want to be just like you!'

I said, 'Well, hopefully, honey, you won't get cancer.'

Maha Koraiem

Sally's sister

When we were little kids, Sally and I used to play teachers and students. Sal always insisted on being the teacher, and despite all my protestations, I had to be the student. 'Please, Sal?' I would beg.

'No, I am the teacher,' she would reply.

Being the younger sister, I was so excited by the fact that Sal even wanted to hang out with me at all, I didn't really mind that I never got to be the teacher. We had a little blackboard with yellow plastic legs. Sally would stand in front of it, and proceed to give me a lesson, speaking to me as though she knew everything about the world. I lapped it up. I completely looked up to her and believed she knew everything. How funny that years later, when she would face cancer, the biggest battle of all, Sal would still be the one to stand up and be the teacher.

It's hard to explain what it's like to watch someone you love more than anything in the world go through cancer, particularly when that person is the strongest person you know, the person who you genuinely believed was invincible. Add to that the fact that it happened at what should have been the happiest time of Sal and Marcus's lives—with the arrival of baby Annabelle, a baby who was so hard-fought for—it was just too much to bear.

The hardest part, after the shock of Sal's diagnosis, was watching her go through chemo. It was terrifying for all of us, but particularly for Sal. And yet somehow she had a way of making us all feel better. 'It's fine, no big deal,' she would say. 'I'll be fine.'

When I told Sal I would come to her chemo sessions, she said, 'Nah, don't come to the hospital. Don't take a day off work just for this.' I knew that deep down she was scared, but there was no way she would let me, her little sister, feel that fear, or worry about her.

But nothing would stop me from going to chemo and hanging out with her. So, I took a day off work every time she had to go in for treatment. Although I went along to almost every single chemo session she had, the truth is, there isn't anything you can do for your loved one. Sure, you can be there, but there is nothing you can say or do which makes it any better, or takes away from the pain they experience when they go through chemo. Nothing can alleviate the physical or emotional pain of cancer.

I remember after the first couple of cycles of chemo, Sal would be well enough for us to stop by a deli on the way home to pick up some food. Salads and fresh fruit, particularly apples, were top of the list. The apples were supposed to be good at removing the metallic taste she was experiencing from the chemo. But over time, as the cycles went on, Sal was too sick for us to stop at the fruit shop. She just wanted to go straight home and lie down and try to forget all the pain.

She would often close her eyes in the car. I was never sure if she was sleeping or simply trying to find some kind of mental escape. I would look over at her sitting in the passenger seat with her bald head, eyebrows and eyelashes gone and her skin, which had turned a very dull grey colour. It was heartbreaking. I thought, 'How can this be happening to you? You are the strong one, the one who has fought so hard for everything. You shouldn't have to fight this too.' It wasn't fair.

During those days, I used to look to Sal for comfort. I know that might sound strange when she was the ill one, but I needed to hear her say that she would be alright, that she would survive, that she wouldn't give up. Because the thought of not having her around was too painful to contemplate, too awful, too terrifying. And Sal being

Sal would say to me, 'It's going to be okay. I am going to be okay, don't worry. I'm not going to die.' Even if she didn't always believe it herself.

Sally had always been determined. When we were young, she would point at the large coffee table in our living room and say to me, 'Do you think I can jump over that?'

'No,' I would reply, worried she would jump and fall flat on her face.

'I will prove to you I can,' she would say. 'I will rise to the challenge.' Then she would leap over the table, landing safely on the other side. I was in awe of her fearlessness.

The expression 'I will rise to the challenge' became a common one for us. Every time Sal wanted to do something (pretty often), she would ask me if I thought she couldn't.

'I will prove to you I can. I will rise to the challenge!' she would bellow. It's still something we laugh about today—Sal's defiance of anything anyone says she can't do, of any challenge she faces.

Sometimes when the chemo got too much we would joke. 'What? You reckon it's tough with cancer and chemo and a baby? I'll show you! I will rise to the challenge!' And she did.

I wasn't surprised when Sal called me before her first chemo appointment to tell me she had written us a to-do list for our time at the chemo clinic. The first thing she mentioned was thankyou cards. I asked what they were for, and though some of them were to thank people who had sent her or Annabelle gifts, it turned out that the majority of them were to thank people for the thankyou cards they had sent her after she had sent them *gifts!*

'I sent so and so a housewarming gift, and they sent me a thankyou, so I want to send them a card,' she would say.

Now I was pissed off. 'You're thanking people for the thankyous they sent you? You have cancer*!' But Sal wouldn't hear of it. So many people had been supportive and amazing, she said, and so she wanted to show her appreciation. That was Sal—thanking people for their thankyous, even in the midst of cancer.*

The other thing that struck me at that time was how interested Sal still was in all the normal everyday stuff. She never ever made me feel like she didn't have the time or the energy to listen to me and my stories and find out what was going on in my life, my worklife, my personal life, even my friends' lives. She was still there, 100 per cent, asking about everything that was happening, there for me whenever I needed it, and even when I didn't. She was still my big sister. And that wasn't just with me, it was with everyone. I received countless emails from her friends saying that they had seen her and despite how horribly sick she was, that in a way she was just the same old Sal, laughing and gossiping and just being . . . well . . . there.

The day Sal's hair was shaved off was tough. When we reached Kenneth's house, I could see the emotional turmoil she was in, but she still chatted away to Kenneth and Belinda, all the while choking back her tears.

When she had her breakdown in the Witchery dressing room later that day, trying to come to terms with the loss of her hair, she sat in there for what seemed like hours, then finally emerged, wiping away the tears. She collected herself and said, 'Right, let's go!' and we went home to show Marcus her new haircut.

But that is Sal, picking herself up off the floor and carrying on. Never forgetting her family or her friends or letting them feel for a moment that what she was going through was any more important than their lives. And teaching me all the way that through grace, humour and humility, you can rise to the challenge, despite all odds. So in time, this too shall pass.

It takes a village

I'm not sure how I would have got through it all without the loving support of my parents, Marcus's parents, Marcus, Maha and my incredible friends.

You hear stories about relationships not surviving this kind of crisis: one partner gets sick and the other one shoots through; or else they stick together just long enough for the sick person to recuperate, and then they shoot through.

That's not Marcus. He chose me—we chose each other—and that really means something. I know I can count on him, no matter what.

When I was first diagnosed with cancer, Marcus offered to leave his job and just be with me, to support me 24/7. I wouldn't let him; I couldn't stand the thought of the three of us, me and Marcus and Annabelle, stuck in the house all day, contemplating how sad it was (and financially it wasn't really an option either, but that's another story). I wanted to have some semblance of a normal life going on. I wanted to feel like cancer was a *part* of our life but not our *whole* life.

Life on chemo was hard on me, but it was terribly hard on Marcus, too. I'm basically an optimist at heart: although I would be struck by the fear that I was going to die every day, I never believed it for very long. I *couldn't* believe it. But Marcus has a different frame of mind to me, and when he was told that I had cancer, he emotionally faced the real possibility of my death. That's a huge burden to bear, especially when he was trying all the time to keep my spirits up, to keep me focused on the fight, help me get through each day and come back for more.

And that's what he did: he was always strong for me, and loving, and supportive. He did his best not to let me know how frightened he was. He didn't really begin to think we'd turned the corner until after my third cycle of chemo, about four months in. That's an awfully long time to be living with that kind of uncertainty—while trying to be the best dad he could be to Annabelle and working incredibly hard in his new job.

When I was pregnant, Marcus had taken a new role with a large finance company. He described his new job as a little bit like being a horse race: the company takes on a lot of new people, and then they all compete to bring in clients and business. Every month, everyone's performance is reviewed, and the lowest-performing people would be let go. Marcus hadn't been in his job very long when I was diagnosed, so he was still trying to make his mark in this highly competitive environment, and, at the same time, being there for me as much as he could be: coming to appointments, talking to doctors, listening to me when I needed to talk or cry, even if it was at one o'clock in the morning and he had to be at the office the next day. He gave me unconditional support—so much love and so much care, no matter how difficult it became—and it did get difficult. He had to watch while the treatment stripped me down: first my hair, then my health, then my breast. He had to watch me suffer through chemo for weeks and months, knowing there was nothing he could do to make it better. And he had to endure the terrible uncertainty of not knowing whether all this pain and misery was actually going to pay off. Would it work? Would it save me? We couldn't be sure.

But through all of it, Marcus stood strong, even though there were times, I'm sure, when he would have liked to just get on his motorbike and ride until all this went away. He gave his all at work, and he gave his all at home, and no-one could ask for more than that.

◆ ◆ ◆

Maha was amazing, too. She has a high pressure full-time job, but when I was diagnosed she was the first one to offer to help out. Along with Maha, Marcus came with me to my first chemo session, but he couldn't take many days off work for that kind of thing, so Maha would accompany me instead. I'd turn up with my to-do list and I'd dictate letters or thank-you cards to her. She used to joke that what I really needed was a PA, not a sister. At other times we'd just chat and not worry about the list.

Those were nice times. And when I was feeling strong enough, she'd take me out to lunch at some of my favourite restaurants and try to give me some special days in among the gloom. Her support meant a lot to me.

Sometimes I'd call Maha and she'd say, 'What are you doing?' And I wouldn't say anything. I'd just cry and cry. Or I'd say, 'It's so boring. Cancer is so *boring.*' And I'd hang up. I couldn't articulate how horrible it was. My life was a nightmare. But a *boring* nightmare.

It was a new phase in my relationship with my sister; not a happy phase, but oddly, it brought us closer together. Although we'd always been close and Maha had been through a lot of ups and downs with me, I'd always tried to be strong around her. Typically, if something was the matter, I'd say, 'No, no, I'll be fine, don't worry about me, I'm okay.'

But as the chemo gradually wore me down, I didn't have the energy for that any more. I was too emotionally fragile to be alone—I needed someone with me who wouldn't make any demands, someone who'd just be there and be easy to be with. I was still traumatised, I think, by the shock of what had happened to us, and I really felt that from one minute to the next, something terrible might happen again. But if I had someone else there with me, I felt protected, as if nothing bad could happen.

The first person I turned to was Marcus, of course, but his work meant that he couldn't always be there. So I'd call Maha and ask her to come over and hang out with Annabelle and me for a few hours, or just watch a DVD. Little things like that. Until chemo, I'd never been able to ask her for what I needed. I'd never wanted to burden my sister or put her out by making demands on her. But with chemo, that changed. It had to.

The other thing Maha did for me, along with my closest friends, was to help anchor me to the normal world. I knew I could ring her and talk about normal things, fun things: we'd talk about whether she'd been shopping and what she'd bought, and when she was going to move house: the ordinary business of daily life.

Different people end up being different things to you at a time like this; I felt I could offload all my emotional pain on Marcus, because, although I knew he was in pain too, he seemed so strong and I thought he could take it. So he was my emotional bedrock.

My friends helped me connect to life as I'd lived it before, the life that was still going on around me, outside of cancer world. I didn't have a job to go to anymore and I wasn't really well enough to socialise, so they became my lifeline to normality.

My parents were also so strong and so wonderful, especially when it came to looking after Annabelle. They've always said 'Whatever you need, whenever you need it, we're happy to do it' and they were true to their lifelong parenting motto. Whenever we asked they were always more than happy to step in and help.

I'd been trying to get Annabelle into a routine because I thought she should have some sort of structure in her life among the mayhem of hospitals and treatment. Mum always said, 'I don't know why you're so obsessed with routines.'

And I'd say, 'Well, didn't we have a routine?'

'Yes, of course,' she'd reply. But I guess it's different when you're a grandparent. Once, Annabelle stayed over at Mum and Dad's place overnight and Mum told me Annabelle woke up at 2 am and wanted to play—so Mum played with her! 'How could I say no to that little face?' Mum said. I pretended to be mortified at such disregard for the routine, but truthfully I was chuffed that they'd bonded so deeply and so strongly. When I see Annabelle run into my parents' arms and cuddle them, it makes me so happy.

It's hard to put in words the love and gratitude I have for my parents. Only now that I have had Annabelle can I even begin to fathom what it would have been like for them to find out that their daughter had cancer. And that it was a rare, aggressive cancer.

Through some of my darkest hours, they helped to care for me and for Annabelle, to keep my chin up and to keep me focused on the future. There were many times after chemo and surgery when Annabelle and I would go around to Mum and Dad's house and I could let go a bit and allow them to look after me. They nurtured me, fed me, let me sleep, took Annabelle for walks and played with her for hours at a time. They gave us both more love than we could ever ask for.

To say that Mum and Dad made things that much easier is an understatement—they would drive across the city to see me as often as I wanted, cook for us (if you know my mum, she likes to show her love through food. We had more food than we knew what to do with!).

There were many days when Marcus would go over to their house just to see them, to have dinner and to share with them what was going on with my prognosis and treatment schedule or to share how he was feeling or how I was doing. And they listened, they supported and they loved.

I don't doubt that Mum and Dad had their many moments of darkness too, fearing for me, my life, the treatment and my surgery. But they never ever let themselves be there less than one hundred per cent for me, one hundred per cent of the time. My love for them and appreciation for how much support they gave us—and still give us—is eternal. Mum and Dad, I love you so much. Thank you for *everything*, I am truly blessed to have you as my parents and grandparents to Annabelle.

I think Marcus's parents, Margitta and Manfred, found it tough being in Canberra and felt as if perhaps they couldn't be there to help us through the daily grind of the treatment. They would call us all the time and give us moral support and encouragement.

Margitta would constantly send me care packages—there would be gifts for Annabelle and motivational and inspirational books and CDs for me. After I completed my chemo she would send me Noni Juice and any vitamins that she thought would help my recovery. She never failed to include a card inside every box with heartfelt words of support and encouragement. I would look forward to the parcels because they were so full of love.

Margitta also gave me tips she found helpful regarding the radiation process as she had undergone radiation herself as part of her breast cancer treatment.

We really appreciated their support and were so grateful they were there to help us in our time of need.

I'm also so very grateful to my girlfriends, because they brought an extra level of support. In a way you expect your partner and your family to pitch in and help—that's what families are for—but you can't expect the same level of commitment from your friends. My friends turned out to be absolutely sensational.

When I was first diagnosed, they all wanted to do something to help, but nobody really knew what to do. Adene, my friend who'd taken over my job while I was on maternity leave, suggested organising a food roster.

At first I didn't like the idea. I didn't want to admit that I needed any help. I was only just back from hospital and I didn't want everyone fussing over me and feeling sorry for me and bringing me food like some kind of invalid. At that stage I hadn't started the chemo and had no sense of how sick I was going to become. I refused their help and said, 'No, I'm just going to carry on as normal. It's fine. If I need a meal here or there Mum'll make it for me.'

'Why don't we try it?' Adene said. 'If you hate it we can stop.'

'No.'

'Don't you think it'd be good for Marcus? He needs to eat, and you'll need to eat, and that way all you've got to worry about is looking after Annabelle.'

'No, no, we'll be fine.'

Eventually Maha made me see sense.

'Why are you saying no?' she asked. 'Everyone is rallying around you, they all want to help. You've just got to tell them what to do. Can we come with you to chemo? Can we look after Annabelle? Can we cook? You can't keep shutting people out.'

'I don't want to shut them out,' I replied. 'I just don't want everyone going "Poor Sally poor Sally, it's just so terrible and here's a meal."'

I didn't want to feel like a victim.

'Yes, but these are the people you love the most, right?'

'Yes.'

'If it was me, and I said can I please cook you a meal, would you say no?'

'No,' I said. 'I would let you cook.'

'Then why not just let them cook for you? They want to help. Why not be happy that they care enough to want to help?'

I realised she was right. So Adene drew up a roster where two people would share a week: someone would do the front half of the week and someone else would do the back half of the week. They brought over fresh salads and meat and fish, meals we could heat up easily. And once the chemo started, those meals were our saviour. It was great in a practical sense because I didn't have to shop, didn't have to cook, and if there were things I couldn't eat, or really wanted to eat, I could tell my friends and they would respond accordingly. We just didn't have to worry about food at all.

And there was more to it than that. Every time I opened that fridge, I felt the love, the love that had made all these people take the time to provide all these beautiful meals for me. I know what a hassle it is to cook a meal. My girlfriends had their own families, their own jobs, their own lives, and yet they made the time and endured the effort to shop and prep and cook all these meals and drive them over. It's actually a big thing when everyone's juggling their own daily demands. But no-one ever made me feel like it was a big thing. Every time I looked in the fridge I felt as if they were there in the house with us. When you're sick, you feel so alone in the sickness. No-one can help you fight the disease. No-one can help you get through the pain. The only thing they can do is love you, and that love is what gives you the strength to keep fighting.

And they helped me by just being normal—reminding me that real life was still going on outside. They'd come over for a chat, and we'd talk about what was happening with the cancer and how I felt. And once we got through that and some tears, we'd start on what was happening in the tabloids. They took me to lunch, we went for walks, gossiped. Normal stuff.

When I was first diagnosed, I was worried that my friends wouldn't want to see me anymore. I don't even understand why I thought that—if one of *my* friends got cancer, *as if* I wouldn't be friends with them anymore. But I was seriously afraid I was going to be ostracised. In fact nothing could have been further from the truth. Looking back, I feel as if the doctors saved my life, but it was the people around me—my parents and Marcus's parents and Marcus and my sister and my girlfriends and close male friends, that core unit of people—who saved my soul.

Because that's what gets damaged. While your body is ravaged, your soul takes a beating. You know that saying, 'It takes a village to raise a child'? I feel like it takes a village to save someone from cancer—I couldn't have done it by myself. I just *couldn't*. For all my strength and for all my passion and determination, truthfully, I could not have done it on my own. I needed my family and friends to love me and support me and encourage me and believe in me and laugh with me. They are the ones who helped me through, day after day.

It's like a boxing match. You've got to keep coming back for more hits. And you need them there cheering you on, yelling, 'You can do it! We believe in you!'

Before I got cancer, I'd taken strength from the idea that I was tough enough to be my own cheer squad. I'd been lucky enough to find a husband who was supportive and thoughtful, loving and smart, and I probably couldn't have got to where I am without him. But still, I really believed the only person I could count on to get me over the line was me. Now I know that's not true—when things get really tough, you need all the loving support you can get. Yes, you still have to fight it out for yourself—no-one can do that for you—but the people who love you are an irreplaceable source of strength when you've run through your own supply. They help you get up again and keep on going.

Sometimes people think, *I haven't studied medicine so I can't help you. I can't save you.* But the sheer act of loving someone is so powerful that reaching out actually helps to save them. I know it's awkward and uncomfortable when someone's sick; it's easier to shy away, to not call and wait till it's over. If you can be brave enough, it's so important to call or email or do whatever you can. It doesn't matter if you don't know what to say, or you're worried they don't want to talk about their illness. It's easy—don't talk about it. Ring them up and say 'Hi', or 'I'm thinking of you', or 'Did you hear what happened at work the other day?' The simple act of making contact will give them strength and let them know they're not alone.

I don't know how people do it if they've got to fight it by themselves. You experience so many gut-wrenching times. You need family and close friends around you to help you get through each stage. My family and friends have been—and continue to be—instrumental in my recovery and I'll forever be grateful. Forever. Because what they showed me was that they loved me not because I'm on TV and not because I interview celebrities but just for being me. I'd never really understood that before. And that was such a powerful thing.

Adene Cassidy

One of Sally's closest friends from Channel Seven

Sally, the bright, beautiful reporter at Today Tonight, *that was my first impression of her. Our friendship was instant. In fact, I can't really remember how it grew so quickly because it feels like Sally has been in my life forever, when in fact we only met in 2009.*

We had a lot in common: we were both career women, focused, busy, the same age. I was a mum and I remember wondering why Sally hadn't had babies yet. Of course, not everyone wants kids, but when you're new to parenthood, which I was, you want every woman to be able to experience the wondrousness of being pregnant, and the ultimate joy of holding their baby for the first time.

Sally loved her job at Channel 7, a new career path after years in finance. She was driven and efficient, but I could tell she felt as though something was missing. One day, over one of our many girly catch-up lunches, Sally opened up to me about her desire to have a baby; she just couldn't figure out how to make it all work. Would it mean the end of her job, the career she'd worked so hard for? It's a common question when you're thinking about having kids, and I felt as though Sally was looking to me to see how it was managed, or should I say, juggled!

Sal seemed understandably daunted by the prospect of being a mum. She talked about wanting to do it and do it well and to really be there for her child but she didn't want to give up on her career either. As a mother and as her friend, the only advice I could give her was to say that it would truly be the best thing she and Marcus would ever do. It's a cliché but there's no other way to describe it.

It was a few months later when Sally finally opened up about her struggle to fall pregnant. As it turned out, she and Marcus had been trying for years and she was terrified that it would never happen. The worst part was that the doctors had no explanation for why she couldn't conceive. I think the fact there wasn't a definitive reason made it all the more difficult. At least if you know what's wrong, you can try to work on it, or make a plan, and if there's one thing I know about my darling friend, it's that she loves to plan!

Sal felt as though time wasn't on her side and the pressure it was putting on her marriage was immense—Marcus was desperate to be a dad; it was something he'd wanted ever since they'd got married. Sal asked me my thoughts about IVF. My reply was that if that's the way to have a baby, then go for it. I knew of other women who had gone through the process and I really felt that Sal wouldn't regret it. But it was a difficult decision, an emotional one too, because it meant Sal admitting that she and Marcus couldn't do this on their own—they needed help.

Eventually, when Sal opted to go ahead with IVF, it turned out to be the best decision of her life. Sally and Marcus fell pregnant on their first attempt. It was a joyous phone call when I received the news. We spent ages talking about pregnancy, motherhood and, of course, work. For all of her early hesitations Sally was super-excited about being a mum. I think she had finally realised you only get one shot at being a parent so you have to enjoy the ride.

When my beautiful friend was diagnosed with cancer, needless to say I was devastated. But in amongst all of the shock, tears and fears for Sal, the one thing I kept thinking over and over was how glad I was that she had made the big decision to go ahead with the IVF, because she and Marcus had been able to have beautiful little baby Annabelle. Sal had been able to experience pregnancy and to hold her baby in her arms. And that was something that could never be taken away from her.

In the months that followed, I was so proud to see Sal become the mum she had wanted to be. The same dogged determination and passion with which she fought to have a baby and fought cancer she also applied to being a mum. Never one to just lie down and take it, Sal remained incredibly hands-on with Annabelle, which was no easy task given how sick she was. That mothering instinct had kicked in when Annabelle was born and it was so deep and so primal that Sal wouldn't—couldn't—be anything but an absolutely devoted, loving, caring mother who did everything in her power, cancer or no cancer, to make sure Annabelle was happy, healthy and loved.

Fundraiser

One of the most amazing things my friends did was organise a fundraiser.

I'd been talking to Sarah about how expensive it was having cancer, there were so many bills.

The year before I was diagnosed, we'd paid for IVF, an obstetrician and all the other costs involved in having a baby. That's thousands of dollars—just to have a baby.

Then cancer came along, and I wasn't prepared for how expensive it would be. I assumed that if you have cancer everything would be covered by Medicare. But since I was a private patient, it wasn't. Chemo is covered substantially by Medicare but there are quite a lot of out-of-pocket expenses. There are injections to boost white blood cells, which are mindblowingly expensive.

And every time you see your oncologist or your surgeon—and you're seeing them constantly—there's another out-of-pocket cost. Some of it will be covered by Medicare but the greater part is not. One visit doesn't seem like a lot, but when you're going 20, 30, 40 times, it all adds up.

Because Annabelle was a newborn while I was having my chemo she was up a lot during the night. There were some nights when I just couldn't get up to look after her, so we sometimes had a night nurse. And night nurses don't come cheap. If I lived in a really big house I guess I could've got an au pair, but I live in a tiny two-bedroom apartment. There was no room for an au pair. And I couldn't leave Annabelle with Mum. I simply wouldn't have been able to sleep if I didn't have my baby near me. I needed to be able to check on her, to tuck her in, to kiss her forehead.

I was also supplementing the chemotherapy with alternative therapies. I found acupuncture was helpful with easing the nausea a little bit, so I had that every two days in each of those first weeks of chemo. And once I finished chemo, I needed to strengthen my immune system, so I went to see a naturopath. You can't take any herbs or vitamins or supplements while you're having chemo—anything that makes you feel better is helping the cancer—but once it is over you need all the help you can get. And, of course, supplements cost money, too.

Then I needed surgery. The cost of the hospital stay was covered by my private health fund, but I had bills for the anaes-thetist, the anaesthetist's assistant, the surgeon, the surgeon's assistant—it's a team of people. And while some of their costs were covered by Medicare, we were actually out of pocket by a large sum of money. And the surgery I needed had to be done in stages. I had a right breast mastectomy, then a left breast mastectomy and reconstruction. Each procedure used different medical teams, and we were paying for them all.

Even after I claimed the expenses back from Medicare and the health fund, we were tens of thousands of dollars out of pocket. That's a huge amount. People think if you're on TV then you must be really rich, but, sadly, unless you're a huge star, you're not rich at all. I earn a normal wage and so does Marcus, and we have to budget for everything. We don't have tens of thousands of dollars sitting around in our 'just-in-case, rainy-day' fund. I mean, who has a spare $50 000 just sitting in their bank account in case they need new breasts?

I came to dread looking in the mailbox because every time I did there'd be more bills—just one more source of stress that you really don't need at that time. And, of course, your normal bills and the mortgage don't disappear just because you've got cancer. We started to go backwards very quickly and tried not to worry about the money, because we had bigger things to worry about, but we couldn't help it.

'We should have a fundraiser,' Sarah Stinson said.

I said, 'No way. I don't want some kind of pity party. I don't want people saying, 'Let's throw five dollars into a hat.' I couldn't think of anything more embarrassing.

'I think we should do it,' Sarah said. 'It's not about the money. It's about showing you that you're supported.'

Reluctantly, I agreed. Privately, I told myself it would just be me, Marcus, Sarah and Maha. We'd have a few drinks and we'd all go home. I didn't think anyone else would show up.

'Do you want to be involved in the arrangements?' Sarah asked. 'Or do you want to just turn up on the night?'

Sarah knows I like things to be done just so. I'd given very specific instructions to my sister and Camilla when they were organising my baby shower, right down to the colour of the invitations. When the fundraiser idea came up it was New Year. I was three months into chemo and as sick as a dog. 'You do whatever. I'll just turn up.'

So Sarah went away and organised it.

It sounds so easy when I say it like that, but it really was a major, major undertaking. Sarah sold tickets and organised gifts, chose songs and organised bands and entertainment, found places to rehearse, arranged a venue, catering, all the countless other things that go into making a special event the night of someone's life. Sarah already had an incredibly demanding full-time job, but she took the time to do this for me—and she did it selflessly. The gift she gave me helped me get through the chemo and the tough months that followed.

The night of the fundraiser was one of the most mind-blowing nights of my life. It ranks up there with my wedding and Annabelle's birth. For me, it came at just the right time: I was deep into my chemo, facing the prospect of more to come, and I was at a seriously low ebb. Even though Maha had warned me the tickets had sold out in a matter of days, I didn't realise what that would actually mean until we walked in the door and saw an astonishing sea of people.

There were 600 people there and another 250 on a waiting list. There were old friends, new friends, work friends, people I'd known at BT and at the recruitment firm, my hairdresser, neighbours, the woman who does the strata management for our building, people I knew who I wasn't necessarily friends with, people I came across as part of my daily life. It seemed like everyone I'd ever, ever crossed paths with was there.

And, as if that wasn't amazing enough, Sarah had organised some brilliant talent to help make the night really special. Larry Emdur was on official hosting duties. Larry and I were already acquaintances through work, but when I was diagnosed he didn't miss a beat. He was there in a second and he never wavered all the way through. We would meet for lunch and he would always find a way to make my situation seem funny. It was actually incredible how much he could make me laugh over the worst things. I would take Annabelle and inevitably the stench would waft over from the pram. 'Urgh,' he'd say, 'your stinky baby's so gross, she's turning me off my gourmet kebab.'

When I first thought about doing this book I told Larry as we were wrapping up lunch one day. 'Good idea,' he said. We went our separate ways and I'd barely walked in the front door when he called me. 'So, have you finished that book yet? God you're lazy,' he quipped. See what I mean? He made such an effort to support me and whenever I tried to thank him he would flatly refuse to acknowledge that he'd done anything. He MC'd the fundraiser and had the crowd in hysterics as he took the piss out of me. I couldn't have asked for anything more.

Sarah had asked Brian McFadden to perform as she knew how much I loved Brian. I know Brian McFadden through work; I've interviewed him a few times. When I first went public about being ill, he rang me to say, 'I can't believe it.' I don't know Brian super-well, yet he took the time and made the effort to reach out, to ring and say, 'I believe in you. You're going to win. You're going to fight. You've got a new baby. I know how special that is. She needs you. We need you. Keep fighting. We love you.' I don't even know if he would remember that call but I remember it so clearly. And then when he came and performed at my benefit, I was just blown away by his kindness and generosity.

Everyone had been so kind and so generous. The fundraiser was held at the Beresford Hotel. Justin Hemmes donated the venue and drinks to make sure it was an amazing night. There was a battle of the bands between the Channel 7 band and the Channel 10 band. I've never worked at Channel 10, but incredibly they came out to support me anyway. I know loads of fashion and beauty people through work, and they donated thousands of wonderful products: watches, make-up, shoes, perfume, creams, clothes. Places I'd worked with at *Sydney Weekender* donated experiences and tickets. It was years since I'd worked there, I would never have imagined they'd remember me. But they did. And Sarah auctioned all this fantastic stuff.

I wore a beautiful Alex Perry dress that Alex had helped me choose. On the night I had no hair, no lashes, no eyebrows, and I looked really grey—not even the best Alex Perry dress could totally distract from how sick I was. No offence, Alex! But everyone who loved me said I looked beautiful.

◆ ◆ ◆

Another really special thing Sarah arranged for me was a photo shoot with Anne Geddes. In true Sarah fashion, she did something amazing but made it seem casual, like she hadn't even pulled off anything. I went around to see her one day, and as I was just getting in the car to leave, she said, 'Oh, did I tell you about the photo shoot I've got for you?'

'No.'

'Oh, yeah, I've got this photo shoot that you'll do with Annabelle. It's with Anne Geddes. Okay. Bye.'

I thought she had to be joking. I always assumed Anne Geddes was American. But she lives and works in Sydney, and she'd agreed to have us spend a morning with her so she could take our photograph. I've grown up with Anne Geddes calendars and cards, and I never imagined my baby might be one of her subjects. Talk about experiences money can't buy: Anne Geddes isn't a photographer for hire—she's an artist. And somehow Sarah made it happen.

A few days before the shoot I went to meet Anne and her team. She wanted to discuss her vision with me. Personally, I didn't care what she was going to do—as soon as I met her, I felt like I was in the presence of greatness and trusted her to create something amazing.

It was really interesting to watch her at work. She studied me for a while—I could tell she was thinking—and then said, 'Yes, okay, I've got it. This is what we're going to do.' She explained she was going to use a gold fabric on a gold background, and Annabelle and I would both be wrapped in it. When I describe it, it doesn't sound that special, but when I turned up on the day, what they'd created was sensational. When she talked about gold fabric, she didn't mean some Spotlight special. It was a stunning piece of organza, and Anne's daughter, Kelly, had pulled out individual threads to create a ripple effect through the fabric. So they wrapped me and Annabelle in the fabric, and they'd made headpieces with more fabric. At that stage I had lost all my hair, eyebrows and lashes, but they had a make-up artist who'd brought along a special product she used to draw on eyebrows so they looked real.

They laid on a lovely morning tea for me and bought me a massive bunch of flowers, which made it feel all the more special. And then the photo shoot itself was amazing. I've done photo shoots for work and they can take hours. Three hours is normal. You'll be posing and posing and smiling and your cheeks hurt and you keep smiling. But that day, I picked up Annabelle and held her really close. And Anne is so incredibly talented, she looked through the lens and went *click click click*. 'Mmmm. Look at me.' *Click click click*. I was just warming up when she said, 'I've got it.' I was amazed.

And the image is just incredible—beautiful but also sad. She captured the sadness in my eyes. I love it.

For the fundraiser, Anne blew up a massive image and printed it on canvas. It's in my bedroom and I gaze at it every single morning. Annabelle looks like a little cherub. She's so little and so cute. I'm so grateful I have that special image to treasure forever, as a memento of that time with Annabelle, and also a reminder of how far I've come.

Funny coincidence: after we'd taken the shot and were having morning tea, I got talking to Kelly, one of Anne's daughters, who's part of Anne's team, and we discovered that I used to train Kelly and her sister Stephanie when I was a personal trainer. Sometimes the world seems very small.

The experience blew me away. I was so touched and so moved that Anne and her team went to such trouble. It wasn't a small thing that they did for me—it took effort and time and work and artistry and thought. It was a gift from deep within the heart.

◆ ◆ ◆

Sarah had many angels who helped pull all these wonderful experiences together, including chief angel Angela Morgan, Executive Assistant for Peter Meakin, who was our Director of News and Current Affairs. And they did it out of pure kindness. An event on that scale needs an awful lot of volunteers to make everything happen. Internally within Channel 7, Sarah had helpers from every possible area of the network—people I knew and people I'd never met. I also posted a note on Facebook, asking if anyone could help Sarah on the night of the fundraiser. And I was so surprised by the people who volunteered—Maxine who works at the strata agency that manages my building, and the PR girls from David Jones. I'd worked really hard to build a good relationship with the DJs girls, but there had been some hiccups along the way. It meant a huge amount to me that they came to my fundraiser. All these people came and stood at an auction desk for four, five, six hours, for no reason other than to help me.

It was a great party and a sensational night, although it was very emotional too. There's no way it couldn't be, given the reason we were there. And many people there hadn't seen me in a long time, certainly not since I fell ill, so that first sight of me came as a big shock. There were plenty of tears. Maha told me afterwards that when she saw so many shocked and upset people, it made her feel really frightened again. She wondered why they were crying, did they know something she didn't? She'd forgotten what a jolt it was seeing me for the first time so intensely and so obviously sick.

I'd do anything for the people I care about, whatever it takes to let them know how much I love them. Until that night, I don't think I really understood that my friends felt the same way about me. There was such an outpouring of love, it was utterly overwhelming—and will stay with me forever. I understood for the first time that these people like me for me, not for my job. I was so hung up on using my work to validate myself—I assumed because that's why *I* liked me that it was why other people liked me too. And, yes, if I didn't work in the TV industry I probably wouldn't have had a fundraiser with Brian McFadden or Larry Emdur. But I'll always remember sitting on the stage with Larry, scanning the room and looking at the faces of all those people. It was so powerful. I could almost hear them thinking, *Do it. We love you. Get better. Get strong.* The atmosphere was incredibly intense, and I could feel their strength and love being funnelled into me. I felt like I could've run a marathon.

Marcus, however, found the night quite difficult. It was hard to reconcile what we were going through—the worst thing that had ever happened to us—with these people turning up for a party. There was a great vibe, people were really going off—but at the same time, people kept coming up to him and saying, 'Mate, I'm so sorry, what a terrible thing to have happen.' For him, it didn't quite compute: what are we celebrating exactly? The fact that my wife's sick? He was just about at his lowest point emotionally, and was finding it difficult to get into the celebratory vibe.

However, seeing how much it lifted my spirits, how much strength it gave me, he was glad I was happy. The love I felt that night was so powerful and so lasting—I was able to carry it with me through the rest of my treatment.

I left the party with Marcus and Maha, feeling like I was floating. Maha and I swapped notes excitedly—Did you see so and so? No, was she here? What about so and so? Wow, I can't believe he was here, that's amazing! There had been too many people to see and thank and talk to, but I felt the incredible power of their love for me.

It's a shame I had to fall ill to have a night like that. I feel everyone should have a night like that in their life, where all the people who know you and love you are there to cheer you on for being the great person you are. Everyone should have an appreciation party. Sometimes we forget what great people we are. But I know I'll never forget what brilliant people my friends are. They've proved it—every single one of them.

I could fill this whole book with stories from that night, sharing every single tidbit that everyone told me, telling you in great detail about the impact the night had on me, not just in getting through the cancer, but as a person. I could bore you for hours with how my heart wants to explode with love and gratitude for that evening. Rarely can I talk about it without crying. It moved me and changed me in a way I didn't think would be possible. It went well beyond the money raised, which, of course, was so helpful. The feeling of love and care and support was so deep and so powerful.

That evening was an absolute gift.

Sarah Stinson

Executive Producer of **The Morning Show** *and one of Sally's best friends*

I will never forget the precise moment I learned just how quickly life's little problems can become completely irrelevant: the issues and distractions that plague our everyday lives, the things we devote so much time and energy to worrying about, those insignificant, stupid moments we stress over. It might be the household bills you're struggling to pay, the personality clash you've had with someone at work, or the ongoing vanity war that's fought every time you look in the mirror. Trust me, while they may consume you one second, they can also vanish in the blink of an eye.

For me, it was being precious about having to take a fifteen-hour flight from Los Angeles to Sydney. I was mentally preparing myself for how punishing it would be and how I needed to 'suck it up' and get through it . . . I know . . . Everyone hates long-haul travel, but I was out of valium and the road ahead was looking bleak. You see, for the previous two weeks I'd been on the adventure of a lifetime with another one of our 'rat pack', Lucie McGeoch. In Thelma and Louise *fashion, we'd terrorised the United States from coast to coast, and I'm sure the Yanks couldn't wait to see the back of us.*

The day began like all the others. We awoke bleary-eyed, swearing never to drink again, and after some futile attempts to piece together the night before, we tried to call Sal. We hadn't heard from her in days—she didn't answer.

Lucie and I were staying at the infamous Chateau Marmont in West Hollywood. To this day I'm not sure how it happened but we managed to score a huge rock star two-bedroom suite overlooking the pool. Letting the environment get the better of us, we recharged for another day in LA. It began with a long lunch with Phil Goyen (60 Minutes *producer), Blair Late (LA-based entertainment reporter) and Joshua Horner (DWTS judge) at Lisa Vanderpump's (*Real Housewives of Beverley Hills*) restaurant SUR.*

Again we tried to call Sally—still there was no answer. We were starting to worry because we hadn't heard from her in days . . . it wasn't like her to be out of touch.

Several bottles of wine later we made our way to the nearby TV studios to meet up with Rove McManus to watch the taping of his show. We had to excuse ourselves from Rove's post-show party as we were running late for another function: the after-party back at Chateau Marmont for Johnny Depp's latest movie, Hunter S Thompson's The Rum Diaries. *It was everything you would expect from a party safely nestled inside Hollywood's most historic celebrity hideaway: hedonistic, loud and loose.*

Lucie was chatting to Hugh Hefner and his entourage while I had somehow drawn a fairly short straw and was locked into a conversation with Marilyn Manson and a dubious movie producer.

I skulked away to call Sally. 'Answer the bloody phone, Sal! We need baby news! You have no idea what's going on . . . Wish you were here!' Still no answer.

Despite being ridiculously out of place in a wash of celebrities, it was still quite glamorous, and that evening, Lucie and I were riding an emotional rum-fuelled high. We decided to have an after-after-show party in our suite.

It was 4 am. Lucie and I were dancing on the coffee table in our suite, being taught moves by a professional chorus line dancer to blaring music. Very showbiz and incredibly camp—as Sal would say, 'Just the way we like it'.

Sally Obermeder

Finally I saw my phone light up with the word. 'SALO'. 'Thelmmmmmmaaaaaa . . . quick it's baby news! Giggling, we stumbled into one of the berooms to take the call.

I can't remember the prelude to the conversation. Maybe it was the rum, maybe it was the shock that was to follow, but I will never forget the delivery, the tone, the words, 'I have cancer.' For those who have never had devastating news from a loved one I hope you never experience it. Every other problem you have in your world is pushed aside, your problems are nothing compared to the challenges that are about to descend on your friend's life. When you first hear the news, everything just stops—not for you, for the one you love. You're completely crushed, completely devastated and completely lost.

I am not sure how it's possible, but suddenly I was completely sober. One of my best friends was scared and needed my support so she could muster the strength to fight. I tried to say something but couldn't speak.

As you search for something to say, you realise someone you love, someone you've laughed with so many times, is on the other side of a vast ocean without you—and with them is the only place you want to be. It's right about then you feel guilty for thinking of your own feelings. Because, after all, you don't have the disease and the person who is scared cannot be you. Your job is to keep your friend's spirits up. You have to be strong, you have to be a rock for them to lean on.

I choked back tears and passed the phone to Lucie. If you ever find yourself in a crisis, you need a friend like her. We call Luce the Oracle. Regardless of the situation she always knows what to say. Calmly taking a pragmatic approach, the Oracle offers reassurance to Sal who is sobbing so loudly I can hear her wails from the balcony. 'I will speak to the best doctors and get you the best information—it is going to be okay, you will be okay.' This went on for a while, Lucie offering sensible, sage advice, then she handed the phone back to me.

Never Stop Believing

'It's f*cking f*cked Sal . . . it's f*cking unfair . . . I can't say anything except I love you and it's f*cked, seriously f*cked' . . . I swear I will do something to make you okay even if I have to cure cancer myself.'

Okay, my irrational rant about curing cancer was no doubt the rum speaking, but I am a woman of my word and I was determined to help my beautiful friend. Feeling helpless isn't something I am used to. If there is a problem, I fix it. Rise, resolve, move on. My mind was racing—what could I do? I may not be able to cure cancer, but I could organise a cracker party. So that's what I did.

There are so many wonderful people who made it happen. I don't want to leave anyone out so I won't mention names, but honestly I cannot take the credit. It was a labour of pure love and over a hundred people pulled together to pull it off.

Media types constantly are bombarded with people asking for help. There are a million great causes and it's very difficult to say no but sometimes we have to. This time I was inundated with people genuinely wanting to give back to Sally, who is widely regarded as one of the kindest, most generous women in television.

Justin Hemmes immediately offered Upstairs at the Beresford, which is one of the best venues for live music in Sydney. The objective was to show Sally how loved she is—to show her she was not alone—and for everyone to let their hair down and have some fun. Tickets sold out in days—there was a huge waiting list. It brought together the people we compete with every day: Channels 10, 7, 9, radio, papers, publishers etc. The night was all about Sally.

A few days before the party Sal and I had dinner. The chemo was making her violently ill, the colour had drained from her face, every hair on her body had fallen out and she had put on a great deal of weight from the treatment. I asked her if she wanted to know anything about the party. She didn't. That's how I knew just how sick she was—Sal has always liked to be in control.

I don't know if you believe in a divine power overseeing the universe, but trust me, you start to have serious doubts when something like this happens. Because what Sally has had to face over the past year is one of the cruellest and most heartless experiences life can inflict.

Her story is one everyone should hear. It is one of darkness, despair, sorrow, but it is also one of joy, promise, hope and triumph. Sally has fought the ultimate battle and won. She is my hero. She has faced the fear and done so with a dogged determination and courage I never knew she had. Sure there were doubts along the way, tears—oh God, there were a lot of tears! In fact, over the last twelve months it seems as if Sally and I have cried in every restaurant in Sydney. There were times when she nearly gave up, but I think it was having her angel Annabelle that kept her pushing through every day.

This is a story of fighting through cancer like no other. Sally was being cared for while giving care. She was a new mother and a patient. I do not know just how Sally and Marcus found the strength they did. You cannot experience two more intense feelings that are so incredibly different than to give life and face death at the same time. yet they did it. They did it together, the three of them as a family.

The world needs more people like Sally and Marcus. The world needs more people who have the courage to fight against adversity. I have watched them over the last year; they are a beacon of hope on the darkest of nights, old friends in the shadows of strangers, and an everlasting comfort when all seems lost.

As brave as they are, even they could not do it alone. They needed the help of their family, friends and an amazing medical staff whose compassion is never sufficiently acknowledged. To all of you who helped and supported Sal's family whether financially, physically, or emotionally, from the bottom of my heart, I say thank you. Thank you for saving the life of one of my dearest friends.

The party was a huge success, the bands rocked, the champagne flowed and yet again we danced on tables. Before Sally left we stood together and looked back at the sea of supporters and once again the tears flowed. She was overwhelmed. 'I don't know what to say, I am just so so grateful.' I hugged her tightly.

'I didnt do all this for a friend who won't be here . . . just get better . . . and if you ever scare us like this again . . . I'll kill you.'

Surgery

When Annabelle was still quite little, I tried to take her to a mothers' group. I knew it was part of the new-mother experience, and I wanted us to experience it. I went only once.

I'd started chemo—it was still early days, and I still had my hair. When I arrived at mothers' group, I felt so different from the other women. On the outside we were all the same: new mums with new babies, grappling with this exciting, overwhelming new experience. I'd wanted to be a part of this world for so long, but I couldn't participate because I had this terrible thing hanging over me and dominating my days. While the other mums were talking about mums-and-bubs yoga, I had a schedule full of chemo appointments. The other mums seemed dazed with happiness—and sleeplessness—but I was dazed with grief. The other mums could give themselves over entirely to this wonderful time, their babies' first precious months of life, but my time would have to be split between my baby and fighting cancer. I didn't feel I could tell them what had happened to me. I didn't want them to have to process grief and terror and imagine what it might be like if it had happened to them. I didn't want to put that on them, but, at the same time I couldn't pretend it wasn't there. That would have been impossible. I felt there was an unbridgeable gap between me and the other mums. It wasn't anybody's fault, but I just didn't feel like I belonged there. And I wondered if I'd ever be able to connect with them.

I remember many of them were talking about the difficulties they were having with breastfeeding—swapping stories, tips and remedies, as mums do— and it reminded me that I'd had to take pills to stop my milk, and soon I was going to lose my breasts. The contrast between the world they were in and the world I was in was just too stark, too cruel. Annabelle and I didn't ever go back to mothers' group.

◆ ◆ ◆

In most early breast cancer cases they do the surgery first and then give you the chemo. Because I had a non-hormonal breast cancer, they chose to give me the chemo first so they could use the tumour as a control factor: if the tumour shrank, they'd know the chemo was working, and that would help prevent more tumours developing somewhere else. Even though I'd had all those big scans to check whether I had any other tumours—and they'd come up clear—I might still have had small cancer cells elsewhere in my body which hadn't been picked up. And the tumours in my breast were growing at such a rapid rate and were so aggressive that although they couldn't see any additional tumours in October, three months later without chemo they might have grown into something really big.

Almost from the very beginning, deep down I'd suspected I'd have to undergo a mastectomy. But while I was doing the chemo I put it to the back of my mind. I had enough to do just getting through the chemo and didn't really give the surgery much thought.

After eight months of chemo, Fran said that I'd had as much as they'd ever given anyone of such high levels of chemo. Eight months of dousing your body in toxic chemicals, is a lot for any body to withstand. My body wouldn't take anymore. It was time for surgery.

I went to see Kylie Snook, my breast surgeon, so we could talk about the surgery and what to expect. I'd hoped, like everyone does, that they'd be able to do a lumpectomy. (A lumpectomy removes the tumour but leaves the rest of the breast intact.) But I wasn't a candidate because there was more than one tumour and they were still spread out over a third of my breast. The whole breast was going to have to come off.

At first I thought, *I don't care.* I'd just finished chemo, and I couldn't believe that anything could possibly be worse.

But Kylie took out a photo album of pictures of women who'd had surgery, and I was horrified. I'd done a few plastic surgery stories about breast implants at *TT*, and foolishly thought I knew what to expect. But these women had massive scars: huge incisions that went straight across and up their chests, where the breasts once were.

'Oh,' I said, 'These are the surgeries that have gone wrong? Yes, these look terrible,' I agreed.

'No, no,' she said. 'These *are* the surgeries. This *is* what it looks like.'

I stupidly thought she was showing me a book of worst-case scenarios.

I began to sob as I turned the pages, thinking, *These women look like they've been massacred. It's like they've walked into a chainsaw. How can modern medicine be so advanced yet this is the best they can do?*

Doctor Kylie Snook is used to me by now. Every time I have an appointment with her I start crying. She explained that it's her job to remove the breast, but then it's up to a plastic surgeon to do the reconstruction. Those scars were not the final destination, they were just a mid-point in the journey.

There are a number of options for reconstruction: one is to have implants. You can also have tissue and blood vessels taken from your stomach or your back so they can use your own tissue to build new breasts. They told me I wasn't really a candidate for implants because in some situations the body can reject the implants and then more surgery is needed to remove the implants or change them. There was still a possibility I might need more chemo down the track and because chemo stops your body healing from surgery, it was decided that it would be a safer option if I had the reconstruction using tissue from my body.

However, Kylie explained that in order for the plastic surgeon to get the skin, tissue and blood vessels they'd need for the reconstruction, they'd have to cut me all the way across from hip to hip, leaving another massive scar. Not only would I have scars from the original mastectomy that went all the way from my armpit to the middle of my chest, but I'd have another scar the same size from the skin graft they did during the reconstruction. Then on the other breast I'd have a big T-shaped scar from where they took that breast off and then I'd have yet another one across my stomach. I was going to look like I'd been hacked at. I sobbed. I felt like the scars were going to be a permanent reminder. Even if in five years I'd recovered from the trauma and shock and crappiness of the whole cancer experience, I'd never really be able to forget it, because every time I looked in the mirror, I'd be reminded of all I'd been through.

In spite of all my talk about wanting to lose five kilos and wishing I was skinnier, I'd never really hated my body before, except perhaps when I was at my heaviest. Now I was afraid that after they'd done all that to me, I was going to be scarred and ugly, that I'd be ashamed to let Marcus see me, and I would never be able to feel good about myself again.

People said things to console me: 'They're only breasts, at least it's not your legs, at least you'll still be able to do everything,' or, 'At least the scars won't be on your face.' But really, that didn't help. What could be more personal than having a whole chunk of yourself cut off? You have to lose a whole body part. And that reminds you just how serious this is. It's not like an infection where they can give you medicine to make you better. To save you, they actually have to cut off a part of your body.

And, of course, it's more than that: your breasts are part of your femininity, they're a part of what makes you feel like you. That's not something you can get your head around quickly or come to terms with easily.

I wanted to have the mastectomy and the reconstruction at the same time. I wanted to go to sleep and wake up with new breasts. They wouldn't be the same as my old ones, but at least

I'd never have to go through that terrible in-between stage of having no breasts at all.

This was what Giuliana Rancic had done. I ripped out an article from *Who* magazine and took it with me to show Kylie.

She looked at the article and said, 'What's this?'

I explained that Giuliana had her mastectomy and reconstruction at the same time and I'd like to do the same thing.

'Right,' Kylie said. 'You know, people often do a lot of research before they come to see me. They'll bring in things from the Harvard medical journals, they'll have scoured the web and looked at cutting-edge research, they'll have analysed the latest surgery options. No-one has ever come in here with an article from a tabloid.'

Well, what did she expect?

Unfortunately, I wasn't a candidate for having both procedures at the same time. In some cancer cases they don't have to have radiation therapy, or they can do radiation on the breast before they remove it. Then once the patient has completed radiation, they can then take the breast off and reconstruct it at the same time. But in my case, the tumours still hadn't shrunk enough—even after eight months of brutal chemo they were alive and well—and if I had a reconstruction at this stage there would be too much breast tissue in the way for the harsh strong radiation they'd planned to be effective. Plus, giving radiotherapy to a natural tissue reconstruction can adversely affect the appearance of the reconstructed breast.

My only option was to have the mastectomy first, then radiation, and wait to finish that before I could have my reconstruction.

And the other piece of bad news? Because my body was so

depleted and shattered by the chemo, my immune system was still struggling to fight off a simple thing like a cold. I didn't have the strength to recover from really massive surgery which is what's involved with a reconstruction. They would have to take off the breast with the cancer in it first, but leave me with the other one still there.

By now I was feeling as if nothing in this whole process had gone the way I wanted it to. I'd hoped that the hair-saving treatment would save my hair—it hadn't. I'd hoped the chemo would work quickly so I wouldn't have to do more—it hadn't. I'd hoped for a lumpectomy—not an option. And I'd hoped I could have a mastectomy and reconstruction combined, but that hadn't worked out either.

Of course, I *was* still alive. And I didn't have cancer anywhere else in my body. So that *had* gone my way. But I still had days when I thought, Come on, give me *something*!

◆ ◆ ◆

When I arrived at the Mater for my surgery I was actually feeling pretty good about everything. I'd finished chemo, I was still in a lot of pain but at least I wasn't horrendously sick every day. I felt like I was moving forward and this was the next stage in my recovery.

Earlier in the year, when I was hospitalised with the infection that caused my fever, I'd been transferred from St Vincents hospital, where I went initially, to the Mater, where I spent a few days recovering. When I returned to the Mater for my surgery they gave me the same room, and I was ridiculously excited about that. 'Oh, Marcus, this is my room!'

'It's not a hotel, babe,' he laughed.

'No, but this is my space!'

Maybe it was silly, but it felt good to be in familiar surround-ings. And I'd done so many hospital visits by then I knew to bring all my things—my candles, magazines and flowers. It was almost like I was settling in for a weekend away. I set myself up and I was super-positive, thinking, *This is great. This is going to be great! It's only surgery. This'll be nothing compared to the chemo. It'll be so fine.*

Idiot!

I was fasting before I had the surgery, and was so hungry while I waited all I could talk about for hours on end to Marcus was food.

'Wouldn't you love to eat some tacos with extra guacamole?'

'Don't keep talking about food.'

'Or what about a pad thai? I'd love a pad thai.'

'Stop torturing yourself.'

'What about a pizza?'

The nurses finally came in and started rolling me away on the bed.

'Make sure you get me a pizza for when I wake up!

'You're not going to want a pizza.'

'Don't tell me what I want! Just make sure there's a pizza waiting for me when I get back, okay?'

They took me into theatre, and when I came out I was drugged and hazy. Marcus was there with me in recovery. I said, 'I don't want a pizza any more.'

'I knew you wouldn't,' he said.

'I really want fried rice. That's what I want!'

Maha was there too and she went and got me some fried rice.

When it came I ate one mouthful, said, 'Oh, I'm so nauseous,' and passed out again.

When I came to I was in a lot of pain, and here's the funny thing: when you've had a piece of you cut out, you'd think you'd feel lighter. But you don't. What I felt was a sensation of immense pressure, as if an elephant had his foot on my chest. It's the strangest feeling.

For the first day and a half I was on morphine and although my chest was really painful, I was in good spirits, really good spirits.

My friends asked me, 'Can we come and visit? Do you want visitors?'

'Yeah! Yeah! Come and visit!'

They'd visit and ask me how I was feeling, and I said, 'Yeah, I'm great! It's fine! The pain of this is actually so manageable and so much better compared to the chemo. I'm really great!'

My oncologist Fran came to see me too. 'So, how are you feeling?'

'I'm great, Fran, I'm great!'

She told me later that after she'd seen me she said to the staff at the Mater, 'She's not herself. She hasn't cried yet.'

She was right. I unravelled pretty quickly after that.

On about day four I woke up and the enormity of it hit me. I thought, *Oh my God, what has happened here? This is actually so terrible and so horrendous.* I had started grieving. It was like a death had occurred. I just couldn't believe that they had chopped off part of me. It was heartbreaking. And no amount of people saying, 'Yeah but you'll get new ones' could make it better. It's actually a little bit annoying. Just imagine if your partner died and they said, 'Don't worry, you can get a new one.' It doesn't help relieve the pain.

I told the nurse, 'I don't want any visitors today,' and spent the whole day lying in bed crying on and off, on and off.

Kylie Snook came to visit me. 'You can go home tomorrow if you want,' she said.

But I couldn't. I was sobbing and saying, 'I can't go home. I don't want to go home.'

I wanted to stay in hospital because it was my safety net. In hospital you're not part of the real world. I didn't have to see anyone. I didn't have to go anywhere. I could lie in bed all day and they'd bring me food, and Mum and Dad would bring Annabelle over, but I wouldn't have to actually *do* anything.

'Well,' Kylie said, 'Why don't you stay another couple of days and see how you feel.'

I just couldn't get my head around what had happened. It was one of the first times I actually felt really sorry for myself. It was so different to the chemo—equally as painful, but in a different way. I felt a deep sense of shame. Other people had told me they'd felt ashamed when they had cancer, and even when I lost my hair, I couldn't really understand that. Losing my hair was shitty, and it made people stare at me, but I didn't feel ashamed about it. Now, however, I understood. I felt disfigured—like I wasn't whole.

Not even the good news that the mastectomy had removed all the tumours within the breast tissue and the margins were clear was enough to make me feel better.

For about a month after my surgery I fell to pieces. I cried a lot, and couldn't see anyone. I spoke only to my family and my closest friends—Camilla, Sarah, Lucia, Adene, Jo, Lizzie, Julia, Tracey, Belinda and Sam. I just wasn't coping. All I could manage was to stay home and look after Annabelle and go to therapy to help me deal with it all. I didn't want to walk down the street to buy milk because I was so ashamed. (Of course I had to: life goes on. I still had to buy groceries and go to the post office and take Annabelle out for walks, even when my heart was breaking.) Wherever I went, I couldn't look anyone in the eye for fear of what I might see there. I was ashamed to be seen. I felt like everyone could see I wasn't whole. Of course, no-one could, no-one knew, because I had a prosthetic. But I knew. And I felt like I wasn't worthy to be out with everybody else.

I knew it made no sense. If I saw someone who was an amputee, I wouldn't think they didn't deserve to be out because they were somehow not complete like everyone else. But I couldn't apply that knowledge to my own situation.

I was so embarrassed I couldn't even let Marcus see it. When I was in hospital, Kylie had come in to check my wound one day when Marcus was there. He'd seen the wound then, but once I got home, I didn't want him to see it at all. I'd get changed with the door shut, and I was crying all the time.

It was weeks before the worst of it passed. Nothing in particular happened that made me feel okay. I guess it's like all grief. If you give it enough time, eventually it passes. I just needed to cry and cry and cry until gradually I noticed that as the days went on I cried less. I cried five times a day and then four, then three, till I reached the point one day when I realised, *Hey, I don't think I cried today.*

I'd turned the corner. Slowly I felt less heartbroken, more able to see the positive side: I'm going to get a reconstruction and, of course, it won't be the same but what matters is that I live to tell the tale. However, I was still vulnerable, and there was always a chance I'd unravel.

A couple of weeks later my friend Tory Archbold, who runs Torstar, a lifestyle PR agency, invited me to an event she was organising for Nespresso. 'You've got to come,' she said. 'You're a coffee fiend, and you've come to Nespresso events since the very beginning.'

So I agreed to attend the event.

They'd hired a photographer who'd worked on the Great Gatsby movie to take photos in black and white. When I saw my picture, I fell apart. I could see that my left breast was there, but on the right side it was a little bit concave—when they remove the breast, it's not flat, it's actually concave—and I could see the top of the prosthetic that I'd put into my bra. Truthfully, I don't know if anyone but me would have realised what it was. But I knew, I could see it, and that was enough. Poor Tory, I slid off to the bathroom with Sarah and hid in there bawling my eyes out.

One of the girls who works for Tory walked in, 'Hi girls!' she chirped. Then she realised I was having a meltdown, 'Okay,' she said, and turned on her heels, and went straight back to let Tory know there was a situation in the bathroom.

I love Tory because she's incredibly kind and driven and hard-working. We met when I started at *TT*, and over four and a half years we've gone from just working together on odd stories to becoming close friends. I also love Tory because she's direct, very direct. 'Right,' she said as she put her hand up to stop the traffic of partygoers, 'no-one else is coming in the bathroom!' And she kept everyone out until I'd pulled myself together.

Finally, we all came out and there was an enormous queue of people waiting. I felt bad. Sarah piped up, 'If you have a drug problem, don't do it at an event!' It was so funny. You really need humour at moments like that.

As time went on I became more accustomed to it, and there were stretches where I forgot about it completely. But there were other times when I would be reminded all over again. Whenever I went out, I was presented with the problem of what am I going to wear. I'd open my wardrobe and think, *I can't wear that because it's low-cut or it's a V-neck or it's got no straps and I have to wear a bra to put the prosthetic in.* And if my top is too tight I can tell that I'm wearing a prosthetic. Your real breast is heavy, but the prosthetic is quite light so if you wear the wrong thing, you can tell that you've got something in there that's not quite the real deal.

I had a prosthetic that was kindly supplied by the Breast Cancer Network Australia. It's a bit like a sponge, a triangular-shaped padded thing that sits in your bra. You can get more lifelike ones, and you can get bras with fitted prosthetics, but I didn't want to invest in anything long term. For me, the prosthetic was only temporary until I could have my reconstruction.

Every time I got dressed, and every time I glanced at myself in the mirror, I'd be reminded. I'd see myself and think, 'Oh. Oh yeah.' It was tough. I also found it tough having one breast taken off, while the other was still there. It was a stark reminder every day of my old life on the left with the healthy breast, and my new cancer life, with no breast on the right. Every day I would see it right there in front of me, the blunt reminder of the disease that had chopped off part of my life. Part of me. And I kept discovering new things I hadn't considered: I wanted Annabelle to start swimming lessons, but I didn't want to get into my cossie and be reminded again that I was different to the other mums. Marcus would have to go to swimming lessons.

Samantha Armytage

Co-host of **Weekend Sunrise** *and one of Sally's close friends*

I wandered around Westfield Bondi for a long time that day trying to find a little gift to take to the hospital. Sal reads every fashion magazine. We TV gals avoid chocolates at all cost and flowers just seemed too naff. She was a hard girl to buy for. She had every-thing . . . except, as of that week, her right breast.

It was August and Sydney was unusually chilly. In a window I saw a mannequin draped in a chunky charcoal Italian wool scarf. Bingo. It's so Sal. So stylish. And in my mind, so damn practical. It will keep her warm and *cover up her entire chest and torso.*

I knew how much she had dreaded this surgery. While saving her life and freeing her of those bastard tumours, it would leave her horrifically scarred and remove part of her womanhood.

It's not my style to use clichés at the best of times. And these were not the best of times. I had made an effort to not *say things to Sal like, 'You do what you have to do', or 'At least you'll get new boobs.' This was a shitty situation. Her old boobs were fantastic. Why had this happened to her? Someone with Sal's good karma didn't deserve this. Marcus didn't deserve this. God forbid, Annabelle didn't deserve this.*

When I walked into Sal's room at the Mater she was sitting alone in the dark. Oh God. I know this is not about me, but what if she's really not handling this? I didn't know what I'd say. How I'd act. I didn't want to cry. She'd set the tone of coolness throughout those eight months of chemo and really made it easier for the rest of us. What if she has a breakdown now?

She looked around and burst into a smile. We hugged and I tried not to squeeze her too tightly. She pulled me into an Obermeder bear hug.

She had a tube coming out from under her t-shirt and through the V-neck I could see the concave of her breast bone. It's polite to exclaim, 'Don't worry, you can't notice' but I didn't say that, because you could. I handed Sal the scarf and told her my reasoning behind this practical present. She burst into tears. She put it on straight away and didn't take it off until October.

It needs to be said, I left that hospital room with more than I'd taken in. That's the thing with Sal. Even when she's going through hell, you leave her feeling better than when you arrive.

I'd complimented her on her nail polish colour (only Sally Obermeder has a full manicure prior to surgery) and she passed me the bottle. 'Here, it's yours.' Apparently her neighbour had just started a new nail polish business. That's the other thing with Sal. She knows everybody. And she cares about them.

Throughout those first eight months, Sal, Annabelle and I would catch up for lunch or coffee on Sal's weeks off from chemo. She had no hair and managed to look impossibly glamorous each time (it turns out she has a really attractive skull shape), carrying a baby in one arm and a designer handbag in the other.

The entire restaurant would stare, part sympathy, part curiosity. We'd start with entrées and how she was coping and feeling. She'd give me all the gruesome chemo details. As is her nature, she was direct and generous in her descriptions of what she was going through behind closed doors. Some days she was barely able to get herself off the bathroom floor to go out. I'd never known anyone who'd had chemo before, so it was a learning experience for me to have my darling friend Sally being knocked for six. In fact, I couldn't believe she made it out of the house at all during that time. I honestly think if it was me I would have called in sick to our lunches. As the months went past, I kept waiting for those calls from Sal, and they never came. She turned up with Annabelle every time.

Never Stop Believing

Sal would often burst in and out of tears during lunch. I think we've cried together at every fine dining establishment in the eastern suburbs. At the time, I have to admit I wondered what the other diners made of us. In hindsight, I love that she owned it. She owned cancer and she beat it. I love that she let her emotion out whenever it came bubbling up. And that meant we all could do the same. If she was sad, she cried, and then three minutes later she was roaring with laughter. And we were too.

During main course, while the waiters entertained the divinely easy-going Annabelle, Sal would turn the tables. 'What's goss at work? How's your love life?' she'd ask. It turns out my love life wasn't so great at the time and my dad was battling cancer of the larynx (no great surprise after forty-five years of smoking—he too has been given the all-clear, thank God!).

But Sal with her heart the size of Phar Lap (so I lied, a cliché!) would nurture me and listen to all my problems.

Afterwards I actually had to remind myself of the ordeal she was going through, such was her pure love and concern for me and all our friends. She was craving 'normal', and didn't our group of mates provide it.

Two days after Annabelle was born, I rang Sal to chat and she didn't answer. I thought it was because she was changing a nappy or something. I can hardly believe what she has been through since then, but I am so proud to call her my friend.

Radiation

Radiation really is much easier than chemo. It doesn't make you sick, and it's very targeted. For five days a week, at the same time every day, I'd go down to the basement of St Vincents Hospital and lie in a big radiation machine and they'd irradiate me. And then I'd go home.

I decided my radiation would mark the beginning of me trying to get some strength and fitness back, partly because I knew I had reconstruction surgery coming up, it was a whopping 16-hour op. You need to be as fit as possible because they cut through all your stomach muscles. You can't use your core and have to do everything using the strength in your legs and arms. I was still pretty weak from all the chemo—it makes your muscles disintegrate—so I had extensive ground to make up. But

I was more than ready to start feeling fit and well again.

I decided that rather than driving to all my appointments I'd walk every day and push Annabelle in the pram. It's a decent walk from my apartment in Bondi to St Vincents Hospital in Darlinghurst, but we really came to enjoy it. For the first time since I was diagnosed, I felt like I had some structure to my days, a regular routine we could follow, and Annabelle loved it. It became an outing for her. We'd stop at the park and I'd put her on the swings, and then we'd keep walking. She was going to the same place, seeing the same nurses, and she thought it was really fun. Sometimes people asked me, 'What do you do with Annabelle while you're having radiation?'

What did I do? The minute I'd arrive, there'd be a flurry of excitement, 'Annabelle's here! Annabelle's here!' they'd squeal. The nurses, the receptionists, the radiation oncologist . . . even the guy in accounts, they'd all abandon their desks and make a beeline for Annabelle. Annabelle would be dragged from my arms as all the staff fight over who will play with her first. I practically had to turn the radiation machine on myself.

So the nurses went out of their way to make me comfortable and happy and they looked after her while I was having my radiation. The whole process was pretty quick. The slowest part is lining up the machine. The radiation nurses rattle off these numbers every day—ninety-seven point five, twelve point two—which is all about lining the lasers up so that the radiation is properly targeted. My radiation was in the breast area but also around my neck and under my armpit, just in case there were any cancer cells there. I'd go in, lie down for a couple of minutes, the machine would be switched on and then I'd walk out.

Before I started radiation, I had to have three little dots

tattooed on my skin to help them line up the lasers. I remember lying in the machine at St Vincents, which was very similar to one of the machines they used to test me at the Mater when I first was diagnosed. Straight away I found myself breaking out in a cold sweat and having a flashback, remembering how I'd felt in that machine and how traumatic it had been. I was reliving that fear all over again. That happened to me a lot just after the surgery. I'd keep having flashbacks to the day I was diagnosed, or the early days of tests at the Mater, and the intensity of the fear and emotion would come flooding back.

Lying in the radiation machine to have the tattoos done brought back so many bad memories, and I cried and cried and cried. Everyone was used to me over at the Mater, but these guys had only just met me and weren't accustomed to me.

Rebecca Chin, my radiation oncologist, looked quite alarmed. She kept asking, 'Should we stop? Do you need to stop?'

I'd sob, 'No. Carry on. I'm fine.'

I went to see Fran a week later and said, 'I felt really bad for Rebecca. I was there last week and I was crying'.

'Yes,' Fran said. 'I heard.'

'Did she ring you?'

'She rang me to say you were crying your eyes out. She wanted to know, should I be worried? And I said, 'Nah, it's fine. Don't worry about her. She cries all the time.'

'How embarrassing.' I'd developed a reputation as a massive cry-baby.

Fran just said, 'Meh, it's all good.'

'You'll see,' I said. 'I'm going to do radiation now and I just won't cry. I've really turned a corner.'

'Mmm, sure,' Fran said.

And sure enough, a while later, one of the nurses at St Vincents told me, 'I'm going on holidays so I won't see you again, because when I'm back you'll have finished.' She was so kind and compassionate and I'd got used to seeing her every day, so when she told me this I burst into tears. 'I'm so sorry,' I sobbed. 'I just get so attached.' And I'd thought I was doing so well!

◆ ◆ ◆

At first with radiation you can't tell anything's happening. You go, the machine does its thing, you leave, your skin looks the same. Then, around the third or fourth week your skin starts to burn. You can see exactly where they've done it because there's a perfect line. Mine was in a sort of U-shape. From then on your skin burns and burns. By about the fifth week, I had two large open wounds rubbing on each other where the radiation had burnt so deep. I wasn't able to use my right arm anymore, I had to lift Annabelle with my left arm and I would drive with one hand because any movement of my right arm caused the open sores to rub against each other and it was immensely painful. In the end, the skin's so burnt. It's like the worst possible kind of sunburn except it doesn't get a chance to heal because you come back every day for more radiation. It was excruciatingly painful.

I'd go to see Rebecca, the radiation oncologist, and say, 'Oh, it's really bad.'

'Well, show me.'

I'd show her, and she'd say, 'That's fantastic. Looks great!'

And everyone'd be smiling and looking at my burns, and I'd be thinking, *You freaks. You're all weird.* They loved how bad it was because it was evidence of a good reaction. The worse it looked the happier the nurses were. I'd look at it and think, *Oh my goodness, how can this be good for me?* But they know what they're doing.

Other people would tell me, 'It looks really painful.' And it does look painful, it's raw and peeling. But actually it was okay because it was the only that part that hurt. The rest of my body was fine, and that was in stark contrast to the torture of chemo.

I cried when they told me I was finished and didn't have to come back.

'I'm going to miss you!' I said.

A new me

Just weeks after finishing radiation, I began the last stage of my journey: a second mastectomy and a full breast reconstruction.

My surgeon, Megan Hassall, is a rock star: she's the Bono of plastic surgery. She's petite, and full of confidence—and rightly so, because she's a superstar. When I think about what she does for work every day—she builds breasts from scratch—it blows my mind. It's incredible and makes such a difference to people's lives. It certainly made a huge difference to mine.

Megan was very different from my other doctors. Fran was very straight down the line and businesslike, particularly in the beginning. It was only later that she softened and I discovered her cheeky sense of humour. We now have many laughs. Kylie was very warm and nurturing, always ready with a hug and a box of tissues. Megan was amazing, but also a tiny bit scary. When I went to talk to her about what my new breasts would be like, I asked her, 'What size breasts will I have? I don't want them too big because I'd like to be able to go running again.'

She said, 'You'll get what I give you and you *will* love them.' She said it in a funny way, but she meant it. What can you say to that? Okay, yep, I'll love them.

My first mastectomy had been emotionally wrenching, even though I knew it was necessary. The decision to have the second mastectomy was surprisingly easy. I didn't have any tumours in my other breast, so I didn't need to do it. It was purely preventative, and my doctors had told me that there was no evidence that having the other breast off leads to a reduction in mortality from breast cancer. But, once I thought about it, there really wasn't a choice. I didn't want to be looking over my shoulder all the time, worrying that the cancer might come back.

One thing's for certain, if it does come back, there's not much that can be done. They don't give you the same chemo, because the chemo used the first time won't work. The rationale is if it worked the first time the tumour would have shrunk down to nothing. But in my case it didn't shrink to nothing, so they know the chemo didn't completely kill that cancer. So if, heaven forbid, it ever came back there would be no point using the same treatment. They could give me other combinations of chemo, but I've already had all the strongest ones they have. Anything else would be milder and therefore less effective. As I saw it, there was no point going through so much pain—the chemo, the first surgery, all the horror—to then leave the job half done. I didn't want to be thinking, *Damn, I knew I should have had that second mastectomy.*

Also, for the purposes of the reconstruction, I was advised that many surgeons feel they get a better, more symmetrical result if the breasts are 'built' from the same tissue, rather than trying to match a reconstructed breast with an original one. It's often necessary to have a breast lift, augmentation or a reduction to get the two breasts to match, so many women feel you may as well just have the mastectomy.

About a week and a half before I went in for my surgery, we got a terrible shock. I was out with Annabelle one morning and got a call from Mum. The first thing she said was, 'Now, don't panic . . .' which of course makes me start panicking immediately. Ever since my diagnosis, I become frazzled when someone says something like that. It's that feeling of living on the edge of disaster; one minute everything's okay, and the next it's really not. The blood drained out of my face and I felt myself go weak at the knees. I had to put Annabelle down because I was afraid I might drop her. I thought, *Oh my God, she's going to say something really bad.* And before she'd even said anything more, the flood of tears rose up.

'Dad's at Royal North Shore Hospital,' she said. 'He's had a heart attack.'

I was panicking, I couldn't take it. My dad's heart attack was so unexpected, and the fear of losing him after everything else that had happened caught me completely off balance.

It was such a shock, too, because I'd seen him only the day before. Annabelle had been at Mum and Dad's for the afternoon, and Dad had dropped her home. He was fine, chatting and joking, talking about the two of us doing something nice together. And then, the next morning he had a heart attack. Ninety per cent of one artery was clogged. They operated straight away. He was in ICU for a day and a half, and then was transferred to the cardiac ward for a few days.

I was really struggling. I love my Dad, and I depended on him so much; I just couldn't cope with the thought that we might lose him.

My parents really were amazing, though they were more concerned about me and were worried about the effect this would have on my improving spirits, and my preparation for the huge surgery which lay ahead. They kept telling me not to worry, it was all going to be fine; I just had to focus on staying strong and getting through my own surgery. Whenever I visited Dad in hospital, he was talking in typical Dad fashion: 'I'm fine, it's nothing.'

I'd say, 'Dad, you had a *heart attack.*'

He'd be dismissive. 'I'll be fine in a couple of days.'

Men can be annoying. When they get the flu, they carry on like the world's coming to an end, but when they have a heart attack they pretend nothing's happened.

Luckily for all of us my dad's getting better. But it was just another reminder—as if I needed it—of how rapidly things can change.

◆ ◆ ◆

I had my second mastectomy reconstruction at Hunters Hill Private Hospital. The mastectomy and reconstruction happen at the same time, in one 16-hour operation. I was having a TRAM reconstruction, using the transverse rectus abdominis muscle. They cut across from hip to hip and take fat, tissue, blood cells and veins and use them to build new breasts. On the left side, where I had the second mastectomy, they would keep the skin of the breast, scoop out the breast tissue, and then create a new breast with the tissue they'd taken from my stomach. On the right side, where I had the first mastectomy three months earlier, I didn't have enough skin to create a breast, so they had to take a skin graft from my stomach and use that to cover my new right breast. That left a gap in the skin of my stomach where they'd taken the piece out, so they pulled my remaining stomach skin down to compensate for that. The scarring is huge. It's a procedure they can only do once, because it removes some muscle and blood supply to the abdominal wall, but it really is phenomenal. They make new breasts out of living tissue! Phenomenal.

When I woke up from the surgery, the first thing I noticed was that feeling of pressure on my chest that I'd had with my first mastectomy, although this time it didn't seem quite so bad. But really the day after surgery is mostly a blur—I was on morphine and slept on and off. The first 24 hours are critical—they have to make sure the blood vessels that they've connected up don't die; if that happened, they'd have to rush me straight back into surgery— a nurse sits outside your room all night. She doesn't attend to anybody else—she's like your own Florence Nightingale, with her little desk and her night lamp—she comes in every 30 minutes to check everything's still functioning. The way nurses look after you is incredible. People talk about heroes and idols—and I'm the first one to idolise a movie star or a musician—but when I look at nurses and what they do every day, I'm amazed. I couldn't get over the quality of care I got at the Mater Hospital and at Hunters Hill Private.

I got safely through the first 24 hours, and when I woke up, the thing I really noticed was that my back was searingly painful. It felt broken. I couldn't move an inch. More morphine, sleeping and general agony in between. The following day I woke up with what felt like a brain clot. The pressure in my head was enormous. It wasn't like a headache, it was not even like the world's worst migraine—and I've had migraines—it was worse than that. I couldn't lift my head. The anaesthetist came to see me, and he explained that my body was desperately trying to adjust to all the changes that had taken place. Because I'd had a mastectomy, my body had suddenly lost a lot of hormones. And I'd had massive surgery—skin and tissue that had been moved around and had to regrow—my body was struggling to find equilibrium, but it couldn't quite get there. And that was causing the headache. That 24 hours of pain in my head was excruciating, and, I think, the worst part of it—along with the fact that it had been three days since I'd moved at all. I felt like I'd done a 70-hour flight in economy. And the pain in my head meant another day of staying in bed. So, I didn't get up until day four.

In the beginning, I didn't feel like I could walk properly—everything felt so stiff I slowly walked five metres up the corridor and five metres back and that's as much as I could do. The next day I walked ten metres, and by day seven, when I left, I was actually feeling pretty good.

My family were worried that I might have another emotional breakdown like the one I'd experienced after my first mastectomy. It was another mastectomy—we'd been warned that I'd be laid up for four to six weeks and the recovery would be really tough. A couple of days in, Maha warned the nurses to keep an eye on me. But the crash never happened. I was in a fair bit of pain, but mentally, I was totally fine.

One awful thing about this surgery is the drains they put in under your skin. When I had the first mastectomy, I had two drains under the right breast area, and at the Mater they gave me a little handbag to put the drains in so that I could walk to the cafeteria. With this surgery, I had two drains on one side, one on the other and two for my stomach—a mass collection of tubes and bottles to collect the blood. It's just disgusting. They're not small things, these drains, they're plastic tubes about a centimetre in diameter, and they were deep under my skin, maybe 20 centimetres. The tubes under my breast were the most painful and my first experience with them at the Mater hadn't been great. They had twisted and the skin had started to grow over them, so when it was time to take them out, they had to tug and tug. It was excruciatingly painful and pretty disgusting to watch.

Megan came in to see me on the last day, and I told her what had happened last time.

She just looked at me and said, 'No-one ever complains when I do it.'

I thought, *No, that's because we're all scared of you.*

But she was right, I didn't complain. I was just thrilled to be free of the mass of tubes and bottles of blood and to actually have my body back to myself.

Once I got home, I took it easy at first. I had to be very careful about lifting Annabelle. For the first few days, Marcus had some time off work, and Mum came to give me a hand. She was astounding: coming from the other side of the city every day to help me with whatever I needed. Sometimes I didn't need anything, just her company and it felt good just to be able to spend time together, the three of us. Even though we were often just doing ordinary things, getting groceries or going to the park, I'd get quite emotional looking at us—three generations—Mum, me and Annabelle, and I thought 'I'm so happy

I'm here'. Sometimes I don't think my parents realise just how much they mean to me. Mum and Dad—I love you.

Within about two weeks, I was feeling, quite honestly, really well. And that came as quite a surprise to me because I'd been warned that the recovery was going to be long and painful.

Before my surgery, I'd had a lot of questions about what to expect. Megan suggested that I visit a patient of hers at Royal North Shore Hospital. She'd just had the operation and Megan thought she could give a patient's-eye view. The nurse showed me into her room. The poor woman was laid up in bed, looking half dead. I was horrified and said, 'Oh, I can come back.' I thought there was no way she was in any condition to speak to me. But the nurse said, 'No, no, she's looking great, she's really turned the corner.' I thought, *Oh my God, if that's great, what did she look like before?*

She said, 'It's the worst surgery, the worst thing you can do. It's so painful. I can't move my stomach, I can't cough, I can't laugh. Don't do it, it's hell!'

I gaped at her, just wanting to get out of there. I did think to ask her one more question: 'Did you do chemo?'

'No, I didn't,' she said.

And I think that explains a lot: my experience of chemo was so horrific it's changed my tolerance for pain. After going through that, other kinds of pain aren't as bad, although the recovery from surgery is certainly traumatic. I had to wear a binder around my stomach for six weeks because I had no stomach muscles. That really restricted my movement. To get up, I had to roll over like a seal and throw myself off the bed. I was also quite numb in my stomach and my breasts were totally numb. They don't use dissolvable stitches, they use the old-fashioned kind, so I had to go back, get the tape and the dressing changed, and then have the stitches taken out slowly as the weeks went on.

It was by no means easy, but after everything I'd been through, I was put back together, I got new breasts and that feels like a reward. I felt more confident, more relaxed, more like myself. Marcus tells me the difference is striking: I'm standing taller, my posture has changed, I'm wearing the kinds of clothes I love to wear. The old me is coming back.

And that has made a huge difference, for both of us. Marcus described what it was like after the first mastectomy: he had a picture in his mind of what I looked like, and then after the mastectomy, I didn't look like that any more. I walked around with my shoulders hunched—it was a physical response to what I was feeling, a self-protectiveness, and a feeling of shame. A mastectomy doesn't just leave a flat chest behind, it leaves a scooped-out hole. It's confronting. And the fact that I'd lost one breast, but kept the other made the contrast even more striking. Every time I saw it, I felt the shock and pain all over again. Every day it was a reminder of all that we were going through. There's our old life, there's our new life. I tried to be strong and courageous and face the world every day but the vulnerability and shame were always there. Now I look like myself again. Of course, my breasts will never be what they were before, but I'm very happy and grateful with what I've got.

Suddenly, so many things feel possible. After my first mastectomy, I couldn't imagine ever going to the beach again—I couldn't bear the thought of myself in a cossie. But I don't feel that way anymore. I actually look forward to beach days, and taking Annabelle to the pool.

I have huge scars from surgery and discolouration from radiation but don't mind if people can see them. In a funny way, I feel quite proud of them because they're the signs of everything I've been through. I find them empowering, and also very human. No-one gets through life without scars, physical or emotional.

It's amazing how getting a bit of time and distance on what's happened can change your perspective. I remember looking at those photos of other women's surgeries and thinking how terrible and mutilated they looked. I was horrified to think that might be me, too. But as the months have passed, none of it seems so horrifying anymore. I look at my own scars and they don't seem that bad. In fact, I think I'm happy with how I look. I've become more comfortable with it all. The pain and the terror are in the past now, and I can get on with living.

◆ ◆ ◆

After the surgery in October, I had a PET scan, a full-body scan to detect whether I had any tumours anywhere in my body. The technician who did the scan told me it would take him at least a day to get the results, and the protocol was that once he had them, he'd call Fran, and then Fran could tell me.

This was my last big test. When it was done, I started wondering, as I had so many times before, whether it had all been enough: the chemo, the surgery and the radiation and the complementary therapies. Had we knocked off this thing?

But I knew I had to wait, so I made plans to go to lunch. On my way there, my phone rang. It was a number I didn't recognise. I answered, and a man's voice said, 'Hi, this is the doctor from St Vincents. I'm calling about your PET scan.'

My heart dropped like a stone, I thought, *Oh my God, why*

is he calling me? This can't be good news. But he said, 'I've rung Fran and she's not there. I've sent her all the details, but I just thought you'd want to know as soon as possible: it's all clear.'

I was standing there on Ocean Street in Woollahra thinking, *Oh my God. Oh my God. I've done it. We've done it! Thank you, universe. Thank you.*

Now, I wish I'd taped that call. It was just the best phone call I've ever had. Possibly even better than the call I got from the IVF clinic telling me I was pregnant.

Marcus has my message telling him the good news. This was amazing news for all three of us. I was in the clear. We had our life back!

Of course, I still wanted to ring Fran, just to check. Eventually I got hold of her and she confirmed the news: it was all good. We were done. Treatment was over.

For the first time in a year, I felt I could breathe. I realised that until that day, I'd been holding my breath, waiting for the next blow to fall. And I don't think I was aware of how stressed I'd been until the stress was finally lifted. Of course I knew I was worried and exhausted . . . but it's only when you don't feel it any more, that you realise how bad it actually was, how afraid you were, and how tired you were from fighting. I went into that surgery feeling so weary . . . battle weary.

I grew so tired of the appointments, and fighting and struggling to get my health back, the see-saw backwards and forwards, living all the time with uncertainty and the fear that at any moment something could kill me. And then when they finally told me it was over, the relief was tremendous. Suddenly I was full of energy and possibility. I started frantically thinking about all the things I wanted to do now: go to the beach, see my friends, throw a party, have a barbecue—not that I couldn't have had a barbecue before. And I wanted to surprise my mum and dad, take them away on holiday and do something good for them because they'd had such a hard year and had been so incredibly supportive of us.

It was almost exactly a year. Not long after that phone call, we celebrated Annabelle's first birthday, which meant it was a year since I'd been diagnosed. Someone asked me whether I'd felt sad on the anniversary of the diagnosis, but I didn't feel sad at all, it was over. It felt like Annabelle's birthday was my birthday too: it was a fresh start, a new beginning. All day Marcus and I were high-fiving each other, saying 'You know what? We did it! Job well done.'

Matt White

***Former host of* Today Tonight *and one of*
*Sally's close friends***

There's a line in a song I know that says 'I can't cry hard enough'.
When I first heard that Sal had been diagnosed with breast cancer
that's exactly how I felt—I just couldn't cry hard enough. No amount
of tears can make the sadness or the shock go away. This was real.
This was scary. This was so incredibly wrong. Cancer, please don't do
this. Not to anyone, especially not to Sally. Cancer, you really have
no idea how wrong this is. Really.

Here's how wrong it is. Your first words to someone who has just
been diagnosed with cancer should not be 'Congratulations', but that's
exactly what I said when I first spoke to Sal while she was in hospital.
I couldn't wait to congratulate her on the birth of Annabelle and, no
matter how strange it sounded or how difficult the conversation was
going to be, cancer wasn't going to deny us the chance to celebrate
the most wonderful moment in Sal's life.

Here's how wrong it is. Sally had spent her last few weeks at work tire-
lessly using her contacts to stock our Today Tonight *office with all sorts*
of goodies so she could raffle them off to raise money for a cameraman
she'd never met, from our Brisbane office, who had just lost his leg—to
cancer. It was so wrong, so hard to fathom and so difficult to comprehend
that this disease had decided to pick on someone like Sal.

Well, cancer, you picked the wrong person because Sally never
stopped smiling. And that's what I love most about my beautiful, brave
friend—she never gave up and never, ever stopped smiling. It's funny,
literally, because laughter often defined our friendship before cancer,
and laughter would be there during cancer.

Sally Obermeder

The first day I met Annabelle I stepped out of the lift at Sal's apartment to see Mum and baby daughter beaming. Sal's chemotherapy had kicked in and her gorgeous trademark long hair was now more like a patchy buzz cut—so, of course, I couldn't help but crack a gag about their matching hairstyles. Sal had every right to push me straight back into the lift—but she laughed, as always.

I'll never forget that day when we walked to what would become our regular catch-up café around the corner from Sal's apartment. It was Sal's first 'public appearance' since she had lost her hair and, despite my bad gags and the obvious feeling that people were looking at her, she held her head up and kept that smile all the way. I remember thinking: courage and humour—that's how Sal's going to face this.

Our coffees and cuddles with Annabelle were great therapy. Even in this most abnormal of times, it was Sal's ability to make things seem normal that was truly incredible and completely inspirational.

Oh, and by the way, cancer, that's another thing you need to know. Sally Obermeder has delivered some of the best one-liners ever to put you in your place.

Marcus is simply amazing: a loving husband and a doting dad who knows that despite all this he's a lucky man with a wonderful wife and a gorgeous daughter. Their lives have changed forever but they've still got what matters the most—each other.

I tried not to cry whenever we were together during those tumultuous, terrible and testing twelve months. But when Sal asked me to write this it finally dawned on me that the battle really had been won—and I lost it. Sally, you did it. And now I can't cry hard enough with happiness.

A recovering perfectionist

Over the past year I've spent a lot of time thinking about my life. When I was first diagnosed, Marcus suggested I see a therapist, just to help me process everything that was going on, and it was the best decision we could have made. Marcus is a wonderful support, and I know I can tell him everything. But going through something like this is so gruelling I eventually felt I couldn't expect him to listen while I processed every emotion, day after day, night after night. It's too much. He had his own emotions to deal with. Having someone who's actually paid to listen, but who isn't in a relationship with you, helps to take some of the pressure off.

In the beginning, therapy was simply about offloading, expressing my shock at what was happening and my fears for the future. But, eventually, a point came when I didn't want to talk about cancer anymore. I didn't need to. I'd said all I needed to say. And that's when I started to reflect more broadly on my life and my personality and why I do what I do. Why do I drive myself so hard? Why do I punish myself so much? Why don't I treat myself the same way I treat other people, with kindness and love?

And therapy helped me. It really is mysterious how it works because my therapist barely says a word. She doesn't tell me what to talk about, she doesn't direct me, she barely even asks any questions. But somehow, that process of sitting there and talking and going from one memory to another made me question things: Why do I do that? Why am I like that? And what is that doing to the people around me?

I began to see very clearly that the little voice in my head, the one that kept saying, 'It's not good enough, you're not good enough, you haven't done it, you haven't made it, you haven't achieved it, you're ten years behind, you've got to do more,' wasn't making me happy. I was spending so much time thinking about the future, ticking things off my to-do list, doing more, achieving more, that I could never stop and just enjoy life. Marcus would ask why I had to give everything a mark out of ten, and I'd say, 'I just have to. Otherwise, how do I know if I'm improving?' I was obsessed with improving myself. Now I look back and think, *Oh my God, no wonder I was always so tired!* but I couldn't even acknowledge that to myself.

Once I started cancer treatment it was about nine months before I actually cooked a meal again. And when I did, it was crap. But I thought it was great: I was thinking, *This is so good! It's so good to be cooking!* I was just enjoying being back in the kitchen, doing something I hadn't been able to do for ages. It didn't have to be perfect, and it wasn't something to beat myself up about. I was happy to enjoy the experience and be able to share a meal that I'd cooked with Marcus and Annabelle.

◆ ◆ ◆

Looking back, there are things I regret. Particularly my stubbornness about IVF. For somebody who prides herself on her willingness to take a rational approach to things, to go out and get educated if I don't know about something, my refusal to really get on board for so long feels so ridiculous. Could the course of my life have been different? Could I have ended up with more children if I hadn't been so closed off? Probably. And that regret is something I have to live with. I look at Annabelle now and I think, *What was I thinking?*

I know my mum will just love to hear me say this, but she was right: I should have started a family much earlier because it's awesome! It's better than you think it's going be. When I was pregnant, I thought, *Oh my God, I couldn't possibly love this baby any more!* and then she came out and I thought *Oh my God, I couldn't possibly love you any more!* Now she's seventeen months, and I think, *Oh please, I hardly loved you before! NOW I really love you!* The feelings just grow, and grow, and grow every single day.

And the strange thing is, I believe cancer has actually made me a better mum. A number of the people who are closest to me were surprised by how relaxed I turned out to be. I think they imagined I'd be as driven about my child as I was about myself—iron-clad routines, learning two instruments and three languages from birth, worrying if she didn't hit every milestone early. But that isn't the kind of mum I turned out to be. I just want Annabelle to be healthy and happy. That's good enough for me.

I do wonder if I'd had Annabelle but no cancer, whether the old manic Sal might have crept back in. I'd start working hard, then harder, worrying more, trying to do more. And however much I loved my daughter and enjoyed my time with her, I might have got sucked back into that whole work-is-everything and I-need-it-to-validate-myself mentality. Cancer has taught me to be present in these moments, to enjoy them and savour them while I can, because I can never take anything for granted.

◆ ◆ ◆

It's easy to say cancer is life-changing, and it does alter you, emotionally and physically. But I'm still 90 per cent the same person I was before I had cancer. I still like Mexican food, I'm still friends with the same people, I still love my husband and I still love fashion and celebrities and tabloids just as much as I did before. It's the ten per cent that's changed that makes the biggest difference. That ten per cent change has affected the flavour of the other ninety per cent. It's like making a big pot of pasta sauce, and then adding lemon juice to it. Even though the lemon juice would be such a small percentage of the whole volume of sauce, that small amount is enough to change the flavour of the sauce completely. Well that's what happened to me: lemon juice in pasta sauce. That ten-per-cent change has affected the rest of me so deeply and so profoundly, so even though I'm the same, I'm different.

When I look back, I can see how much I sacrificed for the

sake of the future. Marcus and I both sacrificed a lot for our careers. Instead of going on a holiday and enjoying each other's company, we'd always do the sensible thing and save the money, because we needed a deposit for a house or we wanted to save for Annabelle's schooling. We went to Europe for our honeymoon and we've always dreamed of going back, but we never let ourselves do it. We were so obsessed with living within our means, planning for the future, and trying to get ahead that we forgot to actually live.

Now I have a life to look forward to, I'm determined that that's going to change. I'm not going to rush out and buy a boat. But I want to make sure that we take the time to be together, and enjoy our lives, and have those other kinds of experiences money can't buy: the ones that come from being with the people you love.

Cancer has taught me to be more present. Just like that first Christmas with Annabelle, when I was determined to soak up every detail in case it was the last Christmas I had with her, I've gradually learned the importance of being in the moment. Before cancer, I'd go to lunch with my sister and we'd have a lovely time, but in my head, there'd be all this background chatter: I'd be thinking I need to finish this lunch because I've got to get home and write some emails. And then after the emails I should really try and test out four new recipes. And after the four new recipes, don't forget to pay the bills. Getting things done, even trivial things like paying the bills, became all-important to me because I needed that feeling of achievement.

It turns out everything is much more enjoyable if you just do it for its own sake, without worrying about what's next.

Even so, while I'm glad the nagging voice has gone, I know

there's still a chance it might return—in fact, I half expect it, like an alcoholic waiting for a relapse. I do wonder if, when I'm back at work and things are in full flight again, that nagging voice will re-appear. I hope it won't. But for now, all I can say is that I'm a recovering perfectionist.

◆ ◆ ◆

I can see how lucky I've been. Not lucky to get cancer, obviously. But lucky in so many other ways.

Lucky to have worked my way into my dream job.

Lucky to have had so many amazing experiences and met so many fascinating and inspiring people.

Lucky to have got pregnant in my first round of IVF.

Lucky to have chosen an excellent and careful obstetrician who said, 'Actually, let's have a look at that lump,' when he could have said, 'Let's leave it for now.'

Lucky to have had such an amazing team of doctors, nurses and health carers looking after me and helping me fight.

Lucky to have such a healthy, happy, beautiful daughter.

Lucky to have such a wonderful husband, such a close, loving family, and so many amazing friends. Because even though it's the doctors who saved my life, it's my husband, my baby, my family and friends, and even a few complete strangers, who together saved my soul.

◆ ◆ ◆

I don't know what the future holds for me.

Maybe my luck will continue and there'll be a brother or sister, or both, for Annabelle. We still have four embryos in the freezer, but there's still a lot of unanswered questions. There's a risk I could go into early menopause and be unable to get pregnant again. There's a risk that if I did get pregnant again, the cancer could return. There are all kinds of risks and dangers and we haven't worked our way though them yet. I would dearly love for Annabelle to have a sibling. But if that turns out to be impossible, I know how lucky I am to have her.

A near-death experience forces you to re-evaluate your life. Forces you to be honest. You think, if I live what kind of life do I want? You realise it is precious; you don't want to take it for granted and you definitely don't want to squander it. You realise you can almost count how many weekends you have left.

The one thing that's for certain is that cancer has made me sure of who I am. Happy with who I am. Proud of who I am. Not my job. Not my looks. Not my clothes. Me. The person inside. That's what I discovered.

There are so many things I want to do and see, places to go, people to meet. The world is an amazing place, and I can't wait to share it all with my husband and my little girl.

And that's why I feel so lucky to be here now, writing this book, and looking forward to the life that is to come.

While I'm optimistic, I know the challenges of life, great and small, are by no means over. I'll always remind myself to never stop believing.

Forty

I've gone to put pen to paper many times to write this update. But the truth is, it was tougher than I thought. Despite the fact that many, many wonderful things have happened in the last twelve months, and I am so incredibly grateful for them all, I can't help but feel a little overwhelmed with emotion, simply for the reason that I am actually here to tell the tale.

Even though I had addressed my mortality during my illness, I had some residual feelings about the possibility of not surviving, and ultimately, turning 40 brought all of those to the forefront. I think deep down I believed I would never live to see that birthday. So when the day finally came, I had what I would describe as a mini-meltdown.

I was overwhelmed with feelings of gratitude and happiness.

When I was sick, turning forty seemed like such a long way off, and when you're living day to day and just trying to survive, sometimes it just feels too hard to look that far ahead. You're so busy in the here and now and just trying to get through—trying to live, trying to look after a baby. So as my fortieth approached, my girlfriends said that I needed to start planning a party. But, I didn't. I couldn't. I didn't dare jinx my luck by planning a celebration. My birthday fell on a Friday so it was just a normal work day, and that's how I wanted it to be. No fanfare, nothing special. I wanted to enjoy the ordinary, which can be so easily taken for granted.

In addition to turning 40, I became a co-host of a national news and lifestyle TV show, tried my hand at dancing, and my blog swiish.com.au has gone from strength to strength.

I first headed back to work in March 2013, starting back in my old role at *Today Tonight*. It was such a strange feeling to walk through the doors of the Channel 7 studios for the first time since my diagnosis. As I sat at my old desk, the enormity of what had happened really struck me, and it felt that although I had changed so much, everything around me was the same. It took me a good month or two to find my feet, and to find my confidence too. My old life was unrecognisable—I was unrecognisable—and it was a while before I got back in the groove.

During that time I was approached to do a screen test for a new afternoon program, *The Daily Edition*. The screen test was with former *Sunrise* and *Sunday Night* reporter, Monique Wright; model Kris Smith; and former *The Great Outdoors* reporter, Tom Williams. Tom and I already knew one another from working on *Sydney Weekender*—we used to share office space with Tom's team at Seven's Epping studios. And although

Kris and I had met a few times before, we didn't know each other that well, and Monique and I were meeting for the first time. Sarah Stinson, who was going to be the Executive Producer for *The Daily Edition*, suggested that Monique and I get together and have brunch. Frankly I was a little unsure because I had never met her, and there wasn't anyone I knew who knew Monique. Well, I needn't have been too concerned— within all of three minutes we were chatting away like old friends and laughing so ferociously that other people in the café kept turning to see what the commotion was. I remember thinking how smart, funny and beautiful Mon is, and that it didn't matter if I lost out on the co-host role to her, because I had just made an incredible friend.

For the screen test, we had to work with scripts that we'd pre-rehearsed, plus others we'd never seen before and the whole thing was so different to anything I'd done at *TT*, where all my celebrity interviews were pre-prepared. This was all about live TV. The producers wanted to know if we could talk off-the-cuff and if we could ad lib, as well as if we could read an autocue (which I had never used before). One minute we were having to talk politics, the next we were covering the ins and outs of Gwyneth Paltrow's latest macrobiotic diet plan followed by having to sing and dance around the studio. It was fun, although it also definitely met the criteria of what screen tests are supposed to do, and that is to push you *waaaaay* out of your comfort zone.

By the end of the day my nerves were shot. Three long, stomach-churning weeks followed before I learned whether the job was mine. Mon and I were calling each other constantly: 'Have you heard anything?' 'No, have you?'

Initially I thought that the new show would be for only two

co-hosts. After that day of screen-testing and having spent more time with Mon, Kris and Tom, I wouldn't have minded who got it, even if it wasn't me. And if I did end up being offered one of the hosting roles, I knew I would be thrilled to work with any one of them.

Every day I would head into the studios thinking: *I wonder if today is the day we'll find out? I wonder if there is any chance they might pick me?* Finally, just when I didn't think I could possibly hold out any longer, I was called into a meeting where I was told the job was mine. I burst into tears on the spot. I know, I know . . . so unlike me . . .! I was so relieved and excited.

I guess I just really felt ready for a new challenge and having been through cancer and come out the other side, I felt so strong. I was ready to apply that strength to something new in a work sense. But given that I had only just come back to Seven, I couldn't believe how lucky I was to even be considered for a new challenge, let alone to be offered it. It was an incredible opportunity.

Then we got the best news possible—we would all be working together. I was so excited. I wound things up at *TT* and started at *The Daily Edition* in June. However, Mon, Kris, Tom and I had had no rehearsal time as a group since that initial screen test. The next time we all sat together was when the first episode was live on air! We were bedding-in on the job (and learning about each other), all the while figuring it out on live television. When small things went wrong we would laugh about it together and so it only served to bind us closer together as a team.

The show is incredibly fun, and the four of us have grown closer every day. We're like a family and are lucky enough to have the incredibly talented Sarah Stinson as our Executive Producer. They say that when you do what you love, it doesn't feel like work and I can honestly say that's how I feel about *The Daily Edition*.

In October, I also appeared on Channel 7's *Dancing with the Stars* (*DWTS*). I had agreed to *DWTS* back before I learned about *The Daily Edition*. Ideally, when you go on *Dancing*, you don't have a job; it *is* your job. The training is absolutely gruelling. Dancers spend years and years practising and perfecting their craft, but contestants have to learn several complex routines in a matter of days. It was intense to say the least.

My fellow competitors were rehearsing 10 hours a day but I could only manage four hours, due to filming on *The Daily Edition* and trying to juggle looking after Annabelle. Each night I'd collapse exhausted into bed, and then sit up for hours watching footage of my dance rehearsals, desperately trying to memorise the steps. On weekends, my dance partner, Carmelo Pizzino would dance with me for six or seven hours each day. I was so unbelievably tired!

In fact, I'd started to feel like I had bitten off more than I could chew, like my body wasn't ready for such a full-on schedule. It was too much, too soon. My final surgery was only completed in February so I was still recovering from that. And even though I felt better every day, I'm not sure I was well enough for the level of training *DWTS* required. It was tough.

I was doing more than I should, and felt myself starting to slip back into old habits. I was constantly criticising myself—I felt as though I wasn't doing my job well at *The Daily Edition*, or being there enough for Marcus and Annabelle. I guess the perfectionist in me is still in recovery.

In all honesty, I wasn't devastated when *Dancing* was over, but like so many tough things, looking back I'm glad I did it. I learned an awful lot about dancing and an awful lot about myself. For instance, what you can't tell from watching *DWTS* on TV is that the studio is really small, so when you're dancing you're close enough to the studio audience that you can hear everything they're saying. You can be happily cha-cha-ing when the woman in the front row will nudge her friend and say: 'Beryl, she's no good. She's no good at all.' And you can hear every word!

It was then that I realised I don't take myself too seriously. I thought I would be really sensitive to any criticism about my dancing but I wasn't. I remember in Week One when, by some fluke we didn't get eliminated, I turned to Carmelo, and said: 'Do you think people misunderstood the voting system? Do you think they're all voting for who they want to *go home* like on *Big Brother*?'

I guess I couldn't believe that people would vote for us to stay in the competition when, let's face it, everyone—including Todd McKenney, who called me on it—could see that I had two left feet!

And then, when *DWTS* was all over, I found I had a spare 35 hours in my week that I previously didn't know existed. Suddenly I had so much time on my hands. I could have found the answer to world peace before I sat down to eat my breakfast each day!

With the extra time, I threw myself into my website, swiish. com.au. Swiish is a fashion, beauty, health and lifestyle blog that's all about luxe for less. Most women have a friend or know some-one who constantly nabs one good buy after another—someone who can spot that on trend dress or shoe or even homewares—and it all looks super-expensive, but yet it never is. You end up harassing them to find out what they paid and where to get it. In my circle of friends, that gifted freak of nature (What? Shopping isn't a gift?) is me. So swiish is a place where readers can get their their daily fix of lifestyle, and true to my skillset, it's all fabulous and affordable.

I launched the site with Maha in November 2012 and by our first anniversary (right when I was finishing *DWTS*), things had really taken off. We spent that first year sharing what we know, and readers rewarded us with almost a million impressions each month. In the blogging world, that is especially exciting when you're a newbie. Plus, the website now hosts our charitable initiative, wish by swiish, which grants wishes to breast or ovarian cancer fighters and survivors.

Like any business, it's been an absolute slog. But for both Maha and I, it's incredibly rewarding—it feels like we're back in our rumpus room as kids playing dress-ups, only now it's for real. We have such a long way to go but we still pinch ourselves some days—like the day Liz Hurley tweeted us!—and then there's no question in my mind that it's all been worth it. And the fact that I share the experience with my sister makes it all the more special.

I also became a style ambassador for Westfield in 2013. I loved working with such a wonderful brand.

And then there is our darling Annabelle. She recently turned two—how *fast* did that come around?! Watching her grow into a little person has been incredible. Marcus and I sit and watch her for hours with such joy. She is the cutest little monkey and every day is a blessing.

As I write this, Marcus, Annabelle and I have just taken to the skies for a holiday in Bali. We're going to hang out and have some time together as a family. It's been a wonderful, happy, jam-packed year and it makes me realise how very fortunate I am.

I often think about the future—what I want the rest of my life to look like. I don't take it for granted, and I'm trying to live life to the fullest. There are days where I am still afraid that the cancer will come back but I don't want to be a prisoner to that fear. At the same time I don't want to be presumptuous and assume that I don't have to worry.

So though I'm constantly challenging myself and trying new things, I'm also taking the time to look after myself. You know the saying 'Live each day like it's your last'? There's another that says, 'Live each day each like you'll live forever.' It's a balancing act and it's one that I don't always get right. But I'm kinder to myself and more patient, and I know that I'm doing the best I can. And that's enough. As long as I have my health, and my family and my friends around me, then I consider myself the luckiest woman alive.

Acknowledgements

Fran Boyle, thank you for persevering with me, for seeing past my hair extensions and my tears. Your calm nature and your incredible smarts saved me. I can never explain the extent of the gratitude in my heart. I can never really repay you for what you did for me. But if I do ever get that Kim Kardashian interview, then yes, you can definitely come.

Kylie Snook, I'm sending you a crate of Kleenex tissues to make up for the thousands of tears I cried on your shoulder. Thank you for holding my hand, saving my life and never once making me feel like a weirdo.

Megan Hassall, yes you scared me, but I was and I still am in complete awe of what you did. Thank you for rebuilding not just my body but my spirit.

Manfred and Margitta Obermeder, thank you for your unwavering support and love. You may not have been close geographically but you were with us every step of the way. We could not have done this without you. I love you.

Camilla Crotty, from commerce to Corsica to cancer, I feel like we've covered it all. You are the most incredible best friend and it was never more obvious than when I was sick. All those cookbooks, all those recipes, all that effort and all that pure love. I am so incredibly blessed. Thank you for being my best friend. Here's to many more years, ideally without the cancer and the commerce. Corsica could be good, though! Should I whip up a spreadsheet? (Starry starry night . . .) Love you.

Julia Bradbury, Lizzie Pettit, Tracy Watson, never, ever, ever did I think a job I hated would bless me with three angels. Remember that first Sunday post diagnosis—none of us wanting to say anything, all of us avoiding the elephant in the room. Then Lizzie, never one to mince words, bursts in with 'So, how do we all feel about Sal having cancer?' I feel like being sick has brought us even closer together and I love you darlings more than you will ever know.

Sarah Stinson and Lucie McGeoch, I thought coming to *TT* would be the best thing to happen in my career. It turns out it was one of the best things to happen in my life. It gave me you two, and I love you darlings so much and not just because you get my love of razzle dazzle, not just because you let me cry at Raw Bar a thousand times over, but because you helped show me I'm so much more than my job. I couldn't love you more if I tried.

Joanne Stennett, Jo Jo thank you for holding my hand and letting me cry on your shoulder. I'll always remember how you and Angus came to see me in the hospital straight away, the three of us just dumbfounded and shell-shocked. Both of you never once stopped cheering me on and you supported and loved Marcus, which makes me love you both even more. Thank you.

Adene Cassidy, When I asked you to fill in for me never did I envisage it turning out like it did. But in a funny way it all turned out the way it was supposed to. Like the universe knew what we didn't. Thank you for your insistence on the food roster, Proof that sometimes what seems like the smallest thing, actually makes the biggest difference.

Matt White, my coffee buddy. I actually think we had more coffees while I was off sick than we did when we worked together. That's how much trouble and effort you went to, to make sure you were there for me. You never made it seem like a hassle. And that whole 'I'm in the area' didn't fool me one bit. Bondi is not in the Northern Beaches 'area'. Thank you.

Samantha Armytage, I'll never forget collecting the mail that Sunday morning. I can't even think about it without falling to pieces. It's actually me who is honoured and so incredibly fortunate to call you my friend.

Larry Emdur , We ate haloumi wraps at every dodgy café in Bondi all the way through my cancer. They were the crappiest lunches, but you were the best company. Thank you. You made me laugh so hard and so much I almost didn't see the lessons in the stories. Almost. I'm grateful I did. They helped me to change and made me see the person I want to be. So much love and gratitude to you. PS. If this book is a flop, it's your fault. I knew I should've asked Karl Stefanovic to write the foreword.

Andy Cichanowski and Jason Hinsch, our lunches were something I looked forward to so much. You're not girls but you loved me and supported me and held me through the darkness as much and as well as any girlfriend. And you built me the most kick-ass garage shelves. I still cannot look at a horsehead without laughing.

Mitch Bailey, thank you for Thailand. I needed it. I needed the space. I needed the break. I needed the massages and boy did I need that chicken, chilli and egg sandwich. I'll always remember and cherish the love that you gave me.

Alan Dungey, Al, you took a chance on me. You gave me my first break, my first opportunity and opened the door to my dreams. You also taught me never to write 'There's something for everyone' in a script. Thank you.

Mike Whitney, Mike, our time filming together in NZ cemented my love for you. Do you know what phrase I use more than ever? 'Come under the wing of love.' From Mama Whitney to you and then you to me—I've never forgotten it and it sums up everything I live for. Now stop crying. You're making me cry.

Guiliana Rancic, darling, you embody everything I admire and respect. Your sincerity, passion and drive and your incredible kindness touched me in the most profound way. I hope we can stay friends long after the cancer is a distant memory.

Peter Meakin, Craig McPherson, Neil Mooney, John Choueifate, the support you gave me, unquestionably helped me get better. Not once did you make me feel anything but supported, loved and encouraged. You cheered me on all the way to the finish line. I cannot ever thank you enough. (Look Craig, no tears!)

Claire Kingston, there's no one else I would rather have done this with. I love that you thought it was perfectly normal that I should call you hours after a major surgery to discuss my highly unrealistic book goals. You understood me. Plus your positivity and energy to deliver two babies was seriously impressive. I hope this isn't our last venture together—it was a joy to work with you.

Siobhán Cantrill, who held me together at the end when my nerves got the better of me. You did. Thank you so much. And for reading, re-reading and re-reading again. And thanks for saving me from the circling sharks. Good call!

My Allen & Unwin family, Mark, Marie, Andy, Amy, Karen, Chris, Claire, Caitlin and Isabella, your belief in me from that very first meeting has been unwavering. Your passion and excitement for this book have been beyond my wildest dreams. Thank you.

My CHIC family, Ursula, Kathy, Jane, Ronia, Jaz, Cara, David—woah! What an intense and shitty year that was! Thank you for supporting me, loving me and caring for me well and truly beyond the job requirements.

The nurses & hospital staff at The Mater Hospital and Hunters Hill Private Hospital, and the radiologists at St Vincent's Hospital, thank you for looking after me so incredibly well. As I said to my mum, I could not have been better cared for if it was you right there looking after me. From the moment I arrived to give birth to Annabelle right through to chemo, radio and my surgeries, you all took me into your hearts and cared for me and nurtured me back to health. I owe you my life.

Belinda Jeffrey, Petra Bergman, Kylie Gillies, Anne Geddes and the whole Geddes clan, Sophie Hull, David Dutton, Naomi Shivaraman, Brooke Martinez, Helen Wellings, Louise Donnelly, Carole and Nikki Menere, Jack and Katrina Chemello, Suzi Kinnane, Karen Gordon, Kylie Alexander, Annie Beverley, Jo Hodgson, Xanthe Robinson, Maria

Never Stop Believing

Kirkpatrick-Jones, Tory Archbold, Napoleon Perdis, Roxy Jacenko, Laura Sparkes, Andrew and Irene Connole, Grant and Chezzi Denyer, Ben Fordham, Kerrie McCallum, Ros Reines, David Richardson, Anthony and Kelly Bell, James and Christiane Duigan, Hannah Devereux, Jamal and Joseph Ajaka, Mark Wilkinson, James Thomas, Darren Ally, Steve and Susie Wrightson, Tania Boswell, Katie Jacocevic, Kerri-Anne Kennerley, Yury and Anna Resnick, Charles and Leah Bates, Leon and Lana Goltsman, Rob and Loretta Vicaro, Andrew Ordish, Jo Joseph, Alex Perry, Brian and Vogue McFadden, Kyle Sandilands and Jackie O, Tracey Baker and, last but not least, my Wellington Street family, you all gave me enormous strength and mountains of love. You took me to lunch at just about every fancy restaurant in Sydney. You cooked meals and dropped them off. You babysat Annabelle. You bought me flowers. You bought me magazines. We went for walks. We went for breakfast. We had play dates with Annabelle. You went out of your way to do whatever you could to help me. It worked. You kept me connected to my old life. You made me feel normal. You made me laugh so hard, I quite often forgot I was sick. My heart was so full of love, love that fuelled my fight. We did this together. Thank you doesn't even scratch the surface.

Mum and Dad, sorry for all the times I said you didn't give me enough. You did. You gave me love. The biggest, hugest, most insane amount of love. More than my little heart could take. You gave me my positivity and strength. You made me who I am. I love you.

Maha, if there was a promotion system for sisters, you'd be promoted to the top. But since there isn't all I can say is that you're at the top of my list. You're the best sister anyone could ever dream of having and I'm quite sure the reason I don't win lotto is because I already have. With you. Thank you for all that you did and all that you are. And sorry I drive you crazy, but seriously would you have it any other way? Don't answer that.

Marcus, babe, how do I sum up all the love in my heart? It's impossible to put it into words. All I can say is I love you. You make my heart sing, you make me laugh and you make my life a better place. I hope we can be just like those couples we see on Bondi Beach, old and grey, holding hands and eating ice cream, having lived a life of love and happiness. There's no one else I'd rather share this ride with.

Annabelle, Cookie, we loved you long before you came into this world. You are my everything. All I want is for you to be healthy and happy. You didn't know what was happening but still, with your little cherub face and your cheeky ways, you helped me fight, you made me smile and you gave me so much love. To be here for you, to be your mum and to watch you grow makes the whole battle unquestionably worthwhile.

To the people whom I'd never met before this nightmare began, but who reached out with such selfless love and compassion, I cannot thank you enough. Your messages, your letters, your flowers, your cards and your gifts—they all touched me in a profound way. To those who stopped me in the street, hugged me and cheered me on, thank you. You all contributed to the mountain of strength that got me through. You showed me the power of the human spirit and the strength that love can bring.

To anyone going through their own battle, whatever it may be, I'm sending you love and encouragement, hope and strength. I hope that you'll keep going, keep fighting, keep pushing through and never stop believing.